Visual Basic
for
AVCE

Derek Christopher

Published by
Payne-Gallway Publishers Limited
26-28 Northgate Street
Ipswich IP1 3DB
Tel: 01473 251097
Fax: 01473 232758
E-mail: info@payne-gallway.co.uk
Web site: www.payne-gallway.co.uk

2001

Cover picture © 'Orange Hour' by Hsiao-Mei Lin
Cover photography © Mike Kwasniak, 160 Sidegate Lane, Ipswich
Cover design by Tony Burton

First edition 2001

A catalogue entry for this book is available from the British Library.

ISBN 1 903112 59 1

Printed in Great Britain by
W M Print Ltd, Walsall, West Midlands

Preface

AVCE

GNVQ Advanced IT was first introduced nationally in 1994. The syllabus and method of assessment of all Advanced GNVQs was completely changed from 2000. It is now called AVCE ICT (Advanced Vocational Certificate of Education or Vocational 'A' level). In 2000 I wrote *Computing Projects in Visual Basic* for the new 'AS'/'A' level Computing specifications. Some of the chapters in that book have been reused in this book (with a few changes) to teach AVCE students the principles of Visual Basic.

Programming in AVCE

This book has been written mainly for students doing AVCE ICT with the Edexcel Board. Students doing the 12-unit award have to do 6 compulsory and 6 optional units.. Those doing the 6-unit award must do 3 compulsory and 3 optional units. Two of these optional units for both the 12- and 6-unit awards could be Units 7 and 22 on programming covered by this book. The other two AVCE Boards offer one practical programming optional unit each. These units are very similar to Edexcel's Unit 7.

Programming in other ICT courses

The standard required for Unit 7 is approximately the same as that for the practical Module 3 of the AQA Board's 'AS' Computing. Students doing 'A' level ICT with Edexcel will find the Unit 7 material useful for Module 5 *The Implementation of event-driven applications*. The material in this book on Unit 22 would be useful for students who need to write larger programs involving file-handling such as those doing BTEC National.

How the book is structured

The book has two main sections, one each on Units 7 and 22. Both of these are divided into two parts:

Part One – teaches you all the Visual Basic skills needed to produce a portfolio for the unit.

Part Two – shows you how to build this portfolio of practical work by using a sample case study and an assignment.

The approach throughout is a very practical one. Running throughout the 11 chapters on Visual Basic skills are 33 programs, with step-by-step instructions explaining how to build them and explanations about how they work. In Part Two of each unit you will build a fully-working program to meet the specifications of the provided case study.

Table of Contents

Unit 22 – Programs: Specification to Production
137

Introduction

AVCE optional units

The Edexcel Board has two optional units, 7 and 22, which ask you to program in a high-level language. Both of these are assessed by portfolio only. For Unit 7 you must use a so-called event-driven language such as Visual Basic. Unit 22 does not stipulate the type of language you have to use. However students who do the two units are likely to use the same language for both since the amount of time it takes to learn a new language is considerable. Also, since the portfolio requirements of the two units have a lot in common, it makes sense to do both units rather than just unit 7. After completing Unit 7 you will have learned many of the Visual Basic skills required for Unit 22 and you will have had invaluable practice at putting together a fairly large workable program.

The syllabus

You are probably aware by now of the two main parts of the 'syllabus' of an AVCE unit - *What you need to learn* and the *Assessment Evidence*. The *What you need to learn* section lists all the material you will need to know about in order to produce a portfolio (or to take an exam for units that are assessed externally). The *Assessment Evidence* lists all the criteria you must meet in your portfolio of work to achieve grade E, C or A for the unit. Your teacher sets an assignment (or more than one if they wish) which allows you to meet these criteria. Both *What you need to learn* and the *Assessment Evidence* for Units 7 and 22 are very similar. So a decision had to be made about which Visual Basic skills to cover in Part One of Unit 22 to make it distinct from Part One of Unit 7. The result is that the following topics are not covered for Unit 7 but are covered for Unit 22:

- General procedures and parameter passing
- Records
- Files

This means that the most complex data structure covered for Unit 7 is the array (but not an array of records which is covered in Unit 22). The case study for the unit makes a lot of use of arrays.

DIDiT

DIDiT is an acronym standing for:

Design

Implementation

Documentation

Testing

If you have done the assessment for Unit 3 (spreadsheets) or for Unit 6 (databases) you had to go through these four stages. Programming is the same. The Implementation stage in programming is writing the code. It is clearly the most important stage, since if it is not reasonably well done there is not much you can do to document or test your program. Part One of each unit in this book teaches you how to code. Part Two teaches you about design, documentation and testing.

The sample case studies and assignments

Part Two of Units 7 and 22 starts with a sample case study and assignment. It then goes though the DIDiT stages for the case study and explains how to answer some of the assignment tasks. One of the differences between Units 7 and 22 is the way in which you find out the user's requirements. For Unit 7 your assessor can give you a case study which includes all the user's requirements, so that you can start on the design of your program at once. The case study used in the book, called *Gina's Groceries*, is of this type. Some of the tasks in the assignment refer to particular things the user (Gina) has requested.

For Unit 22, however, you are expected to find a real user, and through your discussions with them draw up their requirements yourself. If you cannot do this the unit allows your assessor to act the part of the user. You still have to find out through questioning, though, what the user wants your program to achieve. The case study used in Unit 22, *TJ's Tennis*, assumes that this process has been done. So for your own work you will not be given a program specification like the one for TJ's Tennis in Chapter 17. The sample assignment for Unit 22 is therefore independent of any case study, unlike the one for Unit 7 which refers to Gina's Groceries in some of the tasks.

Editions of Visual Basic

Visual Basic has gone through several versions. Recent versions have offered three editions – the **Learning** or **Standard**, **Professional** and **Enterprise** editions. The Learning edition contains all that is required by a student to learn the language and to be able to produce grade A AVCE programs, and a great deal more. The other two editions are really only for professional Visual Basic programmers. Everything in this book can be done using the Learning Edition.

How to learn Visual Basic from this book

The *Visual Basic Skills* section of each unit has chapters on several important topics in Visual Basic programming. Each chapter has one or more sections explaining the main concepts and up to four complete programs to illustrate them. Each program consists of step-by-step instructions telling you how to build it, together with any essential explanation. These programs should be done as practical exercises – you do not learn much programming by only reading about it! There are 33 of these programs and they are summarised in Appendix C.

The *Building your Portfolio* section of each unit takes you through the DIDiT stages of the case study. The chapters on Implementation use a step-by-step approach to tell you how to code the case study in Visual Basic.

Appendix A reviews Visual Basic debugging tools. Debugging is part of the *What you need to learn* section of both Units 7 and 22, and is about tracking down errors in your programs. You should learn how to debug your programs quite early on, certainly no later than Chapter 4. The *Assessment Evidence* does not ask you to demonstrate that you can do this, so there are no tasks specifically on debugging in the sample assignments. However you will find that knowing how to debug can help a lot in getting the code to work in your portfolio program.

Take it from here...

All the chapters in the Part One section of Units 7 and 22 have a *Take it from here...* section. This contains several suggestions for follow-up work related to the topics covered in the chapter. Visual Basic Help is likely to be a useful source for many of the answers. You are encouraged to do these if you have the time and interest. However there is nothing in this section which *must* be understood to do the exercises at the end of the chapter or to understand the sample case studies.

Questions on the programs

Most of the sample programs have suggestions for more practical work to develop a concept further or extend what the program does. It would be sensible to do these as soon as possible after completing the program in the main part of the chapter. These questions are graded using from one to three stars.

End of chapter exercises

The exercises at the end of most of the chapters ask you to build your own programs. A few of these involve something new that has not been directly covered in the current or previous chapters. These exercises are also graded using from one to three stars.

Saving your work

In Chapter 1 you will learn that a saved Visual Basic program consists of at least three files. Only the programs in this chapter prompt you to save your work but it would be sensible to save everything you do. Sometimes a program or an end of chapter exercise may be needed again for another program or exercise, and so should definitely be saved. These are as follows:

Program/exercise	Also required for
Program 2.4	Program 14.1
Program 3.4	Program 8.1
Chapter 3 Exercise 4	Chapter 7 Exercise 2
Program 7.1	Program 14.3

Code

Code extracts are always presented in a shaded format as in the example below.

```
Password = "secret"                          'initialise variables
Attempt = 0
Do                                           'start of loop
   Attempt = Attempt + 1
   InputPassword = InputBox("Enter password. This is attempt " & _
                   "number " & Attempt)
Loop Until (Attempt = 3) Or (InputPassword = Password)   'end of loop
```

This extract illustrates three important coding conventions:

- The 4th line of code has an **underscore character** (_) at the end. This means that the line has been broken into two lines because it is too long to fit into the page width of this book. When copying code into your program you *could* break it into two lines in the same way. Visual Basic accepts the underscore character as the connection between the split lines, but note that there must be at least one space before it. On the other hand you can type the two lines as one line into your program, but remember to leave out the underscore.

- Three lines of code have an **apostrophe** (') followed by a short explanation of what the line means. Such explanations are called **comments** and must come after the apostrophe. In this book the code and the comments are formatted differently. Comments are in italics and are not bold. When you run your program Visual Basic skips over the comments – they are there for human use only. Part of one of the criteria to achieve a grade E for both Units 7 and 22 is to have a reasonable amount of commenting in your code. There are rather more comments provided in the code extracts in this book than you are expected to write in your own programs, but they have the extra role here of teaching you how the code works. You do not have to copy these comments when you write the sample programs, but if you do you will certainly find them helpful when returning to your code later.

- The lines of code between the words *Do* and *Loop* are **indented**. Indenting code in a consistent way is an invaluable aid to understanding what you have written. Visual Basic does not insist on it; like commenting you do it for human use only. In this book indents are two characters in width.

Web site

The publisher's web site contains a variety of support material on www.payne-gallway.co.uk/vbavce that you can download.

Students and teachers can download the following:

- Files for the end-of-chapter exercises:

File	Type of file	Required for
Chap08Ex2.frm	VB form	Chapter 8, Exercise 2
Students.txt	Text	Chapter 16, Exercises 1 and 2

- A Word file (ErrorHandling.doc) on error-handling in Visual Basic. This is about tracking down run-time errors and follows on from the coverage of debugging in Appendix A.

- A Word file (Menus.doc) on how to build menus in Visual Basic. This topic is not covered in the book.

- A Word file (Parameters.doc) on value and reference parameters which extends the material in Chapter 14.

- A Word file (VisualBasicOOP.doc) on object-oriented programming in Visual Basic. This is an advanced topic, not required at all by AVCE, and so only those who want to take their programming further are likely to find this of any use.

Teachers can also download the following:

- A Word file (Guidance.doc) on using this book with your students and with some comments on Units 7 and 22.

- Solutions to the end-of-chapter exercises. These are stored as Visual Basic forms, one for each exercise (e.g. Chap05Ex2.frm). To use a form open a new project and add it to the project. You will also need to tell Visual Basic to use this new form when the program runs because it is set up to run the default form, Form1, provided with a new project.

- A Word file (QuestionsOnPrograms.doc) giving explanations and coded solutions to the exercises on the programs and on the two case studies.

- Visual Basic projects of the two sample case studies. This includes all the forms (.frm) and project (.vbp) files, and for the *TJ's Tennis* case study a standard module (.bas) file. Two versions of TJ's Tennis are provided because the UpDown control used on the Main form may not be available to you (it is not one of the standard controls on the toolbox).

- A Word file (ReadMe.doc) explaining how to use the Visual Basic files provided.

Unit 7 – Programming

Part One – Visual Basic Skills

Chapter 1 introduces you to Visual Basic's **programming environment** – the screen on which you build and run a program. You will learn to use the basic **toolbox** and to adopt a standard way of referring to the controls you use from this toolbox in your code.

Chapter 2 teaches you how to use several controls from the toolbox – **text box**, **list box**, **combo box**, **option button**, **check box**, **frame**, **timer** and **scroll bar**. Of these the text box is the one most commonly used in programs and it is also the easiest. You will use the list and combo boxes a lot in the case study in Part Two, so make sure you understand Program 2.1 well.

Chapter 3 introduces you to Visual Basic's **data types** and how to declare and use **variables** that belong to these types. The concept of the **scope** of a variable is important, and you will learn the difference between **global** and **local** scope. The chapter also covers how to output numbers in the correct **format** and how to **concatenate** strings together.

Chapter 4 takes you through the two **selection** constructs in Visual Basic – **If** and **Select Case**. The If construct is extremely common in programming and is used frequently in the case study in Part Two. You will also learn how to use two important **logical operators** – AND and OR.

Chapter 5 covers **loops**. A loop is a piece of code which is repeatedly executed until a condition is reached (in the code) to make it stop. Three important types of loop which can handle any situation where code must be repeated are covered.

Chapter 6 looks at how to handle **strings**, **dates** and **time**. String-handling is the most common task in programming and Visual Basic has a variety of functions to do this. The case study uses the concepts in this chapter in only a limited way, but other scenarios might rely heavily on them (e.g. a library/video system might require a lot of date-handling).

Chapter 7 covers **arrays**. An 'ordinary' array is a data structure in which you can store large quantities of data belonging to a particular data type. A **control array** is a special type of array that event-driven languages like Visual Basic support. Both types of array are used by the case study.

Chapter 8 tells you how to produce **printed output** from your program. In previous chapters you will have printed output on a form, but sending output to the printer is just as easy. One of the user's requirements in the case study is to have a printed receipt. The chapter has two sample programs. The first one extends Program 3.4. You could do this example as soon as you wish after completing Program 3.4.

Chapter 1 – Introducing Visual Basic

A Visual Basic Project

Event-driven languages like Visual Basic are built using one or more **forms**. On these you place a variety of **controls** and attach code to some or all of them to suit the purpose of your program. All except one of the programs you will do in Parts One and Two of this book have only one form; it is surprising how much you can pack into such a program. The case study for Unit 7 uses only one and the larger case study for Unit 22 uses four.

Figure 1.1 shows a form. In this program the user clicks the Start button and then types as fast as they can in the white area. The number of seconds that have elapsed ticks over on the right, and after 60 seconds they are told how many words they have typed in.

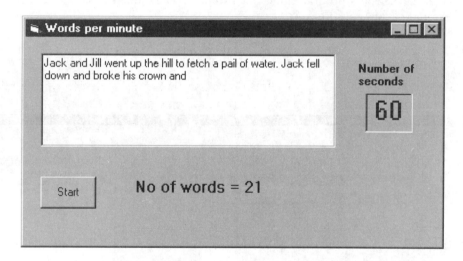

Figure 1.1: A program made up of one form

The example above is a **program**. It has one form with several controls and some code hidden from view which runs when the user clicks the Start button. It is also an example of a Visual Basic **project**. If we called this program WordsPerMinute Visual Basic would save it as a project file called **WordsPerMinute.vbp**. The **vbp** extension means **v**isual **b**asic **p**roject. It would also save the form as a separate file, with a name of your choice, and give it a **.frm** extension.

The Visual Basic programming environment

The programming environment of a language refers to the interface the programmer uses to build a program and then to run and test it. It is the screen in front of you, including all its menus, icons and buttons. Let's have a practical tour of the Visual Basic environment.

Starting a new project

1. Load Visual Basic and you'll get the New Project window shown in Figure 1.2. This will contain two or more icons, depending on which edition of Visual Basic you are using. Select **Standard EXE** and click **Open**.

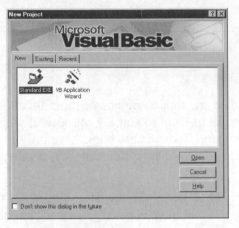

Figure 1.2: The New Project window

2. You're now in Visual Basic's programming environment. The screen has several windows, menus and toolbars. These are shown in Figure 1.3.

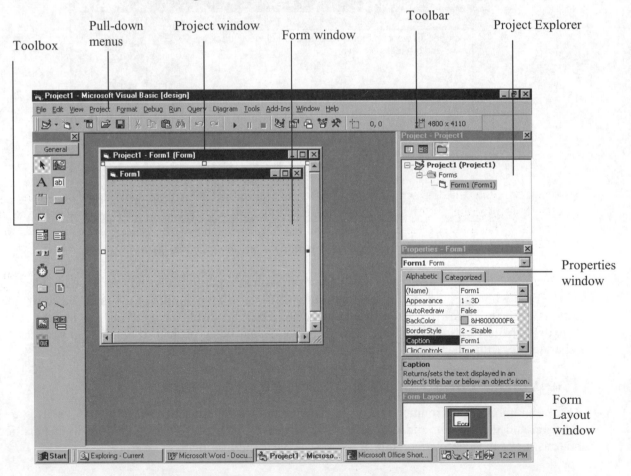

Figure 1.3 – The Visual Basic programming environment

4

The Project and Form windows

The idea that a form is part of a project can be demonstrated by these two windows.

3. Drag the base of the Project window down to reveal the base of the Form window. Resize the Form window and you'll find it cannot be larger than the Project window.

4. Maximise the Project window and you can then make the Form window fill much of the central part of the screen.

The Form Layout window

5. Resize the Form window again and look at the changes in the Form Layout window. This window shows you the position the form will occupy on the screen when the project runs.

The Project Explorer

The **Project Explorer** is the window at the top right of the screen. It contains details of all the forms your project contains. When you start a new project it contains just the one form, which has the name Form1 – twice!

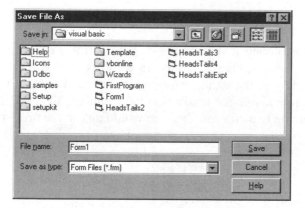

Figure 1.4: Saving a form

6. Select **File/Save Project As** from the menu. You get the Save File As window shown in Figure 1.4 (with a different list of items) and the default file name **Form1**. Because you haven't yet saved the form, Visual Basic insists you do this before saving the project. Save it with the name **FirstProgram**.

7. Now you get the Save Project As window as shown in Figure 1.5. Visual Basic assumes you wish to use the same folder as the one you just saved the form file in. It is a good idea to save the form and project with the same name. Save the project as **FirstProgram**.

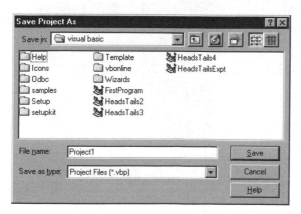

*Figure 1.5: Saving
a project*

8. These names are now listed in the Project explorer, as shown in Figure 1.6.

9. The Project Explorer has three small buttons at the top left. Two of these are named in Figure 1.6. Make sure the form is selected and then click the **View Code** button. You are now in the Code Window for the form where you write the program's code. At the moment it's empty. Click the **View Object** button to take you back to the form.

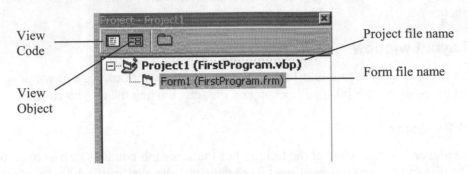

Figure 1.6: The Project Explorer

The Toolbox

The **toolbox** contains icons for each control you can put on your forms. Figure 1.7 shows the controls on the toolbox, but there are several others, known as custom controls, that you will use in this book with more specialised jobs. You add these to the standard toolbox as the need arises. In Figure 1.7 most of the controls have two names. The name inside the brackets is the technical Visual Basic name and the other one is the 'ordinary' way of referring to a control. Thus we would talk in the ordinary way about a list box but the technical term is a ListBox.

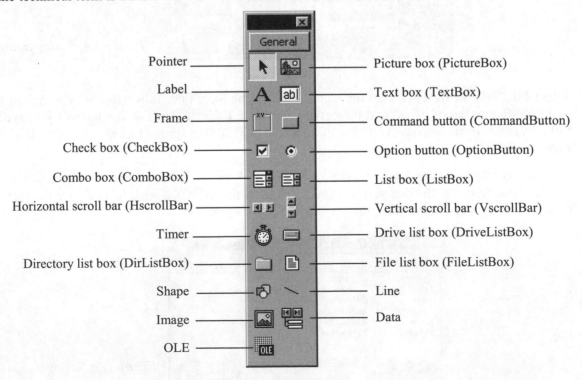

Figure 1.7 – The toolbox

10. Click on the command button control in the toolbox and then draw a rectangle anywhere on the form with the left mouse button down. Release the mouse button to get a command button drawn on the form with the word Command1 in it.

11. Practise placing a variety of controls on the form. Note how the name that appears with some of these controls reflects the type of control. Thus you get Label1, Frame1, Option1 and so on. Place the same control again on the form and the name will be Label2, Frame2 etc.

The Properties Window

When you place a control from the toolbox onto a form it is an example of an **object**. The form itself is also an object. All objects can have **properties**, and most of these can be seen in the Properties window, which is below the Project Explorer. **A property is a descriptive feature of an object.**

12. With the form selected scroll through its 50 properties listed in the Properties window. Some of these are shown in Figure 1.8. These are listed alphabetically but click on the **Categorized** tab and they are arranged by category.

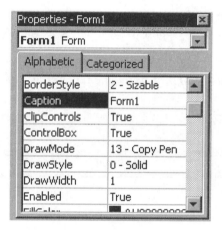

Figure 1.8: Some of the form's properties

13. The selected property by default is the form's Caption. The default value is Form1. Change this to **My First VB Program** and this caption will be displayed in the form's title bar.

14. Find the Name property of the form. This is the most important property you will use in your programs. All controls have a Name property; it refers to the name by which the control is known in your Visual Basic project. Select the form and change its Name property from Form1 to **MainForm**. Names cannot have any spaces.

15. In the Project Explorer the name you gave your form in step 14 appears in front of the file name you gave it in step 6. Note that the Name of the *project* is still the default Project1. You will never need to change the default name of any of the projects in this book.

16. Close the project by selecting **File/Remove Project.** Save the changes if you wish, though the program doesn't do anything.

Menus and toolbar

Along the top of the screen are the pull-down **menus**. You will use many of these as you work through the programs in this book. Below the menus is the **Toolbar**. Nearly all the buttons on the toolbar have a corresponding menu item.

PROGRAM 1.1   *Display your name*

Specification   Display your name on a form in large letters

Designing the form

1.   If you are loading Visual Basic select **Standard EXE** from the New Project window (see Figure 1.2) and click **Open** to start a new project. Otherwise select **File/New Project** and then **Standard EXE**.

2.   Make sure Form1 is selected in the Project Explorer, and then in the Properties window change its Caption property from Form1 to **Print my name**.

3.   Find the form's Font property in the Properties window. Click on the button to the right with the three dots and in the Font window set the font to **30 bold**. When your name appears on the form let's have it in large letters!

Coding

Code may be executed when a particular event occurs. The event in this program is the displaying of the form. The event is called the **Load** event and when it happens your name should appear.

4.   Double-click anywhere on the form and you'll be given the code template shown below. You can tell the type of event from the phrase **Form_Load**. The meaning of the other parts of this template will be explained in later chapters.

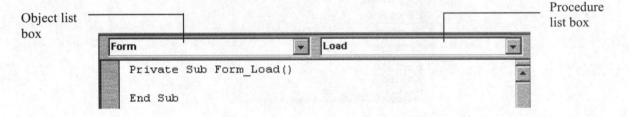

Figure 1.9: The code template for the form's Load event

When you double-click any control on a form, or the form itself, Visual Basic supplies the code template for the event which the makers of the language think is the most common one for that control. For a form they think the Load event should be the default one. Some controls have the Click event as their default one.

5.   To see the events you can have for a form click the small button in the Procedure list box (see Figure 1.9.) It will display a list of 16 possible events associated with a form, from **Activate** to **Unload**.

6.   Between the two lines of the template type two lines of code to tell Visual Basic to print your name on the form. Put your own name between the quotation marks.

```
Private Sub Form_Load()
    Form1.Show
    Form1.Print "Derek Christopher"
End Sub
```

Note the following:

- The two lines of code are **indented**. Indenting code in a consistent way is a very important part of writing good code. It makes code easier to read, as you will appreciate when writing more complex code later. A three-character indent is used in this book.

- **Show** and **Print** are two of the form's **methods**. All objects have methods – **actions you can perform on an object**. Note the dot separator between the name of the object and its method.

Running the program

To run a program its code must be changed from the words you have written, commonly called **high-level** or **source code**, into something your computer can understand. Computers only understand 1's and 0's; this sort of code is called **binary** or **machine** code. The Visual Basic **compiler** changes the source code into binary code and stores this in the computer's memory so that the program can run.

If you select **Run** on the menu bar there are two available options at present. These are:

- **Start** – this will run your program but the program will stop when a line of source code contains an error that the compiler picks out. There are two other ways of doing running a program – press the F5 function key or click the Start button on the toolbar.

- **Start with Full Compile** – the compiler will first check all your code for errors, and only if it can't find any will the program begin to run. The alternative way is Ctrl + F5.

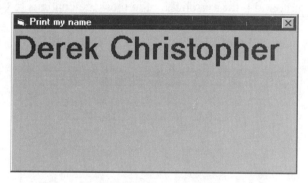

Figure 1.10: Program to display a name

7. Run the program using one of the methods above and your name should appear in 30 point bold font as shown in Figure 1.10. If the program does not run properly check the code you wrote in step 6 above.

8. Close the program by closing its window in the way you would normally close a window – click the small button with an 'x' at the top right or click on the small icon to the left of your form's caption and then click close, or simply press Alt + F4.

9. Select **File/Save Project As** and then save first the form and then the project file using the same name.

> *end of Program 1.1*

Naming objects

Many Visual Basic programmers use a naming convention that adds a lower case three-character prefix to the name they give to a control. For example, if the purpose of a text box is for the user to type in a person's salary then you might name it **txtSalary**. Whenever you come across this in your code you would know it was a text box from the txt prefix, and the 'Salary' part would give a strong clue as to its purpose. The point was made earlier that names of controls are not allowed to have any spaces.

Figure 1.11 lists the prefixes for all the controls on the standard toolbox that you will need to refer to in code in the programs in this book.

Control	Prefix
Check box	chk
Combo box	cbo
Command button	cmd
Common Dialog Control	dlg
Form	frm
Frame	fra
Horizontal scroll bar	hsb

Control	Prefix
Label	lbl
List box	lst
Option button	opt
Shape	shp
Text box	txt
Timer	tmr

Figure 1.11: Prefixes for naming controls

PROGRAM 1.2   *Change a message*

Specification   When a command button is clicked the message "I LIKE Visual Basic" appears. When a second command button is clicked the message changes to "I HATE Visual Basic"

The finished program can be seen in Figure 1.12.

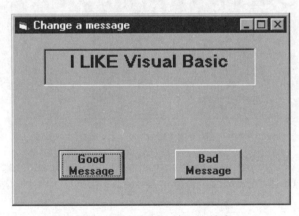

Figure 1.12: Program 1.2

Designing the form

1. If you are loading Visual Basic select **Standard EXE** from the New Project window (see Figure 1.2) and click **Open** to start a new project. Otherwise select **File/New Project** and then **Standard EXE**.

2. Make sure Form1 is selected in the Project Explorer, and then in the Properties window change its Caption property from Form1 to **Change a message**.

3. Click on the Label control in the toolbox, and then with the mouse button down draw a rectangle in the upper part of the form.

4. Find the label's Name property in the Properties window and change it from Label1 to **lblMessage**, using the 'lbl' prefix as explained earlier.

5. Set the label's Caption property to blank by deleting the default value 'Label1'.

6. The default value for the label's BorderStyle property is 0 – None, meaning that no border will be shown when the program runs. To get a border change this to **1 – Fixed Single**.

7. Set the label's Font property to **14 Bold**.

8. Drag a command button from the toolbox and draw a rectangle at the bottom left of the form. Set its Caption property to **Good Message**. Change its Name property to **cmdGoodMessage**.

9. Place a second command button at the bottom right of the form. Set its Caption property to **Bad Message**. Change its Name property to **cmdBadMessage**.

Coding

10. Double-click on the Good Message command button and you'll get the code template for its Click event shown below. The Click event is the one Visual Basic associates most commonly with a command button.

```
Private Sub cmdGoodMessage_Click()

End Sub
```

11. Type the line of code below to set the Caption property of the label to the message you wish to output. As soon as you type the dot separator between the object (lblMessage) and its property (Caption), pause and look at the list of properties which pop up (see Figure 1.13). This very useful feature of Visual Basic is called **Auto list members**. You can select a property from this list by double-clicking it or typing the property name in yourself.

```
Private Sub cmdGoodMessage_Click()
    lblMessage.Caption = "I LIKE Visual Basic"
End Sub
```

The '=' sign means *store or assign the text inside the quotation marks into the Caption property of the label*. Technically it is known as an **assignment statement**.

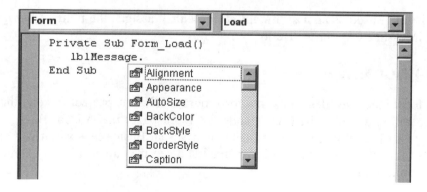

Figure 1.13: Auto list members for a label

12. Get the code template for the Bad Message command button. Do this by returning to the form (by clicking the View Object button in the Project explorer) and then double-click the command button. Alternatively, as you are in the Code window already, just select **cmdBadMessage** from the Object list box at the top left (see Figure 1.9) and its default code template will be provided.

13. Type in a line of code similar to that in step 11 to output the appropriate message when the button is clicked:

```
Private Sub cmdBadMessage_Click()
    lblMessage.Caption = "I HATE Visual Basic"
End Sub
```

Running and saving the program

14. Run the program using one of the methods listed before step 7 in program 1.1. Click on each of the two command buttons to check that the message changes.

15. Save the project and the form using the same file name, e.g. Message.frm and Message.vbp.

> **end of Program 1.2**

Summary of key concepts

- A Visual Basic **project** (program) is made up of one or more **forms**. The project and each form must be saved as a separate file.

- To build a program you place **controls** from the toolbox onto a form. Controls are examples of **objects**. Most controls have many **event procedures**. The code inside these procedures is fired off when the particular event occurs. A common event is the Click event.

- Objects have **properties** and **methods**. A property controls the appearance and behaviour of an object whereas a method is an action that can be done on the object.

- To **compile** a program is to change the **source code** you have written into **machine code** that the computer can understand.

- It is standard practice in this book to prefix the Name property of objects that will be referred to in code by three letters that indicate the type of control, e.g. txt for a text box, cmd for a command button.

- The '=' sign is often used as an **assignment statement**. It assigns the item on its right to the item on its left, e.g. lblMessage.Caption = "Hello"

Take it from here....

1 In Windows locate the two files you saved for Program 1.2 – the project file and the form file. There is a third file called a VBW file ('W' stands for Workspace) that Visual Basic created when you saved the project file. All three are text files which Visual Basic reads when you open the program. Open each of these files in Notepad or WordPad and see if you can identify some of the pieces of information stored in them.

2. Use Visual Basic's Help to find out how it presents information about controls' properties, methods and events. Select the first item in the **Help** menu, select the **Index** tab and then type in the type of control, e.g. **CommandButton**.

3. The few properties looked at in this chapter are all examples of those that can be set at **design** time. Most design-time properties can also be set by your code at **run** time. Choose some controls and compare the properties listed in the Properties window (design-time properties) with those listed in Help. Any extra ones in Help are likely to be run-time properties only.

4. The **Object Browser** is something else you can use to look through the properties, methods and events of controls. Explore this feature of Visual Basic by selecting **View/Object Browser**.

5. Visual Basic comes with a wide variety of sample projects to explore. Where they are stored depends on which version of Visual Basic you are using. The best large-scale project is **biblio.vbp** (a Books project which uses an Access database). If you don't know where they are found click the **Start** button in Windows and then **Find/Files or Folders**. Then enter *.vbp to search for all Visual Basic project files.

6. You can make an **executable** file of a program from the **File** menu. You can run this file from Windows without Visual Basic on your computer. Make an exe file of one of your programs and try this out.

Questions on the Programs

Program 1.1

*1. Add code to display your address after your name on the form when the program runs.

End of chapter exercises

*1. Write a program that changes the title of the form to **Welcome to Visual Basic** when a command button is clicked.

*2. Put two command buttons on a form and set their captions to **Show** and **Hide**. Clicking the Show button should display a label with the message **Hello**. Clicking the Hide button should remove the label and its message. Use the label's Visible property to show and hide it.

**3. Write a program so that the words typed into a text box change to red or blue when an associated command button is clicked (see Figure 1.14). You will need to

- set a property of the text box in the Properties window to allow word-wrapping.

- assign **vbRed** or **vbBlue** in your code as appropriate to the property of the text box that determines the colour of its contents (see **Color Constants** in Visual Basic Help).

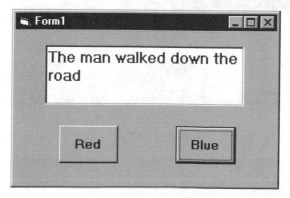

Figure 1.14: Exercise 3

Chapter 2 – Working with Controls

In Chapter 1 you used two controls from the toolbox – a label and a command button. In this chapter you will use another six controls which will allow you to design a wide range of interfaces in your programs. To get these controls to work for you requires an understanding of some of their properties, methods and events.

The Text Box

Text boxes are used for entering and displaying data. The property you will use most commonly is the **Text** property. The commonest method you will use is **SetFocus**, which positions the cursor inside the text box. If you had a text box named txtName, then the code below would print whatever has been typed into it on the form, clear its contents by setting its Text property to blank (**""**), and finally put the cursor in the text box ready for the next piece of data to be typed in.

```
Form1.Print txtName.Text
txtName.Text = ""
txtName.SetFocus
```

The List Box

Use a list box if you want to select one or more items from a list of items. Figure 2.1 shows an example of its use – the query wizard in the database package Access. The list box on the left lists the fields that can be selected. When selected they are moved to the other list box on the right.

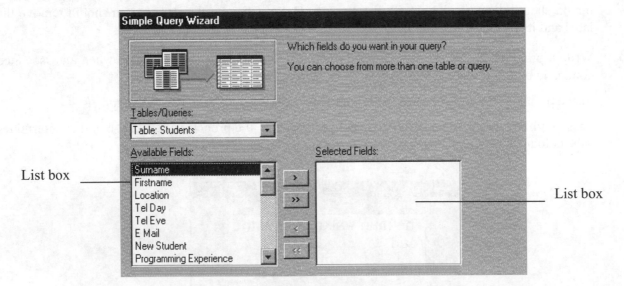

Figure 2.1

The following are the properties and methods of the list box that you will commonly use:

Properties

List	Contains all the items in the list box. The first item is indexed (numbered) by Visual Basic as 0, the next as 1 and so on.
ListCount	Contains the number of items in the list box.
ListIndex	Contains the index or number of the item currently selected. For example, if item number 6 is selected ListIndex contains 5 (since the first item is numbered as 0).
Sorted	Specifies whether the items in the list box are sorted or not.
Text	Contains the currently selected item from the list box

Methods

AddItem	Adds an item to the list box.
Clear	Removes all the items from the list box.
RemoveItem	Removes an item from the list box.

PROGRAM 2.1   *A list box of countries*

Specification	Allow the user to enter the names of countries in a text box. They should be able to click command buttons to display all the names alphabetically in a list box, to delete a selected country from the list box, or to delete all the countries from the list box.

Designing the form

1. If you have Visual Basic open already, select **File/New Project** from the main menu. Otherwise load Visual Basic from Windows. Select **Standard EXE** from the New Project window and then click **OK**.

2. Change the Caption property of the form to **Using a List Box**.

3. Drag a text box, three command buttons and a list box onto the form and position them as shown in Figure 2.2.

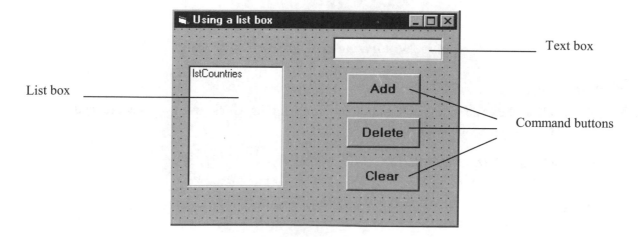

Figure 2.2: Design of program 2.1

4. Set the properties of these controls as shown in Figure 2.3. The purpose of the List property at design time is to populate the list box with items before the program runs. To do this click the small button in the List property and type in the three countries listed in Figure 2.3. Figure 2.4 shows what to do. You must press Ctrl + Enter to get to a new line.

Control	*Property*	*Property setting*
Text box	Name Text	txtCountry blank (i.e. delete *Text1*)
Command button	Name Caption	cmdAdd Add
Command button	Name Caption	cmdDelete Delete
Command button	Name Caption	cmdClear Clear
List box	Name Sorted List	lstCountries True Spain USA Austria

Figure 2.3: Design-time property settings for controls in program 2.1

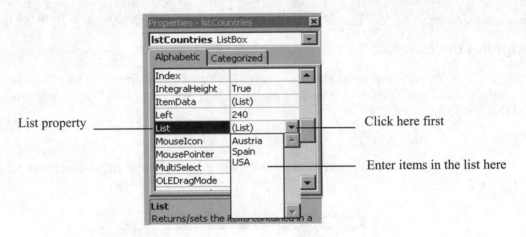

List property — List property

Click here first

Enter items in the list here

Figure 2.4: Entering items into the List property

Coding

5. Double-click the Add command button to bring up its Click event procedure code template. Complete the code as shown below.

```
Private Sub cmdAdd_Click()
   lstCountries.AddItem txtCountry.Text  'add contents of text box to list
                                         'box display

   txtCountry.Text = ""                  'clear the text box
   txtCountry.SetFocus        'put cursor in text box ready for next country
End Sub
```

6. Get the code template for the Click event of the Delete command button. As you are currently in the Code window you can click the Object list box (Figure 1.9) and then click cmdDelete from the drop-down list of controls on your form. Alternatively you could return to the form by clicking the View Object button in the Project Explorer (Figure 1.6) and double-clicking the Delete command button.

7. Enter the code below.

```
Private Sub cmdDelete_Click()
    lstCountries.RemoveItem lstCountries.ListIndex 'delete selected item
End Sub                                            'from list of displayed items
```

The RemoveItem method is told what to delete by giving it the value of the list box's ListIndex property. This contains the number of the current selected item. Items are numbered from 0.

8. Get the code template for the Click event of the Clear command button and enter the following:

```
Private Sub cmdClear_Click()
    lstCountries.Clear              'delete all items displayed in list box
End Sub
```

Running the program

9. Run the program by selecting **Run/Start** or clicking the **Start** button on the toolbar. Enter several country names into the text box and click the Add button after each one. The names will be displayed in alphabetical order in the list box because its Sorted property is set to True. If you fill the list box a scroll bar will automatically be added. Try out the Delete button.

end of Program 2.1

The Combo Box

The term 'combo box' is short for 'combination box' because this control combines the features of the text box and the list box. You use exactly the same properties and methods described earlier for the list box to make a combo box work. The two main differences between combo and list boxes are:

- With some types of combo box you can edit any of the displayed items or type in an item that is not listed.

- The standard combo box must be clicked to reveal its items. It therefore takes up less room on a form.

Examples of combo boxes can be found on Word's Formatting toolbar, and two of these are shown in Figure 2.5. By clicking the small button the list of fonts is revealed. If the one you wish to use is not listed you can type it in the edit part of the combo box and Word might be able to switch to it. The list of font sizes does not include every number. Again you enter the number you want in the edit part.

The Option Button

Option buttons are used to allow the user to select one option from two or more options. A common example is Word's four options when you wish to print a document, as shown in Figure 2.6. You can only select one of these four.

Edit part of the
combo box

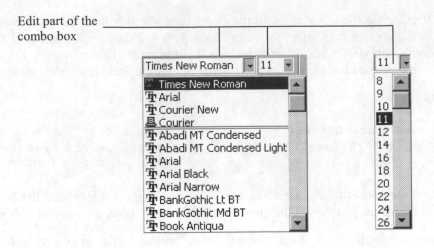

Figure 2.5: Combo boxes on Word's Formatting toolbar

Note the following about the option button:

Properties   Apart from the Name and Caption properties, the most useful property is **Value**. It holds True if the option button is selected or False if it is not selected. You need to understand about selection in Chapter 4 to use this property.

Methods   You are most unlikely to use these.

Events   The **Click** event is the only one you are likely to use.

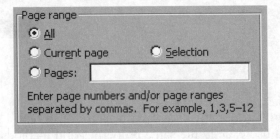

Figure 2.6: Option buttons when printing from Word

The Check Box

The check box is similar to the option button in that you can test its Value property to see if it is selected. Unlike the option button you can select more than one at a time. A common use of check boxes in Windows applications is setting general default values through the **Tools/Options** menu. Figure 2.7 shows an example from the spreadsheet Excel. All but two of the check boxes in this example have been selected.

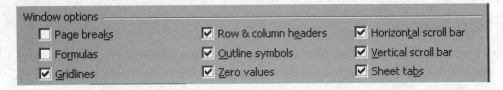

Figure 2.7: An example of the use of check boxes in Excel

The check box has similar properties and methods to the option button. However its **Value** property stores 1 if the check box is selected (and 0 if not selected), rather than True as with the option button. Like the option button, the commonest event you're likely to use is the Click event.

The Frame

The frame is a rectangular shape in which you usually place other controls. In Figure 2.6, for example, four option buttons are contained inside a frame with the caption Page Range. The advantages of using a frame are:

- You can reposition all the controls inside it at design time by moving the frame only.
- You can show or hide all the controls inside it at run-time by showing or hiding the frame only.
- If you want two or more groups of option buttons, so that one can be selected from each group, then you *must* put each group into a frame. Without the frames you could only select one button from all the buttons in all the groups.

You are most unlikely ever to use the frame's methods and events. The **Visible** property can be a useful one. It can hold True or False. Set it to False to hide the frame and all its controls.

PROGRAM 2.2   *Option buttons, check boxes and frames*

Specification   Demonstrate the use of two groups of option buttons and a group of check boxes

1. Open a new project and change the form's Caption property from Form1 to **Option buttons, check boxes and frames**.

2. Drag a frame control from the toolbox and position and size it as shown in Figure 2.8. Change its Caption to **Gender**.

3. Place two option buttons on the frame as shown below. Draw them as rectangles in order to reveal their captions. Change their Names to **optMale** and **optFemale** and their Captions to **Male** and **Female**.

Note: If you had first placed the option buttons outside the frame and then moved them onto the frame, they would not 'belong' to it. You must drag them straight from the toolbox to the frame.

4. Move the frame and both option buttons should move with it.

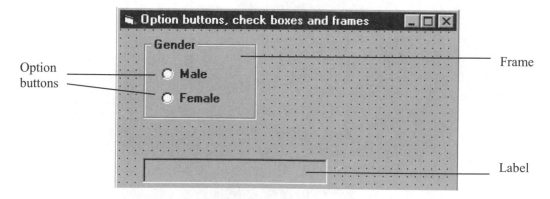

Option buttons

Frame

Label

Figure 2.8: Design of program 2.2

5. Place a label below the frame. Set its Name to **lblSelection**, its Caption to blank and its BorderStyle to **1 - Fixed Single**.

6. Double-click the Male option button to bring up the code template for its default event procedure, the Click event. Type in the code below:

```
lblSelection.Caption = "You selected Male"
```

7. Get the Click code template for the Female option button and enter the code:

```
lblSelection.Caption = "You selected Female"
```

8. Run the program and try out the two option buttons.

9. Place another frame on the form and change its Caption to **Age** as shown in Figure 2.9.

10. Place three option buttons in this frame. Keep the default Names but change their captions to those in Figure 2.9.

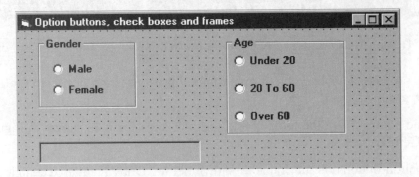

Figure 2.9

11. Run the program to demonstrate that you can select one option from each of the two groups.

12. Place a third frame on the form and change its Caption to **Replies** as shown in Figure 2.10.

13. Place three check boxes on the frame and set their Captions as shown in Figure 2.10.

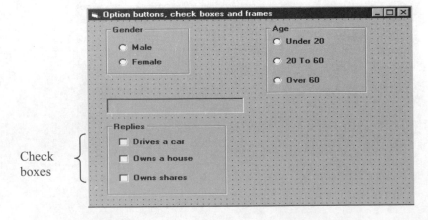

Figure 2.10

14. Run the program and select as few or as many check boxes as you wish.

end of Program 2.2

The Timer

The Timer is one of several toolbox controls that are not visible at run time, which means that you can place it anywhere on the form. It does only one thing: it checks the system clock. It has no methods but two important properties. These are:

Enabled   This holds True or False. An enabled timer is able to carry out what you have coded in its Timer event (see below), but a disabled timer cannot.

Interval   This is measured in milliseconds. A value of 1000 represents 1000 milliseconds or 1 second.

The Timer has only one event, called the **Timer** event. If the timer is enabled, when the time represented by its Interval property has elapsed, it generates its own Timer event. For example, an Interval value of 500 would call the Timer event every half a second.

PROGRAM 2.3   *Displaying the time*

Specification   Display the time to the nearest second on a form

1. Open a new project. Place two labels on the form. Set the Caption of the left label to **The time is**. Delete the Caption of the right label, set its Name to **lblTime** (see Figure 2.11) and its Style property to **1 – Fixed Single**.

2. Place a timer control anywhere on the form. Set its Name to **tmrTimer** and its Interval property to **1000** so that the Timer event is called every second.

3. Double-click the timer to bring up the code template for its Timer event. Add the line of code that follows:

```
Private Sub tmrTimer_Timer()
   lblTime.Caption = Time          'display current time in the label
End Sub
```

Time is the first example of a Visual Basic **function** you have met. A function is a piece of code built into Visual Basic that returns a value, in this case the current time. You will meet many more functions throughout this book.

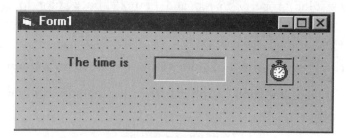

Figure 2.11: Design of program 2.3

4. Run the program. You can't see the timer but the time should 'tick' away to the nearest second.

End of Program 2.3

The Scroll Bars

The toolbox has a **horizontal scroll bar** and a **vertical scroll bar**. They are identical except for their orientation on a form. They are used to increase or decrease a value. They have starting and finishing values, represented by the two ends of the scroll bar, and all the values in between. A scroll box is moved between the two ends to set the value.

Scroll bars have no important methods but the most useful properties and events are:

Properties

Max   The highest value, represented by the right side of a horizontal scroll bar or the bottom of a vertical scroll bar.

Min   The lowest value.

Value   The number represented by the current position of the scroll box – between Min and Max.

Events

Change   Occurs when the Value property changes at run time. This in turn results from the user moving the scroll box. The event is triggered *after* the user has moved the scroll box. This is the scroll bar's default event.

Scroll   Similar to the Change event but is triggered *as* the user moves the scroll box.

PROGRAM 2.4   *Changing a form's colour using scroll bars*

> **Specification**   Use three horizontal scroll bars so that the form's colour changes as the user moves their scroll boxes.

To understand how this program works you need to understand the Visual Basic function **RGB** (which stands for **R**ed, **G**reen, **B**lue). The function provides a colour by mixing proportions of these three primary colours. Each of the three colours can have a value from 0 to 255. So the code

```
Form1.BackColor = RGB(255, 0, 0)
Form2.BackColor = RGB(0, 255, 0)
Form3.BackColor = RGB(125, 125, 125)
```

would set Form1's BackColor property to red and Form2's BackColor to green. Form3 gets equal amounts of the three colours to produce a grey. The three numbers given to the function are called **arguments** or **parameters**.

1. Open a new project and set the form's Caption to **Change the form's colour**.

2. Place three labels and three horizontal scroll bars from the toolbox onto the form as shown in Figure 2.12.

3. Change the Captions of the labels to **Red, Green, Blue**.

4. Name the scroll bars **hsbRed, hsbGreen** and **hsbBlue** as appropriate.

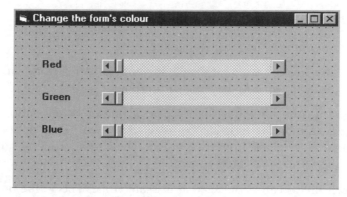

Figure 2.12: Design of program 2.4

5. As the default **Min** property of a scroll bar is 0 leave this alone. Set the **Max** property of the scroll bars to **255**. To set all three at once select one of them and, with the Shift key pressed down, select the other two. When you have two or more controls selected the Properties window lists those properties that the controls have in common.

We will use the Scroll event rather than the Change event for each scroll bar to change the form's colour as this will give a more continuous change. Since the Change event is the default event, double-clicking the control on the form will bring up the wrong code template. There are two methods of getting the code template for an event that is not the default one. Steps 6 and 7 cover both methods.

6. Click the View Code button in the Project Explorer (see Figure 1.6) to bring up the Code window. From the drop-down list at the top left select **hsbRed**. You're given its default Change event template. From the right hand drop-down list select **Scroll** and you'll get the code template you want. You can delete the code template for the unwanted Change event. Make sure the code is as follows:

```
Private Sub hsbRed_Scroll
   Form1.BackColor = RGB(hsbRed.Value, hsbGreen.Value, hsbBlue.Value)
End Sub
```

The three arguments passed to RGB are the numbers (from 0 to 255) stored in the Value property of each of the scroll bars.

7. As an alternative to getting a code template you can type it in yourself. Press Enter a couple of times and then type in the three lines below for the second scroll bar.

```
Private Sub hsbGreen_Scroll
   Form1.BackColor = RGB(hsbRed.Value, hsbGreen.Value, hsbBlue.Value)
End Sub
```

8. Repeat either step 6 or 7 for **hsbBlue**.

9. Run the program and as you move the scroll boxes the form's colour will change. You will use this program again in program 7.1 so make sure you save it.

End of Program 2.4

Summary of key concepts

- The **text box** is used for entering and displaying data.

- The **list box** and **combo box** are used for displaying a list of items from which the user can select an item. With a combo box you can edit the items at run-time.

- Two or more **option button**s allow the user to select an option. If the option buttons are not grouped on a frame only one button on the form can be selected at once. When option buttons are grouped on frames one button can be selected from each group. The **Value** property holds True if the button is selected and False otherwise.

- Any number of **check box**es can be selected at the same time. The **Value** property holds 1 if the box is selected and 0 otherwise.

- A **frame** is often used to hold groups of option buttons or check boxes. If a frame is moved or made invisible, then all its controls move or become invisible.

- A **timer** has a Timer event that is called after an elapse of time equivalent to its **Interval** property value. The **Enabled** property of the timer must be True for the Timer event to be called. An Interval value of 1000 represents 1000 milliseconds or 1 second.

- A Visual Basic **function** returns a value. Some functions do not require any **arguments** or **parameters** to work (e.g. the Time function). Others require one or more arguments (e.g. RGB).

Take it from here...

1. The **Style** property of a list box has two settings. The default one used in this chapter is **0 – Standard**. Experiment using the other style, **1 – Checkbox**.

2. The **Style** property of the combo box has three settings. Experiment using each of these.

3. Drop two option buttons on a form and set their **Style** property to **1- Graphical**. Run the program to find out how this style differs from the standard one.

4. The Value property of the list box and check box can be True or False. The check box also has a third setting. Investigate what this does.

5. Investigate the **SmallChange** and **LargeChange** properties of scroll bars.

6. Investigate the similarities and differences between the **Image** and **Picture** controls on the toolbox.

7. The RGB function has a simpler sister function called **QBColor**. Investigate this function.

8. Three controls that are non-standard and must be added to the toolbox are the **Slider**, **ProgressBar** and **TabStrip** controls. Select **Project/Component** from the menu and in the Components dialog box click the check box with **Microsoft Windows Common Controls** (plus the version of Visual Basic you are using). Note you should not select *Microsoft Windows Common Controls-2*. Click **OK** and several controls will be added to the toolbox, including the three mentioned above. Experiment using these controls using Help to find out about their important properties and methods.

Questions on the Programs

Program 2.1

*1. Run the program and do the following:

- Enter **turkey** (with a lower case 't'). Then click the Add button.
- Enter **austria** (with a lower case 'a'). Then click the Add button.
- With no data in the text box click the Add button.

What can you conclude about the Sorted property of a list box from these three examples?

*2. In Program 2.1 you could select only one item from the list box. The **MultiSelect** property allows you to select more than one. It has two types of multi-selection. Try out both types.

**3. Add labels below the list box to display the number of countries currently in the list box and the name of the country currently selected.

Program 2.2

*1. Add another label below the Age frame to indicate which of its option buttons is currently selected.

*2. Make the Age frame (and the label in question 1 above if you added this) invisible when the program runs. When the user first selects a gender option make this frame (and label) appear.

Program 2.4

*1. To the right of each scroll bar place a label to display the current position of the bar's scroll box (i.e. a value from 0 to 255).

*2. To see the difference between the Scroll and Change events change the first line of **hsbRed**'s Scroll event so that it is a Change event. Run the program and move the scroll box in this scroll bar.

End of chapter exercises

*1. Use a vertical scroll bar to simulate volume control on a radio. Use three option buttons which will position the scroll box at one-third, half and two-thirds the volume when they are clicked.

**2. Build a program using two list boxes as shown in Figure 2.13. One of these, called lstEmployees, lists all the employees in a firm. The other, called lstExcursion, lists those employees taking part in the firm's annual outing. Populate lstEmployees at design time using its List property. When the program runs the user can click a button to copy the selected name from lstEmployees to lstExcursion. A second button should let them delete a name from lstExcursion in case they have made a mistake. Display the number of people on the firm's excursion.

**3. Build a program to implement the two list boxes shown in Figure 2.1. Items can be moved between the two list boxes. You will only be able to move one item at a time rather than the two or more which this actual example allows because you have not done Chapter 4 yet. In Figure 2.1 the lower two buttons, which move items from the right list box to the left one, are dimmed because there are no items to move in this direction. Find out which command button property allows this and disable the appropriate button on your form. As soon as an item is moved into the right list box, allow the button to be used. (You won't be able to enable it when the right list box becomes empty again without knowing about selection, covered in Chapter 4.)

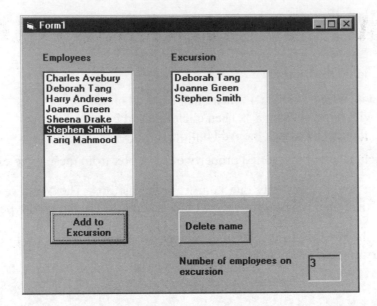

Figure 2.13: Exercise 2

***4.** Build a simple text editor as shown in Figure 2.14. The user writes in the large text box and can change this to bold and/or italics by clicking the check boxes, and they can alter the font size by using a combo box. You need to use the **FontBold**, **FontItalic** and **FontSize** run-time properties of the text box to do this.

To get the command buttons working you need to find out about the **Clipboard** object. In a Windows application when you copy or cut something, it is saved in an area of RAM known as the Clipboard. You will need to use three of the Clipboard's methods called **Clear**, **SetText** and **GetText**. You will also need the **SelTest** property of the text box.

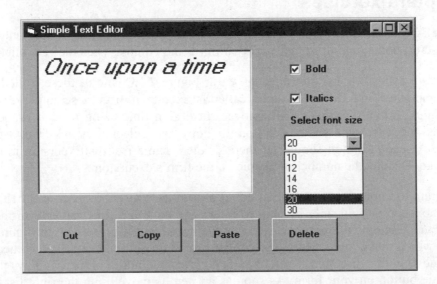

Figure 2.14: Exercise 4

Chapter 3 – Working with Data

Variables

When a program runs, any data that it uses must be stored in RAM. A variable is a name made up by the programmer to identify the address in RAM where a particular piece of data is stored. Our programs so far have managed to avoid using variables but this restricts what can be done. For example, the code

```
Form1.Print txtNumber.Text
```

displays whatever the user has typed into the textbox txtNumber. But to *store* what is in the textbox and use what is stored after the user has typed something else into the text box, we would need a variable.

Data Types

Every variable must be of a given **data type**. The main data types you will use in your Visual Basic work are summarised in Figure 3.1.

Data type	Used for storing...	Possible stored values	Storage required (bytes)
Integer	Whole numbers, e.g.8, 453	-32,768 to +32,767	2
Long	Whole numbers	-2,147,483,648 to +2,147,483,648 (approx. –2 billion to +2 billion)	4
Single	Numbers with decimal places, e.g. 4.76, 98.00	Very large range indeed, from very small to very large	4
Currency	Numbers with 4 decimal places, e.g. 34.8765. Monetary values	Very large range indeed, but not very small numbers	8
String	One or more characters	Any characters	1 per character
Date	Dates and time	Dates from 1 Jan. 100 to 31 Dec. 9999 Time from 0:00:00 to 23:59:59	8
Boolean	True or false values	True, False	2

Figure 3.1: Summary of the main data types

Declaring variables

To declare a variable means to tell Visual Basic two things about it:

- Its name or **identifier**.
- Its **data type**.

The Dim statement

Use the keywords **Dim** and **As** when you declare a variable. The code below declares three variables of different data types.

```
Dim Number As Integer
Dim Payment As Currency
Dim DateOfPayment As Date
```

Note

- Always use meaningful identifiers. The three variables could have been declared as A, B and C but these would tell you nothing about what they are supposed to store.
- Identifiers cannot have spaces. When you use two or more words you could join each by an underscore, e.g. date_of_payment, or you could omit the underscores and make each start with an upper case letter, e.g. DateOfPayment. In this book underscores are not used and single-word variable identifiers will begin with an upper case letter (except when naming controls with their prefix).

Option Explicit

Using the declaration above, suppose you later assigned the following values to your variables:

```
Number = 24                'programmer assigns value to variable
Payment = txtPay.Text      'value assigned from user input
Name = txtCustomer.Text    'value assigned from user input
```

Whether Visual Basic will accept the third assignment given that you have not declared the variable *Name* will depend on whether or not you use **Option Explicit**:

- If you *do not* use Option Explicit you do not need to declare a variable before using it.
- If you *do* use Option Explicit you must declare a variable before using it.

A good rule is always declare a variable before using it. If you don't then your code is more likely to contain errors that are hard to spot. You can do this in two ways:

- Write Option Explicit before declaring your variables, e.g.

```
Option Explicit
Dim Number As Integer
'other variable declarations
```

- Select **Tools/Options** and click the check box **Require Variable Declaration**. Visual Basic will automatically put Option Explicit at the head of the Code window the next time you open this window.

1. Select **Tools/Options** and tell Visual Basic that you want to be made to declare your variables.

PROGRAM 3.1   *Add two numbers*

Specification	Allow the user to enter two numbers and display their sum.

You could get input from the user using two text boxes, but this program will introduce you to another method of getting simple input, the **input box**.

1. Open a new project and get to its Code window by clicking the **View Code** button in the Project Explorer (see Figure 1.6).

2. If you told Visual Basic above to make you declare your variables, the words **Option Explicit** should be there. If you did not then write them in yourself now (see code in step 3).

3. Note the word **General** in the Object list box at the top left. The General part of any form code is where you declare your variables (though see the later section on Scope of Variables). Declare the following:

```
Option Explicit
Dim FirstNumber As Integer        'stores the first number
Dim SecondNumber As Integer       'stores the second number
Dim Total As Integer              'stores sum of the 2 numbers
```

4. Get the form's Load event code template by clicking **Form** in the Object list box (Figure 1.9) and type in:

```
Private Sub Form_Load()
   Form1.Show
   FirstNumber = InputBox("Enter your first number")
   SecondNumber = InputBox("Enter your second number")
   Total = FirstNumber + SecondNumber
   Print "The total is", Total
End Sub
```

Note:

- The words in brackets after InputBox will be displayed in the input box.
- You assign whatever the user types into an input box directly to a variable.
- FirstNumber + SecondNumber adds the contents of the two variables (and not their names!).
- The Print statement has two parts separated by a comma. The part inside quotation marks is output as it stands. The part not in quotation marks, Total, outputs the *contents* of this variable.

5. Run the program. The input box below will appear first (Figure 3.2). Type in a small number and click **OK**. Another input box appears asking for the second number.

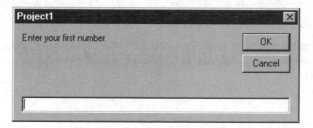

Figure 3.2: The first input box

6. Run the program again and this time enter a number that is too big for FirstNumber to hold, (Figure 3.1 shows that Integer values can go up to 32767), a situation called **overflow**. You will get a run-time error message. Click **Debug** and you'll be taken back to the code, with the line that caused the error highlighted in yellow. Select **Run/End** to stop the program or **Run/Restart** to start it again.

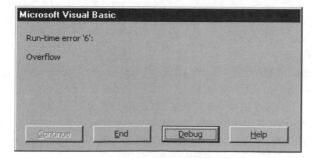

Figure 3.3: The run-time error message indicating overflow

To add numbers that are too large for Integers you must declare the variables as Long instead.

end of Program 3.1

Scope of variables

The **scope** of a variable refers to the part of the program that can use it. There are two main types of scope:

- **global**
- **local**

Global scope

A form variable with global scope can be used anywhere on the form, i.e. in any of its event procedures. In program 3.1 the variables were declared in the General part of the program and this gives them global scope throughout Form1. The code inside the form's Load event used them, and so could code in any other event procedure we might have on Form1.

Local scope

Local variables are declared inside a procedure and can be used only by code inside that procedure. In program 3.1 we could have declared the variables inside the form's Load event instead of in the General part of the code. A good rule is **always declare variables with as narrow a scope as possible**. It will lead to fewer errors.

It is possible to give a global variable and a local variable the same identifier. Program 3.2 shows what happens in this situation.

PROGRAM 3.2 *Illustrating global and local scope*

Specification Demonstrate the difference between a global variable and a local variable

1. Open a new project. Place a command button on the form and name it **cmdOK**.

2. In the General section of the Code window declare a global variable:

```
Dim Surname As String
```

3. In the form's Load event procedure make sure the code is as follows:

```
Private Sub Form_Load()
   Form1.Show
   Surname = "Green"
   Form1.Print "The global variable stores "; Surname
End Sub
```

The semi-colon (;) in the Print command prints the contents of Surname directly after the part inside quotes (rather than leaving a few spaces which was the output in program 3.1).

4. In the Click event procedure of the command button declare a local variable using the same identifier as the global one and display its contents:

```
Private Sub cmdOK_Click()
   Dim Surname As String
   Surname = "Brown"
   Form1.Print "The local variable stores "; Surname
End Sub
```

5. Run the program. The name 'Green' is printed on the form, since the global variable is being accessed by the form's Load event. Click the button and 'Brown' is now printed since the local variable is now being used (Figure 3.4).

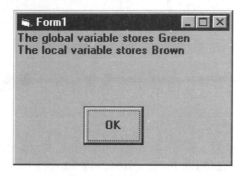

Figure 3.4: Program 3.2

Static variables

Variables no longer exist when they go out of scope. A global variable ceases to exist when the form is closed and a local variable ceases when its event procedure has finished. Sometimes you need to keep the value stored in a local variable until the next time the event in which it is declared is called. You need to declare the local variable as **static** as the next program shows.

PROGRAM 3.3   *Using a static variable*

Specification   Demonstrate the use of a static variable

1. Open a new project. Place a command button on the form and name it **cmdOK**.

2. Make sure the button's Click event code is as follows:

```
Private Sub cmdOK_Click()
   Dim Number As Integer
   Number = Number + 1                    'add 1 to Number
   Form1.Print "Number of clicks = "; Number  'display number of clicks
End Sub
```

3. Run the program and click the button a few times. The printed message will keep saying you have only clicked the button once (Figure 3.5 left). Between each click Number ceases to exist and its contents are lost.

4. Change the word **Dim** to **Static** and run the program again. This time the correct number of clicks is displayed (Figure 3.5 right).

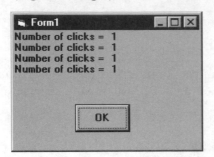 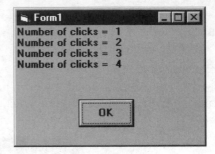

Figure 3.5: Program 3.3

end of Program 3.3

Constants

You can store a new value in a variable whenever this is appropriate. In program 3.3 the value of Number increased by 1 each time the user clicked the button. Instead of a variable use a **constant** when

- the user does not provide the value, and
- you don't want the value to change.

For example, if the basic tax rate is 25p in the pound then you could declare it as a constant as follows:

```
Const TaxRate = 0.25          'use = sign when declaring a constant
```

If you try to assign to TaxRate another value such as 0.28 later in the program, an error results.

Arithmetic operations on data

Arithmetic can be done with variables belonging to all the data types listed at the start of this chapter except String.

Types of operation

There are 8 of these, as listed in Figure 3.6.

Operator	Visual Basic	Order of precedence
Addition	+	6=
Subtraction	-	6=
Multiplication	*	3=
Division	/	3=
Integer division	\	4
Modulus	Mod	5
Negation	-	2
Exponentiation	^	1

Figure 3.6: The arithmetic operators

The program below would produce the output shown in Figure 3.7:

```
Private Sub Form_Load()
   Const A = 6
   Const B = 4
   Form1.Show
   Form1.Print "A + B = "; A + B
   Form1.Print "A - B = "; A - B
   Form1.Print "A x B = "; A * B
   Form1.Print "A / B = "; A / B
   Form1.Print "A \ B = "; A \ B
   Form1.Print "A modulus B = "; A Mod B
   Form1.Print " A to the power B = "; A ^ B
End Sub
```

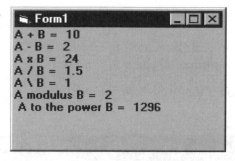

Figure 3.7

Note the following:

- Ordinary division (/) produces a number with a decimal place.
- Integer division (\) produces a whole number. The decimal part is removed.
- Modulus gives the remainder after the first number is divided by the second number, e.g. 6 Mod 6 = 0, 6 Mod 8 = 6, 12 Mod 5 = 2.

Order of precedence

This is shown in Figure 3.6. It tells us the order in which Visual Basic carries out the operations. Look at the following program and the output in Figure 3.8.

```
Private Sub Form_Load()
   Const A = 10
   Const B = 4
   Const C = 6
   Form1.Show
   Form1.Print "B + C * A = "; B + C * A
   Form1.Print "A / B * C / B = "; A / B * C / B
   Form1.Print "(A / B) * (C / B) = "; (A / B) * (C / B)
End Sub
```

In the first expression C * A is done first rather than B + C. In the second expression the three operations are done in the order written since division and multiplication have equal precedence. In the third expression the divisions are done before multiplication because of the brackets.

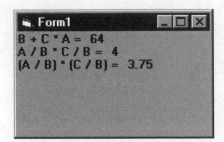

Figure 3.8

PROGRAM 3.4   *Calculating the average exam mark*

Specification   Allow the user to enter as many exam marks as they wish and display them in a list box. The program finishes when the user clicks a button to show the average mark

Although the processing in this program is quite simple, we'll use this example as an opportunity to learn more about how the interface of a form can behave at run-time

1.   Open a new project. Place on it the two labels, two text boxes, three command buttons and a list box as shown in Figure 3.9.

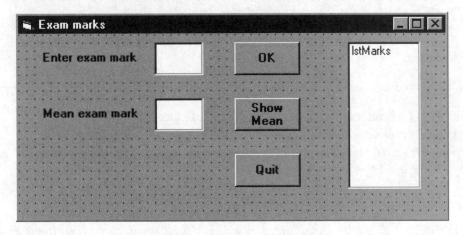

Figure 3.9: Design of program 3.4

2.   Set the properties of these controls as listed in Figure 3.10. Note:

- The OK button processes a mark but the user should not be able to click it until they have entered a mark. Setting its Enabled property to False does this. The same applies to the Show Mean button.
- Before the user enters a mark the text box (and label) to display the mean can be hidden. Setting its Visible property does this.

3.   Two variables will hold the number of marks entered and the total of all the marks. These must be global because they will be used by the Click event procedures of two of the command buttons. Declare them as follows in the General section:

```
Option Explicit
Dim Total As Integer            'stores running total of marks
Dim NumberOfMarks As Integer    'stores number of exam marks entered
```

Control	*Property*	*Property setting*
Form	Caption	Exam marks
Label	Caption	Enter exam mark
Label	Name Caption Visible	lblMean Mean exam mark False
Text box	Name Text	txtMark Blank
Text box	Name Text Visible	txtMean Blank False
Command button	Name Caption Enabled	cmdOK OK False
Command button	Name Caption Enabled	cmdShowMean Show Mean False
Command button	Name Caption	cmdQuit Quit
List box	Name	lstMarks

Figure 3.10: Design-time property settings for controls in program 3.4

4.   Since these two variables store running totals **initialise** them to 0 in the form's Load event:

```
Private Sub Form_Load()
   Total = 0
   NumberOfMarks = 0
End Sub
```

Strictly speaking this is not necessary since Visual Basic initialises Integers to 0 when it creates them. It is a good practice to adopt, however, since you may wish to initialise numbers, or variables of other data types, to something other than 0.

When the OK button is clicked the following must happen:

- The Show Mean button must be enabled so the user can find the mean.
- The exam mark entered by the user must be removed.
- The cursor must be positioned ready for the next exam mark

5.   Type in the code below for the Click event of the cmdOK button.

```
Private Sub cmdOK_Click()
   Dim Number As Integer
   Number = txtMark.Text                      'read exam mark
   lstMarks.AddItem Number                    'copy it to list box
   Total = Total + Number                     'add it to running total of marks
   NumberOfMarks = NumberOfMarks + 1          'increase number of marks by 1
   cmdShowMean.Enabled = True                 'enable the Show Mean button
   txtMark.Text = ""                          'clear out the old exam mark
   txtMark.SetFocus                           'place cursor ready for next mark
End Sub
```

Note in the second line that Visual Basic automatically converts the mark entered by the user in txtMark, which is stored as text in its Text property, into an Integer.

6. When the Show Mean button is clicked, the text box (and label) to display the mean must be made visible. If the user clicks the OK button again there will not be a number to process and a run-time error will result. We should disable it. So type the following into the Click event of cmdShowMean:

```
Private Sub cmdShowMean_Click()
   Dim Mean As Single           'declare local variable
   Mean = Total / NumberOfMarks 'calculate mean mark and
   txtMean.Text = Mean          'display it
   txtMean.Visible = True       'show text box which displays mean
   lblMean.Visible = True       'and show its label
   txtMark.Enabled = False      'disallow more marks to be entered
   cmdOK.Enabled = False        'and disable OK button
End Sub
```

7. When the Quit button is clicked the program should close. In the Click event procedure for cmdQuit type in:

```
Private Sub cmdQuit_Click()
   Unload Form1                 'removes form from memory
End Sub
```

8. Run the program and enter an exam mark. There's a problem – the OK button is disabled so the mark cannot be processed! We disabled it at design time so that the user could not accidentally click it before a mark had been entered. The **Change** event for the text box where a mark is entered can handle this. This event occurs as soon as the first digit is typed in.

9. In the Change event procedure for txtMark enter the code below and then run the program again.

```
Private Sub txtMark_Change()
   cmdOK.Enabled = True
End Sub
```

The program outputs the mean with up to 6 decimal places. It's unlikely you'd want more than one decimal place displayed here. The next section tells you how to do this.

end of Program 3.4

Displaying output

In this section we'll look at formatting numbers and currency and at a method for joining strings together. Chapter 6 looks at formatting dates and times and reviews a number of string-handling functions.

The Format function

The **Format** function is used for formatting numbers and currency. Give it two arguments:

- The expression to be formatted. This would usually be a numeric constant such as 45.86 or a variable.
- An indication, inside quotation marks, of how to format the expression. This could be a **named numeric format** or a **user-defined numeric format**.

The program below uses a variety of named and user-defined numeric formats and it produces the output shown in Figure 3.11. If you wish to run this program type it in the form's Load event procedure.

```
Const Number = 52478.3296
Form1.Show
Form1.Print "Using named numeric formats"
Form1.Print "    General Number    "; Format(Number, "General Number")
Form1.Print "    Fixed             "; Format(Number, "Fixed")
Form1.Print "    Standard          "; Format(Number, "Standard")
Form1.Print "    Percent           "; Format(0.175, "Percent")
Form1.Print "    Currency          "; Format(Number, "Currency")
Form1.Print
Form1.Print "Using user-defined numeric formats"
Form1.Print "0                     "; Format(Number, "0")
Form1.Print "0.00                  "; Format(Number, "0.00")
Form1.Print "###.00                "; Format(Number, "###.00")
Form1.Print "#,##0.0               "; Format(Number, "#,##0.0")
Form1.Print "###.00                "; Format(Number, "###.00")
Form1.Print "£#,##0.00             "; Format(Number, "£#,##0.00")
Form1.Print "0.0%                  "; Format(0.175, "0.0%")
```

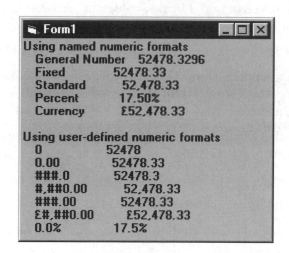

Figure 3.11

There are enough examples here for you to find or work out a format that covers any numeric output you are likely to require. Use this as a reference to return to when the need arises.

In program 3.4 to output the average exam mark with one decimal place, you could not use any of the named formats as these output at least two decimal places. The third user-defined format above shows how to display one decimal place. So in the Click event for cmdShowMean you would write:

```
txtMean.Text = Format(Mean, "0.0")
```

Joining strings together (concatenation)

To **concatenate** two or more smaller strings to form one larger one you use the ampersand operator (&). The code below concatenates two names into one.

```
FirstName = txtFirstName.Text
Surname = txtSurname.Text
lblFullName.Caption = FirstName & " " & Surname    '2 ampersands needed
                'to produce a space between the two parts of the full name
```

Summary of key concepts

- A **variable** is a name made up by the programmer to identify the address in RAM where a particular piece of data is stored.

- Every variable must be of a particular **data type**. The main data types are **Integer**, **Long** (for storing whole numbers), **Single** (decimal numbers), **Currency** (monetary values or numbers with a fixed number of decimal places), **String** (text), **Date** (date and time) and **Boolean** (true or false).

- To declare a variable use the syntax **Dim *identifier* As *data type*,** e.g. Dim Number As Integer.

- Always use **Option Explicit** as this forces you to declare variables before using them.

- **Overflow** is caused by trying to store a number that is too large for its data type. It will result in a run-time error.

- The **scope** of a variable refers to the part of the program that can use it. **Global** variables on a form can be used by all procedures on a form. **Local** variables are declared inside a procedure and can only be used by code within that procedure.

- A good rule is always declare variables with as narrow a scope as possible.

- Form global variables exist until the form closes. Local variables exist until the procedure in which they are declared finishes. However a **Static** local variable keeps its contents between calls to the procedure in which it is declared.

- A **constant** holds a value that cannot be changed during the program. The declaration syntax is **Const *identifier* = *value*,** e.g. Const Number = 20.

- **Arithmetic operators** have an order of precedence. You can change the order by using brackets.

- Use the **Format** function to display numbers and currency.

- Joining strings together is called **concatenation**. Use the ampersand (&) operator to do this.

Take it from here...

1. Four data types not covered in this chapter are **Byte**, **Double**, **Object** and **Variant**. Investigate these.

2. Until Visual Basic 6 the Format function was the only one available for formatting numbers. This version introduced three more – **FormatCurrency**, **FormatNumber** and **FormatPercent**. If you have the appropriate version of Visual Basic investigate these functions.

3. There is a right and wrong way to declare two or more Integers (or any data type) on the same line:

```
Dim FirstNumber As Integer, SecondNumber As Integer    'correct way
Dim FirstNumber, SecondNumber As Integer               'incorrect way
```

The incorrect way would not store FirstNumber as an Integer. Which data type would it be stored as, and how might you prove that is was not stored as an Integer?

4. You could replace the word Dim when declaring a form's global variable with **Public** or **Private**. Find out how these would affect the variable's scope.

5. There is an alternative concatenation operator to the ampersand – the plus sign (+). It usually works well but what would happen in the following situation? Explain the result.

```
Dim Number As Integer
Dim RoadName As String
Number = 10
RoadName = "The High Street"
Form1.Print Number & " " & RoadName
Form1.Print Number + " " + RoadName
```

6. Visual Basic has a range of functions to convert numeric variables from one data type to another. One of these is **CInt** which converts a non-Integer to an Integer (if possible). Investigate these.

Questions on the Programs

Program 3.1

*1. Change the program to add three numbers rather than two.

Program 3.2

*1. Change the output to a single line –**Your name is Joe Black**. The first name should be stored during the form's Load event and the surname during the button's Click event. You will need to use the concatenation operator for the output.

Program 3.3

*1. Using your knowledge of scope, there is another way of displaying the correct number of times the user has clicked the button without using the keyword Static. Change the code to do this.

Program 3.4

*1. If the user enters a lot of exam marks it can be tiresome having to click the OK button after each one. It would be easier to press Enter instead. Find out which property of the command button to set at design time to allow this.

**2. The user can enter one set of exam marks, find their average and then the program ends. Change it so that the user can enter as many sets of marks as they wish. Add a Clear command button to begin the new set of marks. Display only the current set of marks in the list box.

***3. The marks are displayed in a list box. Add a text box and display them here too. The problem is getting the marks displayed on separate lines. If you know about ASCII codes (covered in Chapter 6) use the **Chr** function with the code for a new line (you'll have to research into this). If you get the text box working, fill it with numbers and compare it with a list box for displaying output.

End of chapter exercises

Note: in questions 2 and 3 you will need to repeat code in some of the event procedures. This is not considered good programming, but the way of avoiding this is not covered until Chapter 14.

*1.   Users are asked to enter the names and ages (whole numbers) of their two children. Display a message such as **Sally and Paul have an average age of 11.5 years**.

*2.   Allow the user to enter a series of numbers in a text box (like the exam marks in program 3.4). Clicking a button between numbers displays their running total. Use a static variable for the running total.

**3.   Figure 3.12 shows the program in action. Allow the user to enter the numeric values for A, B and C. They can then click one of three option buttons to display the result of an expression. Format the results of the first two expressions to two decimal places.

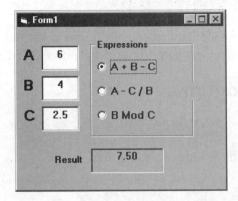

Figure 3.12: Exercise 3

***4.   Build a simple calculator as shown in Figure 3.13. The user enters two numbers and then clicks one of the four arithmetic operators to display the result. The whole calculation is also displayed in the list box. Clicking the Clear button allows all this to be repeated. Since the calculator has no memory, to calculate 6 + 8 − 2 for example, the user would need to look in the list box or at the displayed result of 6 + 8 to find the first number (14) to enter for the next calculation. In Figure 3.13 the user is ready to click the subtraction button to complete this calculation.

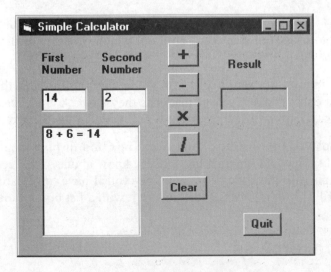

Figure 3.13: Exercise 4

Chapter 4 – Selection

What is selection?

Selection means that one or more lines of code may or may not be executed depending on whether a condition is true or false.

Types of selection in Visual Basic

Visual Basic has two selection constructs:

- **If**
- **Select Case**

The **If** construct has three variations:

- **If Then**
- **If Then…Else**
- **If Then…ElseIf**

If Then

Read the following code and then note the points made after it:

```
Dim Age As Integer
Age = txtAge.Text
If Age > 16 Then                               'age greater than 16?
   Form1.Print "You are old enough to drive"
End If
```

- The condition to test is *Age > 16*. If it is true the message is printed, and if false the message is skipped.

- The '>' sign means 'greater than' and is an example of a **relational operator**. Visual Basic has several of these, which are listed in the *Summary of key concepts*.

- Because the condition is either true or false it is called a **boolean** condition. (Boolean was one of the data types listed at the start of Chapter 3.)

- An **If** must always have a matching **End If** to tell Visual Basic where the construct ends.

If Then…Else

The **Else** part of the construct is executed if the boolean condition is false. For example:

```
If Age > 16 Then                               'age greater than 16?
   Form1.Print "You are old enough to drive"
Else                                           'age 16 or less
   Form1.Print "Sorry, you are too young to drive"
   Form1.Print "You must be 17 years old"
End If
```

If Then…ElseIf

In the previous example there were two routes through the **If** construct. With three or more possible routes you can use an **If Then…ElseIf**. For example:

```
If Age > 16 Then                                'age greater than 16?
   Form1.Print "You are old enough to drive"
ElseIf Age = 16                                 'age 16 exactly?
   Form1.Print "Sorry, you are too young to drive"
   Form1.Print "You only have to wait less than a year though"
Else                                            'age 15 or less
   Form1.Print "Sorry, you are too young to drive"
   Form1.Print "You must be 17 years old"
End If
```

There are three routes through this example and two boolean conditions to test. If Age stores 16 the first condition *Age > 16* is false. The second one, *Age = 16*, is then tested, and since it is true the next two lines of code are executed. The Else part would be skipped.

PROGRAM 4.1   *Deciding exam grades*

Specification   Ask the user to enter an exam mark from 0 to 100. Display the grade it represents – Merit (60 or more), Pass (40 – 59), Fail (under 40)

In Chapter 3 you met the input box as a way of getting data from the user. Its output equivalent is the **message box**. We'll use both in this program.

1.   Open a new project, double-click on the form to bring up its Load event code template and type in:

```
Private Sub Form_Load()
   Dim Mark As Integer
   Mark = InputBox("Enter an exam mark from 0 to 100")
   If Mark >= 60 Then                           'mark 60 or more?
     MsgBox "Merit"
   ElseIf Mark >= 40 Then                       'mark 40-59
     MsgBox "Pass"
   Else                                         'mark under 40
     MsgBox "A mark of " & Mark & " is a Fail"
   End If
End Sub
```

Note that

- Mark is declared as a local variable (though it could have been a global one since there is only one procedure on the form).

- To display a message box use **MsgBox** followed by the message you wish to output in quotation marks. The third message uses two ampersands (&) to concatenate two strings inside quotes and the contents of Mark into one string.

- Another relational operator (>=) is used, meaning **greater than or equal to**. Note that the condition *Mark >= 60* is the same as *Mark > 59*.

1. Run the program three times and test each of the three routes through the **If** construct by entering, for example, marks of 70, 50 and 30.

end of Program 4.1

Testing multiple conditions

The boolean condition has so far consisted of one test. A multiple boolean condition has two or more tests and each one is either true or false. For this you need to use Visual Basic's **logical operators**. The two important ones are **And** and **Or**.

An AND condition

In the example below there are two conditions to test, *Age > 18* and *Gender = "F"*. Each of these is either true or false. **When you AND two or more conditions each one must be true for the overall condition to be true. If just one of them is false the overall condition is false.**

```
Dim Age As Integer
Dim Gender As String
Age = txtAge.Text
Gender = txtGender.Text
If (Age >= 18) And (Gender = "F") Then      'females 18 and over
   Form1.Print "Allow into nightclub"
Else                                        'everybody else
   Form1.Print "Do not allow into nightclub"
End If
```

The two conditions have brackets. This is optional, but as it can help readability the practice is used in this book.

An OR condition

Members of a ten-pin bowling club get an award if, during one season, they score at least 240 points on 5 or more occasions, or they score 200 points on 10 or more occasions:

```
Dim TwoForty As Integer      'VB does not allow identifiers 240 or 200
Dim TwoHundred As Integer    'since they must not start with a digit
'assume data input
If (TwoForty >= 5) Or (TwoHundred >= 10) Then
   Form1.Print "Give award"
End If
```

When you OR two or more conditions, then if at least one of them is true the overall condition is true. They must all be false for the overall condition to be false.

PROGRAM 4.2   *Selecting cutlery*

Specification	Write a program for a mail order cutlery company. The form should have a list of cutlery brands, a list of different cutlery items and a list of purchase quantities. The user must select one item from each of the three lists and then click a button for the price to be calculated. (N.B. the cost calculation is not relevant to the concept of multiple conditions and will not be coded.)

This program provides an opportunity to practise using some of the controls you covered in Chapter 2. Figure 4.1 shows the program in action. The user has selected a brand of cutlery but not the item(s) or quantity. If the Price button is then clicked the message in Figure 4.2(a) appears. When all three things have been selected the satisfactory message in Figure 4.2(b) appears.

The Items are selected using check boxes. If the Full Set check box is selected the other three should automatically be selected. The Quantity is selected using option buttons, but note that the mail order company has decided it does not want any of these selected by default.

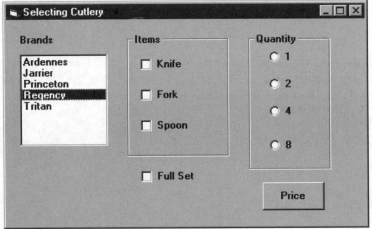

Figure 4.1: Program 4.1

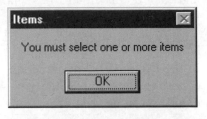

Figure 4.2 (a) above (b) below

1. Open a new project and design the form using figures 4.1 and 4.3. Frames are used to contain three of the check boxes and the four option buttons. Recall that you must place the frame on the form first before placing the controls inside it if you want the controls to "belong" to it.

We don't need variables in this program and only two event procedures need to be coded:

- When the Full Set check box is clicked the other check boxes must be selected automatically.
- When the Price button is clicked an appropriate message must be displayed.

2. Double-click the Full Set check box to get its default Click event procedure. The **Value** property of a check box indicates whether or not it has been selected, so type in the following:

```
Private Sub chkFullSet_Click()
   If chkFullSet.Value = 1 Then      'Full Set selected
      chkKnife.Value = 1                'select other 3 check boxes
      chkFork.Value = 1
      chkSpoon.Value = 1
   Else                              'Full set not selected
      chkKnife.Value = 0                'deselect other 3 check boxes or
      chkFork.Value = 0                 'leave them deselected if in
      chkSpoon.Value = 0               'that state already
   End If
End Sub
```

Control	*Property*	*Property setting*
Form	Caption	Selecting Cutlery
Label	Caption	Brands
List box	Name	lstBrands
	List	*See 5 brands in fig 4.1*
Frame	Caption	Items
Frame	Caption	Quantity
Check box	Name	chkKnife
	Caption	Knife
Check box	Name	chkFork
	Caption	Fork
Check box	Name	chkSpoon
	Caption	Spoon
Check box	Name	chkFullSet
	Caption	Full Set
Option button	Name	optOne
	Caption	1
Option button	Name	optTwo
	Caption	2
Option button	Name	optFour
	Caption	4
Option button	Name	optEight
	Caption	8
Command button	Name	cmdCalcPrice
	Caption	Price

Figure 4.3: Property settings for the controls in program 4.1

3. Get the event procedure for the command button and enter the code below. As there are three parts of the form for the user to make selections from, there are four routes through the **If** construct. Two **ElseIf**s and an **Else** handle this. Note that as **VB does not allow comments on the same line as a joining underscore character** the comments below on the ElseIfs are written on the previous line.

```vb
Private Sub cmdCalcPrice_Click()
  If lstBrands.Text = "" Then                  'has a brand been selected?
    MsgBox "You must select a brand", , "Brand"
          'brand has been selected but has an item been selected?
  ElseIf (chkKnife.Value = 0) And _
         (chkFork.Value = 0) And _
         (chkSpoon.Value = 0) Then
    MsgBox "You must select one or more items", , "Items"
              'brand and item selected but has a quantity?
  ElseIf (optOne.Value = False) And _
         (optTwo.Value = False) And _
         (optFour.Value = False) And _
         (optEight.Value = False) Then
    MsgBox "You must select a quantity", , "Quantity"
  Else                                  'Everything has been selected
    MsgBox "All 3 things have been selected!", , "Cutlery"
  End If
End Sub
```

This code illustrates several things:

- The Value property of an option button is 1 if it is selected (unlike the check box which stores True).

- In program 4.1 we gave the MsgBox function only a message to display. You can also give it several other optional arguments or parameters. One of these, used in the examples here, is a title (e.g. "Brand"). As this is the second optional parameter, and we are not supplying the first optional one, you must indicate this by having the two commas and nothing between them. The *Take it from here...* section asks you to explore these parameters further.

- The **ElseIf**s have several conditions to test and only if they are all true should the message be displayed. Therefore **And**s are needed. The conditions have been written on separate lines here because they will not fit on one line in this book. Recall from the Introduction that you use the underscore character (_) to join lines in Visual Basic code, and that there must be at least one space before the underscore.

4. Run the program and try out the four routes through the code.

end of Program 4.2

Nested If structures

A nested **If Then** is an alternative to using multiple AND conditions. Using our earlier example of the nightclub we could write:

```
If Age >= 18 Then                              'aged 18 or over
   If Gender = "F" Then                        'and female?
      Form1.Print "Allow into nightclub"
   Else                                        'all other people
      Form1.Print "Do not allow into nightclub"
   End If
End If
```

A nested **If Then...Else** could be used for the exam mark example. It looks very similar to the earlier code but note that the original **ElseIf** has been split over two lines and has become a nested **If** instead.

```
If Mark >= 60 Then                             'mark 60 or more
   MsgBox "Merit"
Else
   If Mark >= 40 Then                          'mark 40-59
      MsgBox "Pass"
   Else                                        'mark under 40
      MsgBox "A mark of " & Mark & " is a Fail"
   End If
End If
```

The common feature of both these examples is the pair of **End If**s to match the two earlier **If**s. It's for you to decide whether to use nested **If**s in your code. Again readability should probably be the deciding factor.

Complex multiple conditions

When you are coding a large program you might have to use quite complex multiple boolean conditions made up of a mixture of ANDs and ORs. In Chapter 3 you saw that arithmetic operators have an order of precedence. So do logical operators – AND is done before OR. Program 4.3 illustrates how you must take great care in writing more complex multiple conditions.

PROGRAM 4.3   *Rent a property*

Specification   Illustrate the order of precedence of the AND and OR logical operators

Look at Figure 4.4 showing the program in action. A customer wants to rent a holiday property which has 4 or more bedrooms, and it must be a cottage or a detached house. On the left a detached 5-bedroom property has been selected, the Correct button clicked and the appropriate message **Rent it** displayed. On the right, a one-bedroom cottage has been selected (not what the customer wants), but clicking Incorrect also says rent it. The Correct button has the properly coded multiple condition.

1. Open a new project and place two labels, two list boxes and two command buttons on the form. Set the captions of the labels and buttons to those shown in Figure 4.4

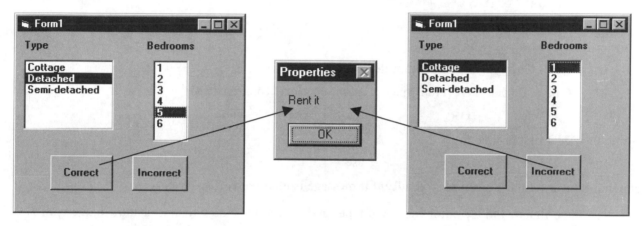

Figure 4.4: Program 4.3

2. Name the list boxes **lstTypes** and **lstBedrooms** and add the items shown in Figure 4.4 using their List property.

3. Name the command buttons **cmdCorrect** and **cmdIncorrect**.

4. In the General part of the form's code declare two global variables:

```
Option Explicit
Dim PropType As String      'stores selected item from Type list box
Dim Bedrooms As Integer     'stores selected item from Bedrooms list box
```

5. In the Click event procedure for cmdCorrect enter the correct coding as follows:

```
Private Sub cmdCorrect_Click()
   PropType = lstTypes.Text
   Bedrooms = lstBedrooms.Text
   If (PropType = "Cottage") And (Bedrooms >= 4) _
                Or (PropType = "Detached") And (Bedrooms >= 4) Then
      MsgBox "Rent it"
   End If
End Sub
```

If the user selects **Detached** and **5** from the list boxes the multiple condition becomes

(PropType = "Cottage") **And** (Bedrooms >= 4) **Or** (PropType = "Detached") **And** (Bedrooms >= 4)

        False   **AND**   True   **OR**   True   **AND**   True

Since ANDs have precedence over ORs these are done first, which produces

        False   **OR**   True

Finally the OR produces True, and the message **Rent it** is displayed.

6. In the Click event procedure for cmdIncorrect enter an example of incorrect coding as follows:

```
Private Sub cmdIncorrect_Click()
  PropType = lstTypes.Text
  Bedrooms = lstBedrooms.Text
  If (PropType = "Cottage") Or (PropType = "Detached") _
            And (Bedrooms >= 4) Then
    MsgBox "Rent it"
  End If
End Sub
```

If the user selects **Cottage** and **1** the multiple condition becomes

(PropType = "Cottage") **Or** (PropType = "Detached") **And** (Bedrooms >= 4)

       True   **OR**   False   **AND**   False

Doing the AND first produces

       True   **OR**   False

which produces a final True, and so the **Rent it** message is incorrectly displayed.

7. Run the program and try out a variety of types and bedrooms. You will find that a cottage with 1, 2 or 3 bedrooms incorrectly displays the message.

end of Program 4.3

Select Case

In the examples so far the largest number of routes through the **If** structure has been four. If you have more than this the **Select Case** structure is probably a better alternative.

Suppose you wished to output the name of the month corresponding to a number from 1 to 12 input by the user. If this value is stored in Month then you would code this as follows:

```
Select Case Month
  Case 1
    MsgBox "January"
  Case 2
    MsgBox "February"
  Case 3
    MsgBox "March"
            'and so on up to........
  Case 12
    MsgBox "December"
End Select
```

Visual Basic would look for the value of Month in one of the 12 **Case**s and execute the appropriate code. If it cannot find a match, because the user has entered 13 for example, nothing happens. You can cover this situation by adding an optional **Case Else**:

```
    Case 12
       MsgBox "December"
    Case Else
       MsgBox "You did not enter a valid month number"
 End Select
```

PROGRAM 4.4   *Wards and Patients*

Specification   Present the user with two list boxes. One of these lists the wards in a hospital. Clicking on one of the wards displays the names of its patients in the other list box.

Figure 4.6 shows the program. Selecting a ward changes the patient list on the right. This is a technique with many applications in computer projects. Examples include courses and students, departments and employees, authors and books and so on.

1.   Open a new project. Design the form using figures 4.5 and 4.6. Note that you only have to put items into the Wards list box, not the Patients list box too.

Control	Property	Property setting
Form	Caption	Wards and Patients
Label	Caption	Wards
Label	Caption	Patients
List box	Name List	lstWards *See the 3 wards listed in Figure 4.6*
List box	Name	lstPatients

Figure 4.5: Property settings for the controls in Program 4.4

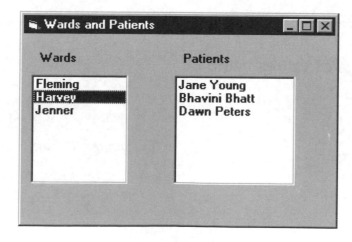

Figure 4.6: Program 4.4

2. Get the Click event procedure for the wards list box and type in the following code:

```
Private Sub lstWards_Click()
  Dim Ward As String
  Ward = lstWards.Text                'selected item from ward list box
  Select Case Ward
    Case "Fleming"
      lstPatients.AddItem "Fred Jones"    'AddItem method used to
      lstPatients.AddItem "John Green"    'populate patients list box
      lstPatients.AddItem "Imran Shah"
    Case "Harvey"
      lstPatients.AddItem "Jane Young"
      lstPatients.AddItem "Bhavini Bhatt"
      lstPatients.AddItem "Dawn Peters"
    Case "Jenner"
      lstPatients.AddItem "William Black"
      lstPatients.AddItem "Michael Jones"
      lstPatients.AddItem "Darren Campbell"
  End Select
End Sub
```

3. Run the program and click on two different wards. After clicking the second ward the list box has patients from both wards. We need to remove the patients from the first ward before the new names are added. Add the following line before each of the three AddItem lines in each Case:

```
lstPatients.Clear
```

Note that the method of populating the patients list box is not the way you'd do it in a real project. These names would be stored in a file. Files are covered in Chapter 10. With **Case** "Fleming", for example, the code would copy details of those patients in this ward from the file. However you would still need the AddItem method to get them into the list box.

end of Program 4.4

Extensions to Select Case

So far the **Case** values have all been simple single ones – months (1-12) and ward names. There are several extensions to this. Here are some examples:

A continuous range of values using *To*

```
Select Case Mark
  Case 0 To 39                  'value ranges from 0 to 39
    MsgBox "Fail"
  Case 40 To 59                 'value ranges from 40 to 59
    MsgBox "Pass"
  Case 60 To 100                'value ranges from 60 to 100
    MsgBox "Merit"
End Select
```

A continuous range of values using *Is*

The code below does the same as the previous example. As relational operators are used the keyword **Is** must follow **Case**.

```
Select Case Mark
  Case Is < 40                  'value is under 40
    MsgBox "Fail"
  Case Is <= 59                 'value ranges from 40 to 59
    MsgBox "Pass"
  Case Is >= 60                 'value is 60 or over
    MsgBox "Merit"
End Select
```

A non-continuous range of values

```
Select Case Month
  Case 1, 3, 5, 7, 8, 10, 12
    MsgBox "This month has 31 days"
  Case 4, 6, 8, 11
    MsgBox "This month has 30 days"
  Case 2
    MsgBox "This month has 28 or 29 days"
End Select
```

Summary of key concepts

- Visual Basic has two selection constructs – **If** and **Select Case**. Both have several variations.

- With an **If** structure a boolean condition is tested. If it is true the associated code is executed, otherwise control passes to the optional **Else** if there is one.

- No matter how complex a multiple **If** condition is, it must reduce to an overall single true or false.

- Visual Basic supports the following **relational operators**:

=	equal to	<	smaller than
>	greater than	<=	smaller than or equal to
>=	greater than or equal to	<>	not equal to

- Visual Basic's two main **logical operators** are **And** and **Or**. The following rules apply:

  * When you AND two or more conditions each one must be true for the overall condition to be true. If just one of them is false the overall condition is false.

  * When you OR two or more conditions, then if at least one of them is true the overall condition is true. They must all be false for the overall condition to be false.

  * ANDs have precedence over ORs.

Take it from here...

1. In this chapter you gave the **MsgBox** function two parameters. It can accept more, and one of these refers to the type of buttons to display in the message box. Investigate some of the button types you can display.

2. Visual Basic has an **IIf** function equivalent to If Then…Else and a **Switch** function equivalent to Select Case. Find out how you might use these functions in code.

3. Only two logical operators, And and Or, were covered. Visual Basic has four more, although only one of these, the **Not** operator, is ever likely to be of use to you. Find out about this operator.

Questions on the Programs

Program 4.1

*1. When you click to remove the message box, the empty form seems to appear. Add one line of code to stop it appearing.

*2. Extend the code so that a mark of 80 or more gets a Distinction.

Program 4.2

*1. Originally the mail order company did not want any of the Quantity options selected by default when the program runs. Now they have changed their mind. Change one of the properties of optFour to make quantity 4 selected when the program starts.

Program 4.3

*1. Add a second Incorrect button so that if you select a Detached property with 3 bedrooms or less it will tell you (wrongly) to rent it.

Program 4.4

*1. Add two more wards and write code to display three patients in each of them.

**2. Rewrite the code using the ListIndex property of the wards list box rather than the Text property.

End of chapter exercises

*1. Ask a salesperson to input the total value of their sales this year to the nearest whole pound. If it exceeds £100,000 their bonus is £10,000. If it is from £70,000 to £99,999 the bonus is £7,000 and if it is £50,000 to £69,999 the bonus is £4,000. Sales less than £50,000 receive no bonus. Output the salesperson's bonus.

*2. A person wishes to attend an overnight conference. They cannot afford to pay more than £40.00 for their hotel, which must be no more than 3 km from the conference hall. Ask the user to input these two data items and then display a message to indicate whether they should book or not.

**3. Write a program that calculates total weekly pay as shown in Figure 4.7. The user enters the number of hours worked and selects the hourly rate of pay from a list box. If overtime has been done, the number of hours is also entered. Overtime hours are paid at double rate. A check box handles overtime. Clicking this should make visible the text box for inputting the number of overtime hours.

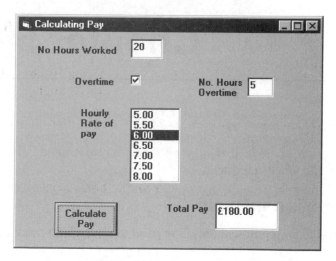

Figure 4.7: Exercise 3

**4. A sports club has three categories of membership charge. Juniors (aged up to 18) pay £60 per year, Seniors (19-49) pay £120 and Veterans (50 and over) pay £80. Juniors who have been a member for 2 years or more get a £20 reduction. Seniors and Veterans who have been members for 10 years or more get a £30 reduction. Write a program that asks for the member's age and the number of years they have been a member, and outputs their category of membership and how much they must pay. Use input boxes to get the data.

**5. The Shipshape Packing Company wants a program for their Orders Department to calculate and display the price of an order. The order clerks enter the number of units ordered, whether a customer is a wholesaler or retailer, and whether or not the customer is a special customer. Use a variety of controls for this data entry. The price the customer pays per unit depends on these three things. The prices are as follows:

Wholesalers		Retailers	
No. units	Price per unit (£)	No. units	Price per unit(£)
1-5	50	1 – 3	60
6-10	45	4-8	55
11-20	40	9-15	50
21-50	35	16-40	45
over 50	30	over 40	40

Special customers get a 10% reduction on the prices above.

***6. Write a program to simulate the changes of a set of traffic lights. Use the Shape control in the toolbox to put three circles on a form. Set the BackColor property of the top one to red and the other two to white. With each click of a button the traffic lights should change continuously through the sequence: Red, Amber and Red together, Green and finally Amber You may need to look back at how you used the RGB function in program 2.4 in order to code the colour changes.

If you get this working, now try to meet a different specification. When the button is clicked the traffic lights colour changes should go automatically through the cycle. For this you need to use a Timer control. Its default Interval setting is 0: change this to any positive value or you may not get the colour sequence to start. A value of 1000 (i.e. 1000 milliseconds or 1 second) will be fine.

Chapter 5 – Loops

What is a loop?

A program loop is a section of code that may be repeatedly executed. The loop contains a Boolean condition that will determine when it terminates.

Types of loop in Visual Basic

Visual Basic has six types of loop, but you only ever need to understand three of them. These are:

- **For…Next**
- **Do While…Loop**
- **Do…Loop Until**

The code, known as the **loop body**, is inserted in place of the three dots. Each loop works in a slightly different way and is useful in different circumstances.

For…Next

You use this type of loop when you know exactly how many times the code must be repeated. For example, the code below prints the numbers 1 to 10, as shown in Figure 5.1. Assume that Number has been declared as an Integer.

```
For Number = 1 To 10
    Print Number
Next Number
```

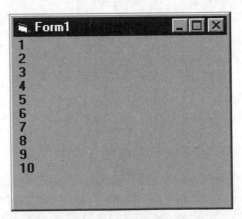

Figure 5.1

The first time the line

```
    For Number = 1 To 10
```

is executed the value 1 is stored in Number. The statement in the loop body is then executed and the number 1 is printed. The line

```
Next Number
```

indicates the end of the loop and control passes back to the first line. Number is automatically incremented to 2 and the loop body executes again, this time printing 2. This process continues until the loop has been executed exactly 10 times, when control passes to the first statement after the loop.

The general form of a **For…Next** loop is

> **For** *variable identifier = start value* **To** *end value*
>   *statement(s)*
> **Next** *variable identifier*

Note that:

- Start and end values may be integer constants, variables or expressions.
- The variable identifier in the last line of the loop is optional, but it is good practice to include it.

PROGRAM 5.1   *Multiplication table*

Specification Ask the user to enter a number from 2 to 12 and then output the multiplication table for their number. If the user enters 5 then the output is
$$2 \times 5 = 10$$
$$3 \times 5 = 15$$
$$4 \times 5 = 20$$
$$\cdots\cdots$$
$$12 \times 5 = 60$$

1. Open a new project and drop a label, textbox and command button on the form so that it looks like Figure 5.2. Name the textbox **txtNumber** and the command button **cmdOK**.

2. Double-click on the command button to bring up the Code window. Type in code so that its event procedure is as follows:

```
Private Sub cmdOK_Click()
   Dim Number As Integer
   Dim Index As Integer
   Dim Result As Integer
   Number = txtNumber.Text
   For Index = 2 To 12
     Result = Index * Number
     Print Number & " x " & Index & " = " & Result
   Next Index
End Sub
```

3. Run the program and if you enter 5 into the text box you should produce the output shown in Figure 5.3.

The first line in the loop

```
For Index = 2 To 12
```

stores the value 2 in Index. When Result is calculated by multiplying this by Number (e.g. 2 x 5), the concatenation operator **&** is used three times to output one line on the form (e.g. 2 x 5 = 10) with

```
Print Number & " x " & Index & " = " & Result
```

Next is then read and control returns to the first line of the loop. When Index has the value 12 the loop runs for the last time.

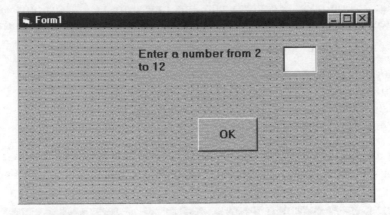

Figure 5.2: Design of program 5.1

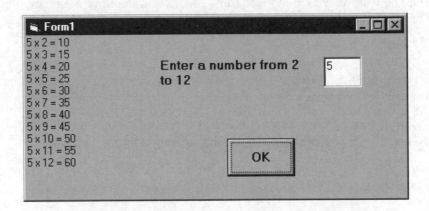

Figure 5.3: Output from Program 5.1

End of Program 5.1

The Step parameter

In the examples we've looked at so far, the value of the variable which controls whether or not the loop is executed has increased by 1 each time round the loop. However it doesn't have to increase by 1. For example, the code

```
For Index = 1 To 10 Step 2
    Print Index
Next Index
```

sets the values of Index to 1, 3, 5, 7 etc. by using the **Step** parameter and giving it a value of 2. The last execution of the loop occurs when Index has the value 9 because the next value, 11, would be bigger than the 10 allowed. You can even give **Step** a negative value. Thus

```
For Index = 20 To 0 Step -5
```

would successively store the values 20, 15, 10, 5 and 0 in Index and make the loop run five times.

A nested *For...Next* loop

A nested loop is when you have one loop inside another. The general structure of a nested **For...Next** loop is:

For.........	*start of outer loop*
For.......	*start of inner loop*
....	*body of inner loop*
Next	*end of inner loop*
Next	*end of outer loop*

Think of the outer loop as a large cog driving a smaller cog which is the inner loop. Every time the larger cog revolves once (one repetition of the outer loop), the inner cog usually revolves more than once. Have a look at the code which follows.

```
For OuterNumber = 1 To 4
   Print "Outer control variable is " & OuterNumber
   For InnerNumber = 1 To 2
      Print "        Inner control variable is " & InnerNumber
   Next InnerNumber
Next OuterNumber
```

This will produce the output in Figure 5.4. The outer loop is run four times, and each time you go round the outer loop the inner loop runs twice.

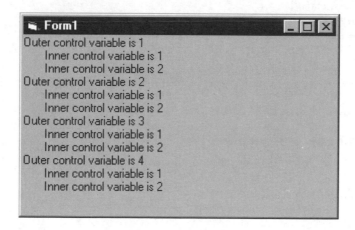

Figure 5.4

PROGRAM 5.2 *Addition Table*

Specification	Write a program to display the sum of row and column numbers

The running program is shown in Figure 5.5.

1. Open a new project and double-click on the form to get the form's Load event code template.

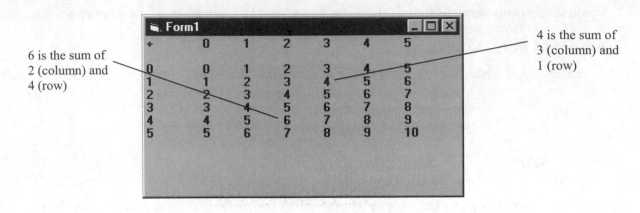

Figure 5.5: Program 5.2

2. Declare the following:

```
Const Max = 5
Dim ColNumber As Integer
Dim RowNumber As Integer
Dim Sum As Integer
```

3. In the form's Load event type in the following code to produce the addition table. Note the three new formatting commands **Space**, **vbNewLine** and **NewLine** and the use of the semi-colon (;).

```
Form1.Show
Print "+" & Space(12);               'print table heading
For ColNumber = 0 To Max             'simple For...Next loop
   Print ColNumber & Space(8);       'print column value and 8 spaces
Next ColNumber
Print vbNewLine                      'print empty line
For RowNumber = 0 To Max             'start of outer loop
   Print RowNumber & Space(12);        'print first number in the row
   For ColNumber = 0 To Max           'start of inner loop
     Sum = ColNumber + RowNumber
     Print Sum & Space(8);              'print addition
   Next ColNumber                     'end of inner loop
   Print NewLine                      'get to next line
Next RowNumber                       'end of outer loop
```

4. Run the program. Then remove one of the semi-colons and run it again. You should see that the semi-colon's job is to keep the cursor on the same line.

end of Program 5.2

Do While...Loop

The general form of **Do While...Loop** is

Do While *condition* is true
    statement(s)   = body of loop
Loop

This type of loop executes as long as the boolean condition in the first line of the loop is true, otherwise it exits. Consider the following code:

```
Number = 5
Do While Number <> 10          '<> means not equal to
   Print Number * Number
   Number = Number + 1
Loop
```

This will produce the output in Figure 5.6.

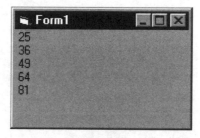

Figure 5.6

Note that:

- If you omitted the line

```
Number = Number + 1
```

  the loop would never end, since Number would never equal 10. This is called an **infinite loop**. This is a common mistake and a good reason to always save your program before running it, because you will not be able to get out of an infinite loop without exiting Visual Basic and thus losing your code. However there is one way to escape an infinite loop – include the line **DoEvents** somewhere inside the loop. This tells Visual Basic to respond to events while the loop is executing; closing the program is the event you'll want it to respond to.

- If the first line of code was

```
Number = 10
```

  then the condition *10 <> 10* would be false, and the loop would not be executed at all. This is one key feature of Do While…Loop which distinguishes it from Do…Loop Until.

PROGRAM 5.3   *Driving Test*

Specification   Ask the user to enter "Y", "N" or "Q" (quit) in response to the question "Has the person passed their driving test?" Continue asking this question until the user answers "Q". Output the number and percentage of people who have passed their test.

1.   Open a new project and design the form using figures 5.7 and 5.8.

Control	Property	Property setting
Label	Caption	Number who have passed driving test
Label	Caption	Percentage who have passed driving test
Text box	Name	txtNumberPassed
	Text	Blank
Text box	Name	txtPercentPassed
	Text	Blank
Command button	Name	cmdOK
	Caption	OK

Figure 5.7: Properties of the controls in program 5.3

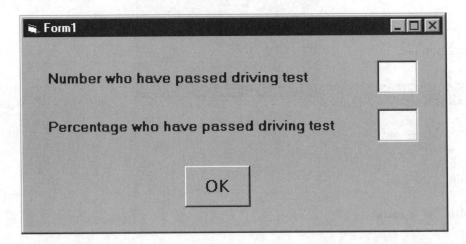

Figure 5.8: Program 5.3

2. Double-click the command button and type the following code into its click event procedure:

```
Private Sub cmdOK_Click()
  Dim TotalNumber As Integer
  Dim NumberPassed As Integer
  Dim Response As String
  TotalNumber = 0                    'initialise variables
  NumberPassed = 0
  Response = "Z"        'set to anything except Q so that loop is entered
  Do While Response <> "Q"
     Response = InputBox("Has person passed driving test?.Y/N " & _
                "or Q to quit")
     If Response <> "Q" Then              'user has entered Y or N
        TotalNumber = TotalNumber + 1
        If Response = "Y" Then            'person has passed driving test
           NumberPassed = NumberPassed + 1
        End If
     End If
  Loop
  txtNumberPassed.Text = NumberPassed
  txtPercentPassed = Format(NumberPassed / TotalNumber * 100, _
                     "###.00")
End Sub
```

3. Now for a really useful piece of advice mentioned earlier. Always save a program with an untested **While** or **Until** loop in it before you run it. If you have written your loop incorrectly so that it won't stop executing – the infinite loop – you will not be able to get back to the Visual Basic environment and you will lose your code. So save it now and then run it.

end of Program 5.3

Do...Loop Until

The general form of this loop is:

> **Do**
>> statement(s)   =   body of loop
>
> **Loop Until** *condition* is true

Since the condition is at the end of the loop, the loop body must be executed at least once.

PROGRAM 5.4   *Password Entry*

Specification   Allow the user up to three attempts at entering the password "secret". Inform the user which attempt they are currently on (1, 2 or 3). Inform the user that the password is correct if they get it within the three attempts, otherwise inform them that their password is invalid.

1. Open a new project, drop a command button onto the form, set its Name to **cmdOK** and its Caption to **Enter Password**.

2. Double-click the button to bring up the Code window and enter the following code into its Click event procedure:

```
Private Sub cmdOK_Click()
  Dim Password As String
  Dim InputPassword As String
  Dim Attempt As Integer
  Password = "secret"                            'initialise variables
  Attempt = 0
  Do                                             'start of loop
    Attempt = Attempt + 1
    InputPassword = InputBox("Enter password. This is attempt " & _
                "number " & Attempt)
  Loop Until (Attempt = 3) Or (InputPassword = Password) 'end of loop
  If InputPassword = Password Then
    MsgBox ("This password is valid")
  Else
    MsgBox ("This password is invalid")
  End If
End Sub
```

The body of the loop asks the user for the password and then adds 1 to the number of attempts the user has had. The condition at the end of the loop is a multiple one:

```
Loop Until (Attempt = 3) Or (InputPassword = Password)
```

The condition is true if either the user has had three attempts or they have entered the correct password. It will also be true if they have entered the correct password at the third attempt since both parts of the multiple condition are true.

3. Run the program to check that it works.

end of Program 5.3

Summary of key concepts

- The general forms of the three loops covered in this chapter are:

For...Next	**For** *variable identifier* = *start value* **To** *end value* statement(s) **Next** *variable identifier*
Do While...Loop	**Do While** *condition* statement(s) = body of loop **Loop**
Do...Loop Until	**Do** statement(s) = body of loop **Loop Until** *condition*

- Use a **For...Next** loop when you know how many times the loop must be executed.

- Use **Do While...Loop** if there is the possibility that the loop body should not be executed.

- An **infinite loop** is one that never stops running. The program will just hang. It is caused by not allowing the condition tested in **Do While...Loop** to become false or the condition in **Do...Loop Until** to become true.

Take it from here...

1. It is possible to force a loop to terminate early by using the **Exit** statement. Find out how to exit early from the three types of loop covered in this chapter.

2. The beginning of this chapter said that Visual Basic has six types of loop, but that you only need to know three of these. Find out about the three that were not studied. These are **Do Until...Loop**, **Do...Loop While** and **While...Wend**. For each of these loops find out how the tested condition works. Also find out whether they must be executed at least once or whether they may be 'skipped' the first time.

3. There is a seventh type of loop called the **For Each...Next**. It has a special job in a Visual Basic program and is used only on arrays and collections (control arrays). Arrays are covered in Chapter 7. A collection is a set of related objects. For example, if you had six text boxes and three command buttons on a form you would have a collection of text boxes and a collection of command buttons. Find out about how you might use the **For Each...Next** loop.

Questions on the Programs

Program 5.1

*1.   In this program the user is expected to type in a number from 2 to 12. As the code stands they can type any number into txtNumber. Add a loop to the code in the event procedure cmdOK_Click to ensure that the user enters a value from 2 to 12. Making sure that input data satisfies certain conditions is called **validation**. All you are doing here is validating an inputted number. If the user entered one or more characters by mistake you would get a run-time error.

Program 5.3

*2.   Rewrite this program using **Do...Loop Until** instead of Do While...Loop.

End of chapter exercises

In questions 2, 3 and 6 use an **input box** to get data from the user.

*1.   Ask the user to input two different numbers. Print all the numbers between the two values they enter.

*2.   A disco can hold 500 people. Allow the user to keep entering the number of people in each group as the group comes through the door. Display the running total and how many more people are allowed in before it becomes full. When the running total first reaches 500 display a message that the disco is full or, if 500 is exceeded, a message that the current group of people cannot go in.

*3.   Allow the user to enter as many positive whole numbers as they wish, and to enter 0 to indicate they have finished. Then display the number of even values and number of odd values entered by the user. Use the **Mod** operator to work out whether a number is odd or even.

**4.   Use nested loops to output the cell references found in the top upper left part of a spreadsheet, within the range A1 to E5, as shown in Figure 5.8. You may wish to use two Visual Basic functions, Asc and Chr, to convert characters to their ASCII values and vice-versa.

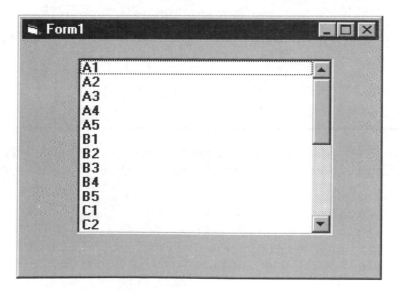

Figure 5.8: Output from Exercise 4

5. Write a program that outputs all the dates in one year in a list box when the user clicks a button. The output is shown in Figure 5.9. Use a **For…Next loop to handle the whole year and inside this a **Select Case** to handle each month. You will need to set the Column property of the list box at design time to allow multiple columns.

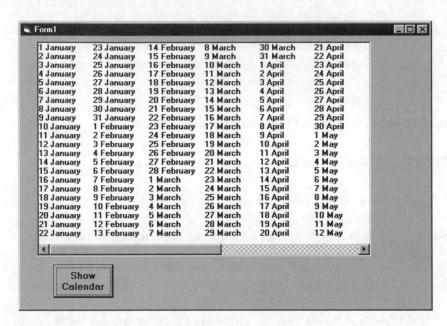

Figure 5.9: Output from exercise 4

***6. People have been surveyed in a shopping centre about the main holiday they had in the past year. They were asked the following questions:

1. Have you had a holiday in the past 12 months?   Yes ☐   No ☐

2. If Yes, was it in Britain or abroad?   GB ☐   Abroad ☐

3. If Yes, how many weeks did it last?   Up to 2 weeks ☐   More than 2 ☐

Allow the user to enter data for as many respondents as they wish. Validate the items of data entered. When all the data has been entered display the number and percentage of respondents who

- did not take a holiday.
- took a holiday in Britain of up to 2 weeks.
- took a holiday in Britain of over 2 weeks.
- took a holiday abroad of up to 2 weeks
- took a holiday abroad of over 2 weeks.

Chapter 6 – Handling Strings, Dates and Time

Introduction

String handling is probably the most common task in programming. Handling dates and time is less common but when the need arises is very important to understand.

Declaring strings

Two types of string can be declared:

- **Variable-length strings**
- **Fixed-length strings**

The code below shows an example of each.

```
Dim Surname As String                'variable-length string
Dim EmployeeNumber As String * 6     'fixed-length string
```

The examples in this book so far have been variable-length strings. The size of the variable (in bytes) depends on how many characters are stored. If Surname above stores "Smith" it would be 5 bytes in size. With a fixed-length string the variable is always the size you declare it to be. Use a fixed-length string when you know exactly the number of characters needed. In the example above, employees always have a 6-character employee number. However fixed-length strings are optional – the only time you *must* use them is when storing records in a file (see Chapter 16).

ASCII

Most computers use the American Standard Code for Information Interchange (ASCII) for storing characters. Each character is stored as an integer from 0 to 255. The following are useful to know:

- Upper case letters ('A' to 'Z') are stored as numbers 65 to 90.
- Lower case letters ('a' to 'z') are stored as numbers 97 to 122.
- Numeric digits ('0' to '9') are stored as numbers 48 to 57.
- The space character is number 32.

Processing strings

Using relational operators

The code below outputs two strings, Name1 and Name2, in alphabetical order:

```
If Name1 < Name2 Then
   Print Name1 & "   " & Name2
Else
   Print Name2 & "   " & Name1
End If
```

Visual Basic does this by comparing the ASCII value of the first character in each string. A lower value indicates that this character comes alphabetically before the other one. If they are the same then the next character in each string is compared and so on. Note that since upper case letters have lower values than lower case letters, **J**ones is alphabetically before **b**rown.

Searching for a substring using *Instr*

The **Instr** function returns the position in the main string of the substring being searched for. Thus the code below

```
MainString = "The man looked up and saw the moon"
SearchString = "man"
Position = InStr(MainString, SearchString)
```

would store the value 5 in Position. If the substring is not present the function returns 0. By default InStr is case sensitive. You must add a third parameter, 1, to make it case insensitive.

Processing individual characters using *Mid*

The **Mid** function returns a substring from the main string. Using the MainString variable in the previous example, consider the following:

```
Dim OneCharacter As String * 1
Dim Characters As String
MainString = "Keep on looking ahead"
OneCharacter = Mid(MainString, 9)          'returns 9th character i.e. 'l'
Characters = Mid(MainString, 9, 4)         'returns 4 characters starting
                                           'at position 9 i.e. 'look'
```

You need to state the position in the main string, and there is the option of specifying how many characters to return (4 in the example above).

PROGRAM 6.1   *Ensuring a person's name has only one space*

Specification   Ask the user to enter a person's surname and then their first name into a single text box. Check that only one space character has been used between the names.

1.   Open a new project and design the form using Figure 6.1. Name the textbox **txtName** and the command button **cmdOK**.

2.   In the Click event procedure for the command button enter the following code:

```
Dim Spaces As Integer
Dim EmployeeName As String
Dim Index As Integer
Dim Character As String * 1               'declare a one-character string
EmployeeName = txtName.Text
Spaces = 0
For Index = 1 To Len(EmployeeName) 'Len returns no of characters in string
   Character = Mid(EmployeeName, Index)   'extract one character
   If Character = " " Then                'is this character a space?
     Spaces = Spaces + 1                  'if yes, increment Spaces
   End If
Next Index
```

```
If Spaces >= 2 Then
  MsgBox "Too many spaces"
End If
```

The function **Len** returns the number of characters stored in the string passed to it. So the **For...Next** loop must be repeated that number of times in order to process each character.

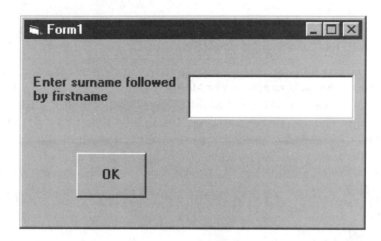

Figure 6.1: Program 6.1

3. Run the program and test it several times by entering a name with one space between the surname and first name, more than one space, a space before the surname and between the names, and a space after the first name.

Breaking strings up with *Left* and *Right*

The **Left** function returns a substring from the main string starting with the first character. One of its parameters is how many characters to return in the substring. **Right** is similar but returns a substring from the end of the string. In the example below each function is passed the string itself and the number of characters to extract. The result is shown in Figure 6.2.

```
Dim Message As String
Message = "Printers are not expensive"
Form1.Print "The first 5 characters are    " & Left(Message, 5)
Form1.Print "The last 7 characters are    " & Right(Message, 7)
```

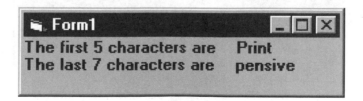

Figure 6.2

Removing spaces with *LTrim*, *RTrim* and *Trim*

The function **LTrim** removes any leading spaces at the left side of a string. **RTrim** does the same thing for trailing spaces on the right side of a string, and **Trim** does the job of both LTrim and RTrim. The only parameter each of these needs is the string itself. In program 6.1, where the user is asked to enter a surname and first name with one space between, you could use LTrim and RTrim to remove any accidental spaces before the surname and after the first name. Using Trim would (wrongly) get rid of the space between the two names also.

Changing case with *UCase* and *LCase*

The **UCase** function converts all characters in a string into their upper case equivalents. **LCase** converts them all into lower case. The only parameter needed is the string itself. If any of the characters are not letters they are ignored. Therefore UCase would change "Hello" into "HELLO" and "He**o" into "HE**O". The code below shows a possible use of UCase.

```
Dim Reply As String * 1
'user has just been asked to enter Y(es) or N(o) into a text box
Reply = txtReply.Text
Reply = UCase(Reply)        'ensure user reply is upper case
If Reply = "Y" Then
    'do something
End If
```

PROGRAM 6.2 *Extract the area telephone code*

Specification   A telephone number is input in the form (01442)-12345, where the number in brackets is the area code. The area code may have a varying number of numeric digits. Output the area code without the brackets.

1.   Open a new project and use Figure 6.3 to design the form. Name the text box, command button and label for displaying the area code, **txtTelNumber**, **cmdDisplayAreaCode** and **lblAreaCode** respectively.

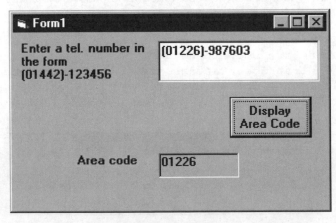

Figure 6.3: Program 6.2

2. Double-click the command button and make sure its code is as follows:

```
Private Sub cmdDisplayAreaCode_Click()
  Dim TelNumber As String
  Dim AreaCode As String
  Dim Index As Integer
  Dim Character As String * 1
  AreaCode = ""                        'initialise area code to blank
  TelNumber = txtTelNumber.Text
  Index = 1                  'set to 1 rather than 0 to skip first bracket
  Do
    Index = Index + 1
    Character = Mid(TelNumber, Index, 1)
    AreaCode = AreaCode & Character   'build up code character by character
  Loop Until Character = ")"          'stop when bracket found
  lblAreaCode.Caption = Left(AreaCode, Len(AreaCode) - 1)  'remove bracket
                                                    'from area code
End Sub
```

The first repetition of the loop processes the first digit after the opening bracket because Index has the value 2. Each repetition of the loop extracts a character using **Mid** and concatenates it to the area code. Because **Do...Loop Until** is used, in which the condition is tested at the end of the loop, the area code will have the closing bracket when the loop finishes. The first line of code after the loop uses **Left** to remove it.

3. Run the program to check that it works. Try it out with the brackets and then without an opening bracket. Without the bracket the first digit of the code is not displayed.

end of Program 6.2

Handling dates

Visual Basic has a wide range of functions for handling dates. The following are the most useful.

Date

The **Date** function simply returns the current date in the format set in Windows Control Panel. The UK format is day/month/year.

Month and Year

The **Month** function must be passed a date and it returns the number of the month from 1 to 12. **Year** returns an integer representing the year in the date passed to it as a parameter. Thus

```
MyDate = #16/04/1990#          'assign a date using # sign or "
Form1.Print Month(MyDate) & " " & Year(MyDate)
```

would print **04 1990**. Note that version 6 of Visual Basic introduced a **MonthName** function which returns the name of a month. However you can display this through the ordinary Format function (see below).

Formatting date output

In Chapter 3 you learned how to format numbers with named and user-defined formats using the **Format** function. You can use this function in a similar way with dates. Figure 6.4 shows the result of running the code below.

```
Const TheDate = "12/6/2001"     'date assigned using " rather than #
Form1.Show
Form1.Print "Using named date formats"
Form1.Print "    General Date   "; Format(TheDate, "General Date")
Form1.Print "    Long Date date   "; Format(TheDate, "Long Date")
Form1.Print "    Medium Date   "; Format(TheDate, "Medium Date")
Form1.Print "    Short Date   "; Format(TheDate, "Short Date")
Form1.Print "Using user-defined date formats"
Form1.Print "    d/mm/yy   "; Format(TheDate, "d/m/yy")
Form1.Print "    dd/m/yyyy   "; Format(TheDate, "dd/mm/yyyy")
Form1.Print "    dddd   "; Format(TheDate, "dddd")
Form1.Print "    dddddd   "; Format(TheDate, "dddddd")
Form1.Print "    dddd/dddddd   "; Format(TheDate, "dddd dddddd")
```

The full range of named formats is used above but only a small sample of possible user-defined ones is shown. The full range can be found by searching on **Format** in Help, clicking **See Also** and then selecting **UserDefined Date/Time Formats**.

Note that Visual Basic 6 introduced the **FormatDateTime** function but this provides no more ways of displaying dates than Format does.

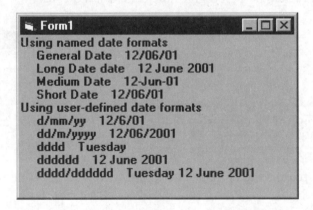

Figure 6.4

PROGRAM 6.3   *College Library issue desk*

Specification	Allow the issue and return of books in a school or college library. Books can be borrowed overnight, for 3 days, 10 days or 1 month. When a book is returned enter the date due back, select its loan period and, if it is overdue, display how many days overdue and the fine. For the issuing of books select the loan period and display the date due back in the form Saturday 09 June 2001.

1. Open a new project and design the form using Figure 6.5. Set the captions of the four display labels to blank.

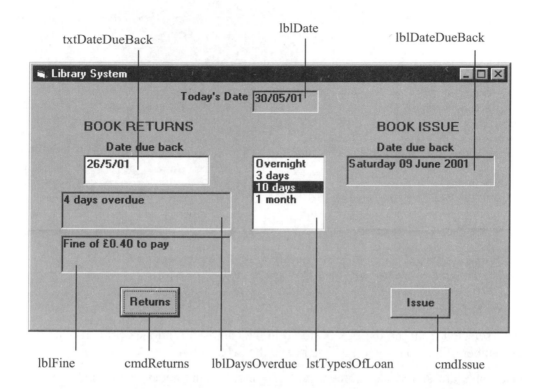

Figure 6.5: Program 6.3

2. In the General section declare a single global variable:

```
Dim DaysLoan As Integer
```

3. In the form's Load event procedure display the current date with:

```
lblDate.Caption = Date
```

4. In the Click event of cmdReturns declare the following local variables:

```
Dim DateDueBack As Date
Dim Overdue As Boolean
Dim DaysOverdue As Integer
Dim FineRate As Currency
Dim Fine As Currency
```

5. Complete the code for the Click event for cmdReturns:

```
DateDueBack = txtDateDueBack.Text
Select Case lstTypesOfLoan.ListIndex
   Case 0                                 'overnight loan
     DaysLoan = 1
     FineRate = 0.5                       'fine is 50p per day
```

```
      Case 1                              '3-day loan
         DaysLoan = 3
         FineRate = 0.25                  'fine is 25p per day
      Case 2                              '10-day loan
         DaysLoan = 10
         FineRate = 0.1                   'fine is 10p per day
      Case 3                              '1 month loan (=30 days)
         DaysLoan = 30
         FineRate = 0.05                  'fine is 5p per day
   End Select
   DaysOverdue = Date - DateDueBack       'eg of arithmetic on dates
   Overdue = Date - DateDueBack > 0       'if date due back is earlier than
                                          'today's date, set Overdue to True
   If Overdue Then                        'Does Overdue store True?
      Fine = FineRate * DaysOverdue
   Else
      Fine = 0
   End If
   lblDaysOverdue.Caption = DaysOverdue & " days overdue"
   lblFine.Caption = "Fine of " & Format(Fine, "currency") & " to pay"
```

Take note of the following:

- The item selected from the list box is stored in the control's ListIndex property and this is used to set the number of loan days and the fine rate in the **Select Case**.

- Because dates are stored as numbers one date can be subtracted from another to calculate the number of days overdue.

- Since Overdue is a Boolean data type, storing True or False, it can be assigned the result of a condition that yields a true/false result. The condition is *Date – DateDueBack > 0*.

- The **If** condition could be written as *If Overdue = True*, but writing just *If Overdue* makes it a little more readable.

6.   Now for the code for the Click event of cmdIssue:

```
   Dim DateDueBack As Date
   Select Case lstTypesOfLoan.ListIndex
      Case 0
         DaysLoan = 1
      Case 1
         DaysLoan = 3
      Case 2
         DaysLoan = 10
      Case 3
         DaysLoan = 30
   End Select
   DateDueBack = Date + DaysLoan
   lblDateDueBack.Caption = Format(DateDueBack, "dddd dddddd")
```

Note the user-defined formatting to display the full form of the date due back.

7.   Run the program. Select a loan period from the list box and click the Issue button. Then enter a date due back in the Book Returns section earlier than today's date, click the Returns button and the number of days overdue and fine should be displayed.

end of Program 6.3

Handling time

Visual Basic has several functions to handle time. The most useful are:

Time and *Now*

The **Time** function is the counterpart of Date. It returns the current time e.g. 07:42:25. Depending on the time setting in Windows you may get AM or PM displayed after the time. **Now** returns both the date and time and is equivalent to using the Date and Time functions together.

Second, Minute and *Hour*

These functions return an integer in the range 0 to 60 for Second and Minute and 0 to 24 for Hour. For example, if the current time is 10:45:12 then

```
Form1.Print Minute(Time)
```

would print 45.

Calculations with time

As with dates you can use the addition and subtraction operators. Consider the following examples which use the **Minute** function in calculating the number of minutes between two times. The output is shown in Figure 6.6.

```
Dim Time1 As Date
Dim Time2 As Date
Dim Time3 As Date
Dim MinutesDiff As Integer
Form1.Show
Time1 = "6:10:30"
Time2 = "6:18:40"
Time3 = "8:30:10"
MinutesDiff = Minute(Time2) - Minute(Time1)
Form1.Print "Minutes difference between " & Time1 & " and " & Time2 & " _
        is   " & MinutesDiff
MinutesDiff = Minute(Time3) - Minute(Time1)
Form1.Print "Minutes difference between " & Time1 & " and " & Time3 & " _
        is   " & MinutesDiff
```

Figure 6.6

The first output in Figure 6.6 is correct because the hour (06) is the same, but the second output, with different hours (06 and 08), does not show the correct total number of minutes difference. To calculate this you need to use the **Hour** function too. The following code would produce the correct answer of 140:

```
HoursDiff = Hour(Time3) - Hour(Time1)
MinutesDiff = (HoursDiff * 60) + (Minute(Time3) - Minute(Time1))
```

Summary of key concepts

- Strings can be declared as **variable length** or **fixed length**.

- Use the relational operators (>, < etc.) to compare strings.

- Use the **Mid** function to process individual characters in a string.

- Use the addition and subtraction operators to increase or reduce a date, or to find the number of days difference between two dates.

- Use the **Format** function to format the output of dates and times.

Take it from here...

1. Two string functions not covered are **StrComp** and **Like**. The former compares two strings to see if they are the same and the latter compares patterns of characters within strings. Find out how these functions work.

2. If you assigned the string "15 Jun 38" to a Date variable, would Visual Basic store this as 15/06/1938 or 15/06/2038? Write a piece of code to demonstrate which century would be stored. Use this code to find out which is the boundary two-digit year for storing a date as 20th century or 21st century.

3. Find out about the following date functions not covered in the chapter – **DateSerial**, **DateAdd** and **DateDiff**.

Questions on the Programs

Program 6.1

**1. The program outputs only one message, if two or more spaces are found. Extend it to output appropriate messages if one or more spaces are found

- before the surname.
- after the first name.

Program 6.2

*1. Run the program but do not enter a closing bracket for the area code. Depending on the speed of your computer's processor the program may seem to hang. It may seem that you have an infinite loop because the loop condition cannot become true. After a short time you'll actually get a run-time error message displaying **overflow**. Click the **Debug** button and the offending line will be highlighted in yellow. Place the cursor over the word *Index* and you'll be given its current value. Can you explain the error?

*2. Assume that the area code always consists of 5 numeric digits. Use the Left and Right functions instead of Mid to extract the area code.

*3.   Rewrite the code using Do While…Loop instead of Do…Loop Until.

**4.   Extend the program so that, if an area code without brackets is entered, an appropriate message is displayed.

Program 6.3

1.   The program uses the Format function to display the full date for the return of issued books. If you have a version of Visual Basic more recent than 5, use the **MonthName and **Month** functions to handle this instead of Format. If you have version 5 or earlier, MonthName is not available, so use Month and a Select Case to convert Month's return value (1 to 12) to a month.

End of chapter exercises

*1.   Ask the user to enter a string and then display it in reverse using a function called **StrReverse** (available from Visual Basic version 6). For example "Hello there" would be displayed as "ereht olleH". There is a harder way to do this using **Mid**. If you use Mid count this as a two-star exercise.

**2.   Ask the user to enter a string and then tell them whether or not it is a palindrome. A palindrome is a string that is the same backwards and forwards. For example "level", "star rats", "eee" are all palindromes.

**3.   Write a program that reads a string from the user and displays only those words beginning with the letters 'd' or 't'.

**4.   Write a program that asks the user to input some text and to indicate which word to search for in the text. Output the number of times this word occurs.

5.   Ask the user to enter some text and change it into upper case without using the UCase function. You will need to use two functions not covered in the chapter, **Asc and **Chr**.

***6.   A manufacturer of sawn timber sells to a large number of timber yards and DIY shops. Assume the user is processing payments from these customers. Allow the user to input the date an invoice should have been paid by and the total value of the invoice. Calculate how many days late, if any, the payment has been made. If payment has been made 15 or more days before the due date give a 10% discount, otherwise give a 5% discount if it has been paid on time. Output details about whether payment has been made on time, any discount given and the total amount due.

***7.   Write a program that counts up and displays how many words the user can type in a minute. The running program can be seen in Figure 1.1. Use a Timer control to display how many seconds have elapsed. At the simplest level you could count the number of spaces in the text to calculate the number of words. But for a 3-star exercise you should handle other possibilities. What if two or more spaces are entered by mistake between words? What if the user starts by accidentally pressing the space bar?

Chapter 7 – Arrays

What is an array?

To store a single number you would declare one Integer variable. To store three numbers you would need three variables:

```
Dim FirstNumber As Integer
Dim SecondNumber As Integer
Dim ThirdNumber As Integer
```

What about storing hundreds or even thousands of numbers? Clearly things get difficult if not impossible! An array is a **data structure** that stores as many items as you require using a single variable. All the items must be the same data type. Thus you can store an array of integers, an array of strings and so on. The only way to mix the data types is to store records in the array, but this is the subject of the next chapter.

You have already used the array data structure, probably without realising it. For example, in program 2.1 you used the ListIndex property of a list box to identify which item in the list box is the currently selected one. Visual Basic numbers the items from 0. So, if you had a list box named lstEmployees, Visual Basic stores the 4th item as lstEmployees(3).

How to declare an array

To declare an array that can store 5 numbers you could write either of the following:

```
Dim Numbers(4) As Integer
Dim Numbers(1 To 5) As Integer
```

The first method numbers the items in the array from 0 to 4 and the second from 1 to 5, as shown in Figure 7.1. The storage 'slots' in the array are called **elements**. The variable *Numbers* stores all the data. Numbers(4), for example, refers to the *contents* of element 4, i.e. 60 in the right-hand diagram.

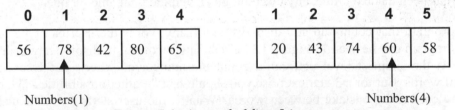

Figure 7.1: Arrays holding 5 integers

Which method you use may depend on what you are storing in the array. For example, if you were storing the annual birth rate in the UK from 1880 to 1960 (81 years in total) you could use any of the following three declarations, but the third one is likely to be the most meaningful.

```
Dim BirthRates(80) As Single
Dim BirthRates(1 To 81) As Single
Dim BirthRates(1880 To 1960) As Single
```

Static and Dynamic arrays

A static array is one whose size is fixed throughout the program. A dynamic array can grow and shrink in size as the program runs. To change its size you must use **ReDim** at the point in your code where you want it to change. For example:

```
Dim Names() As String        'use empty brackets for first declaration
   'code to do something unrelated to the array goes here
ReDim Names(1 To 30) As String        'resize to store 30 items
   'code to add names to the array goes here
```

If we later ReDim the array again to hold more than 30 items, its contents will be lost unless we use the keyword **Preserve**:

```
ReDim Preserve Names(1 To 60) As String
```

Processing an array

Suppose you have declared an array to hold exam marks as follows:

```
Dim ExamMarks(1 To 40) As Integer
```

To store an exam mark in the 4th element of the array you could write:

```
Mark = txtExamMark.Text
ExamMarks(4) = Mark
```

Numeric literals, such as 4 in the above example, are not often used to identify an element in the array. More often you use a variable. Assuming NumberOfMarks stores how many numbers are in the array, the code below prints the array's contents:

```
For Index = 1 To NumberOfMarks
   Form1.Print ExamMarks(Index)
Next Index
```

PROGRAM 7.1   *Array to hold numbers*

Specification	Allow the user to enter up to 5 numbers and store them in an array. Output an appropriate message if the user attempts to store a 6th number. Allow the user to display the contents of the array at any time and to enter a number to be searched for in the array. Display the result of this search.

1. Open a new project and design the form using Figure 7.2. The form has three frames: recall that to make the controls 'belong' to a frame you must first put the frame on the form and then put the controls directly onto it from the toolbox. Name the command buttons **cmdAddToArray**, **cmdDisplay** and **cmdFindNumber**, the text boxes for input and searching **txtNumber** and **txtSearchNumber** respectively, the list box for output **lstNumbers**, and the label to display the result of the search **lblDisplaySearch**.

2. Declare global variables in the General section of the code. These must be globals because they are used in two event procedures.

```
Dim Numbers(1 To 5) As Integer
Dim Index As Integer                        'element of the array
```

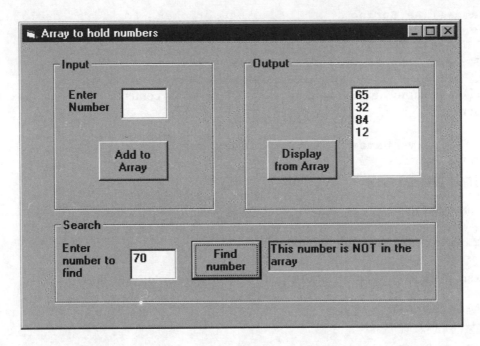

Figure 7.2: Program 7.1 – Four numbers have been stored and a number searched for

3. In the form's Load event procedure initialise Index:

```
Index = 0
```

Index is set to 0 because, as step 4 shows, the code to add an item to the array starts by adding 1 to the value of Index. The first time this is done it will set it to 1, which is the first element in the array.

4. In the Click event for the button to add a number to the array you need to check if the array is full. If it is not full store the number in Numbers(Index), i.e. in the current (free) element.

```
Private Sub cmdAddToArray_Click()
  Dim Number As Integer
  Number = txtNumber.Text
  If Index = 5 Then              'array is full (has 5 numbers in it)
    MsgBox "The array is FULL!"
  Else                           'array not full
    Index = Index + 1            'move to next free element in array
    Numbers(Index) = Number      'and store the number in it
    txtNumber.Text = ""          'clear text box ready for next number
    txtNumber.SetFocus           'and place cursor in it
  End If
End Sub
```

5. Because Index also stores how many numbers there are in the array, it can be used to control a **For...Next** loop to display the array's contents. In the Click event of the other command button type in:

```
Private Sub cmdDisplay_Click()
   Dim Element As Integer
   lstNumbers.Clear      'clear contents of list box else current numbers
                         'in array will be added to list box items
   For Element = 1 To Index   'go through each used element in array and
      lstNumbers.AddItem Numbers(Element) 'display its contents in list box
   Next Element
End Sub
```

6. Run the program and check that the storage and display of numbers works.

7. To search the array for the number entered by the user, the content of each array element must be examined until either you find what you're looking for or you reach the last number in the array without finding it. A Boolean value, Found, is initialised to false and switched to true if the number is found. It is used as part of the multiple condition to get out of the loop. The algorithm used here is the standard linear search and is one that you might find very useful in your project.

```
Private Sub cmdFindNumber_Click()
   Dim Element As Integer
   Dim Found As Boolean
   Dim SearchNumber As Integer
   Element = 1
   Found = False     'searching hasn't started yet so Found should be false
   SearchNumber = txtSearchNumber.Text
   Do While (Found = False) And (Element <= Index)   'one repetition of
                             'the loop processes one number in the array
      If Numbers(Element) = SearchNumber Then
         Found = True
      Else        'current element does not have number being searched for
         Element = Element + 1   'so go to the next element in the array
      End If
   Loop
   If Found Then                        'i.e. if Found = true
      lblDisplaySearch.Caption = "This number IS in the array"
   Else
      lblDisplaySearch.Caption = "This number is NOT in the array"
   End If
End Sub
```

8. Run the program and test the search code with a number that is present in the array and then with one that is not.

end of Program 7.1

Two-dimensional arrays

All the arrays so far have been one-dimensional. Suppose you wished to store a firm's quarterly sales figures for the decade 1990 – 1999. This requires 4 (quarters) x 10 (years) = 40 pieces of data. You could declare a two-dimensional array to hold this data as follows:

```
Dim SalesFigures(1990 To 1999, 1 To 4) As Currency
```

After running the following code

```
SalesFigures(1990, 3) = 56800
SalesFigures(1998, 4) = 96400
```

the array would look like the matrix shown in Figure 7.3. The years are the rows and the quarters the columns because they are declared in that order.

You can have arrays with more than two dimensions but it's unlikely you would ever need to use one. Two-dimensional arrays are useful for storing data for some mathematical problems but in 'business' type problems they are less useful because all their data items must be of the same data type. An array of records (covered in the next chapter) is a more convenient data structure.

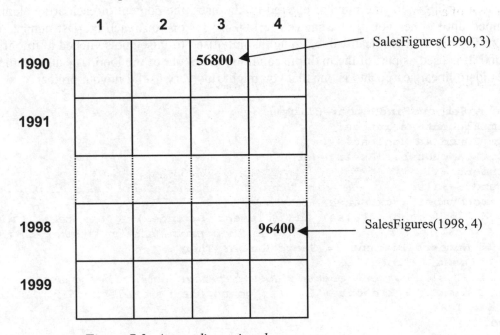

Figure 7.3: A two-dimensional array

Control arrays

A control array is a group of controls which are all of the same type. You can have a control array of text boxes, of command buttons and so on. There are two main advantages in grouping controls this way:

- They all share the same name. For example, five text boxes used for inputting numbers could be named txtNumber(1), txtNumber(2), and so on. If they were not part of a control array each text box would need a different name. Name sharing can often reduce the amount of code you have to write, as program 7.2 illustrates. This technique is used to great effect in the case studies for Units 7 and 22.

- Each control array element has its own properties but, as program 7.3 shows, shares its event procedure code with the other control array elements.

PROGRAM 7.2   *A control array of text boxes*

Specification   Use a control array to store five numbers entered by the user. When all the numbers have been entered, copy them to an 'ordinary' array and display the contents of this array in a second control array.

Figure 7.4 shows the program in action. Five numbers have been entered into a control array of text boxes on the left and then copied to an 'ordinary' array. The control array of labels on the right displays the contents of this ordinary array.

There are two ways of building a control array. Steps 1 and 2 build the text box array using one method and steps 3 and 4 use the other method to build the array of labels.

1.   Open a new project and place the first text box on the form. Name it **txtNumbers**. Set its **Index** property to **1**. The Properties window now shows this control is stored as **txtNumbers(1)**, i.e. element 1 of a control array of text boxes called Numbers.

2.   Position four more text boxes. Set their names to **txtNumbers** and their Index property to **2, 3, 4, 5** as appropriate.

3.   Position the first display label and name it **lblNumbers**.

4.   Copy and paste this label and Visual Basic will display a dialog box asking you if you want to create a control array. Click **Yes**.

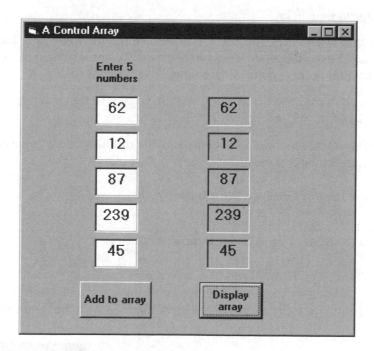

Figure 7.4: Program 7.2

5.   In the Properties window you can see that Visual Basic stores these two labels as lblNumbers(0) and lblNumbers(1). When you create a control array using this method the element numbering starts from 0. To keep it in line with the numbering of the text box elements change the Index property of lblNumbers(1) to **2** and of lblNumbers(0) to **1**. Then place three more labels, name them lblNumbers and set their Indexes from **3** to **5** as appropriate.

6. Add the label instructing users to enter 5 numbers and the two command buttons. Name the buttons **cmdAddToArray** and **cmdDisplayArray**.

7. Declare the 'ordinary' array in the General section:

```
Dim Numbers(1 To 5) As Integer
```

8. Type in the following code for the Click event of the command button to copy the numbers from the control array to the ordinary array.

```
Private Sub cmdAddToArray_Click()
  Dim Index As Integer
  If (txtNumbers(1).Text = "") Or (txtNumbers(2).Text = "") _
        Or (txtNumbers(3).Text = "") Or (txtNumbers(4).Text = "") _
        Or (txtNumbers(5).Text = "") Then
    MsgBox "You have not entered 5 numbers"
  Else
    For Index = 1 To 5
      Numbers(Index) = txtNumbers(Index).Text 'eg number in element 3
                 'of control array copied to element 3 of ordinary array
    Next Index
  End If
End Sub
```

There are two things to note here:

- A multiple OR condition is used to check that the control array contains 5 numbers. If there had been 20 or 30 text boxes this code would become cumbersome. The question on this program at the end of the chapter points you towards a simpler solution to such a situation.

- A **For...Next** loop copies the data from the control array to the ordinary array by matching the elements of the two arrays.

9. The Click event of the command button to copy from the ordinary array to the control array of labels uses a similar **For...Next** loop to the previous one:

```
Private Sub cmdDisplayArray_Click()
  Dim Index As Integer
  For Index = 1 To 5
    lblNumbers(Index).Caption = Numbers(Index)
  Next Index
End Sub
```

10. Run the program. Try it out with less than 5 numbers and then with the required number.

end of Program 7.2

PROGRAM 7.3   *A control array with a shared event procedure*

Specification   Represent the 4 tennis courts owned by a small tennis club by labels on a form. They should be coloured green when the program starts. Clicking any of these should colour it red to show that the court is now in use. The name of the club member responsible for the court should be displayed next to it.

Figure 7.5 shows the program in action. Courts 2 and 3 are in use.

1.   Open a new project and build a control array of 4 labels. Name each one **lblCourts** and set their Index property to **1, 2, 3, 4** as appropriate so that they are stored as lblCourts(1) to lblCourts(4). Set their Font to **14 bold**. Set the Alignment of each to **2 – Center** and the BorderStyle to **1 – Fixed Single**. Set their BackColor to green by clicking the small button in this property, clicking the **Palette** tab and selecting a green colour of your choice.

2.   Put 4 further labels to the right of the tennis court labels and name them **lblNames**. Set their Index properties to **1** to **4** as appropriate so that the control array consists of lblNames(1) to lblNames(4).

3.   Position the text box for inputting a member's name and name it **txtName**. Add the other two labels and set their captions as shown in Figure 8.6.

4.   Double-click any of the tennis court labels and you'll get the following declaration in the code template:

```
Private Sub lblCourts_Click(Index As Integer)
```

Visual Basic has supplied a single parameter, Index. Because the four labels share this procedure, Index is used to identify which one has been clicked.

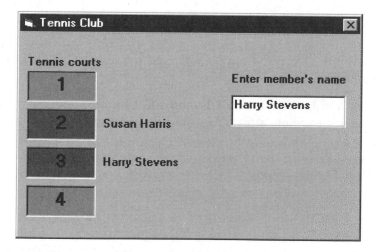

Figure 7.5: Program 7.3

5.   Complete the code for this Click event as follows:

```
Dim Name As String
Name = txtName.Text
lblCourts(Index).BackColor = vbRed        'change tennis court to red and
lblNames(Index).Caption = Name            'display member's name next to it
```

The new thing here is the use of **vbRed**. This is one of 8 **color constants** that you can use to set the colour of an object rather than using the RGB function that you used in Chapter 2.

6. Run the program, enter a member's name and click one of the tennis courts to check that it works.

end of Program 7.3

Summary of key concepts

- An **array** can hold any number of items of the same data type.

- A **static** array cannot change in size at run-time. A **dynamic** array can grow or shrink in size. To change its size redeclare it with the **ReDim** keyword, followed by **Preserve** if you wish to retain the array's contents.

- The storage 'slots' in an array are called **elements**. Thus Numbers(5) and Numbers(24) are two elements of an array called Numbers. Any array element can be read or written to directly.

- Arrays can have two or more dimensions. A **two-dimensional array** can be viewed as a matrix with rows and columns.

- A **control array** is a group of controls or objects which are all of the same type. The controls share the same name and event procedures. For example, a control array of text boxes might be stored as txtNumbers(1) to txtNumbers(10).

Take it from here...

1. If you declare an array with

```
Dim Numbers(9) As Integer
```

Visual Basic numbers the elements from 0 to 8. Find out about **Option Base** and how you can change the lower default boundary.

2. Two functions not used in the chapter are **UBound** and **LBound**. Find out what these do and how you might use them when handling arrays. Also find out about the **UBound** and **LBound** *properties* of a control array.

Questions on the Programs

Program 7.1

*1. When a number is added to the array a check is made to see if it is full. Remove this check by commenting out all the code in the If statement body except the four lines which currently belong to Else. Run the program and enter 6 numbers. Try to understand the error message you get when you try to store the 6th number.

*2. Using the initial static array declaration so that 5 numbers can be stored, increase the size of the array by 1 each time the user clicks to store another number when they have entered six or more numbers.

**3.   Add command buttons to do two things:

- Find and display the highest number in the array. Hint: store the first number in the array into a variable *Highest* and then loop through the rest of the numbers comparing each with the current value of *Highest*.

- Calculate and display the mean value of the numbers in the array.

Program 7.2

1.   A compound If statement is used in the Click event for cmdAddToArray to check if any of the five text boxes have not got a number. Rewrite this using a **For Each…Next statement. You may have found out about this special loop in doing question 3 of *Take it from here...* in Chapter 5. It allows you to process each element in a control array. Visual Basic has a range of data types to handle controls or objects in your program and you will need to use one of these here. Declare a variable of a TextBox data type, for example:

```
Dim MyTextBox As TextBox
```

End of chapter exercises

*1.   In a program you could have a control array of command buttons instead of using option buttons. Build a simple program to illustrate this. Use an array of three command buttons to represent how much a person is satisfied with a particular service on a scale of 1 to 3. When one of the buttons is clicked an appropriate message should be displayed, e.g. for button 3 display the message *You are very satisfied with the service*.

**2.   Exercise 4 at the end of Chapter 3 asked you to build a simple calculator. You will have needed separate event procedures for each of the four arithmetic operator command buttons. Now group these buttons into a control array and rewrite the program using a single event procedure.

**3.   Write a program to store product codes in an array. Product codes have 6 characters and each code must be different from all the other codes. After the user enters a product code check that the code has not been used already and output an appropriate message if it has.

**4.   Write a program to help children learn their capital cities. Use two arrays – one for country names and one for their capitals. Store about 6 items in each array (or more if you wish) in the form's Load event procedure and use two list boxes to display the contents of the arrays when the program starts. The child should select a country from one list box and its corresponding capital from the other. When a command button is clicked tell the child if the answer is correct. If the answer is wrong display the correct one.

***5.   Write a program to input, for up to 20 students, their name and the marks they achieved on each of three exams. Store this data in a two-dimensional array. Because the names must be stored as Strings, the marks must also be of this data type rather than Integer, since all items in an array must be of the same data type. Allow the user to display all the names and marks at any time (in a list box). This part of the program is shown in Figure 7.6.

When you have this working extend the program so that the user can select one of the exams and see its average mark. Use option buttons for selecting the exam.

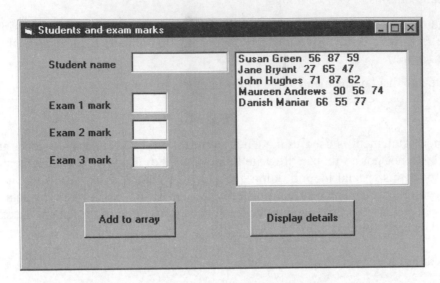

Figure 7.6: Program for the first part of exercise 5

***6.** Write a program to build a more realistic calculator than the one in exercise 2, as shown in Figure 7.7. Use two control arrays of labels. One of these has the 10 digits plus the decimal point. The other has the 4 arithmetic operators and the '=' sign. Clicking any of the labels in the arrays sets off the relevant control array's Click event procedure. The C button clears the display and allows a new calculation to start. The Off button simulates switching the calculator off, i.e. the program closes. Use the form's Unload event to close the program (see step 7 in program 3.4).

Figure 7.7: The calculator for exercise 6

Chapter 8 – Printing

Printing to a form

In earlier programs we often used the Print method of a form to display output. We did this as a quick method of confirming that our code was doing what it was supposed to do. Most of these programs, 3.1 to 3.3 for example, simply printed the result of something at the left margin of the form. Program 5.2, however, used one or two other ways to position the printed output on a form. Whatever the display looks like, in real applications it is unlikely that you will wish to print much data on a form.

Printing to a printer

To send output to a printer you need to use the Printer object. Like all objects it has a range of properties and methods. The most important ones are:

Properties

Orientation   The page orientation. Use the constants **vbPRORPortrait** and **vbPRORLandscape**.

Page   Visual Basic keeps track of how many pages have been printed.

Methods

EndDoc   Terminates a print operation sent to the Printer object. For safety call this method at the end of a print operation.

Font   FontSize, FontBold, FontUnderline, FontItalic are the important varieties. Set FontSize to a number and the others to True or False (e.g. Printer.FontSize = 15).

NewPage   Forces output to a new page, Increments the Page property by 1.

Print   Prints the listed item(s) after this method call and moves the printing position to the next line. To get a blank line call the method alone.

PROGRAM 8.1   *Printing exam marks*

Specification   Extend Program 3.4 so that the exam marks and the mean mark are printed out.

Program 3.4 allowed the user to enter any number of exam marks. These were displayed in a list box and the mean mark was displayed in a text box when the user clicked a command button. In this program we will run through the data in the list box, print it and print the mean displayed in the text box.

1. Open Program 3.4 and add another command button. Change its caption to **Print** and its name to **cmdPrint**.

2. Enter the code below for the Click event of the command button. Always use the Print method of the Printer object (i.e. Printer.Print) to print something. If you do not add what to print then it prints a blank line. Tab is used to position what is printed. For an even-spaced font, like the one used for code, the value in brackets after Tab means that printing starts that number of characters from the left. For a proportional font the relationship between the Tab value and the number of characters is more complex. Note that you do not *have* to state which font to use when using the Print method.

```
Private Sub cmdPrint_Click()
  Dim Index As Integer
  Printer.Font = "Courier"                   'this is an even-spaced font
  Printer.Print "Exam marks"
  Printer.Print                              'prints a blank line
  For Index = 0 To lstMarks.ListCount - 1 'ListCount stores how many
                                             'items list box contains
     Printer.Print Tab(12); lstMarks.List(Index) 'List(0) is first item in
                                         'list box, List(1) the second item etc.
  Next Index
  Printer.Print
  Printer.Print "Average"; Tab(12); Format(txtMean.Text, "0.0")
  Printer.EndDoc                             'terminate printing correctly
End Sub
```

3. Run the program. Your printed output should look something like that in Figure 8.1

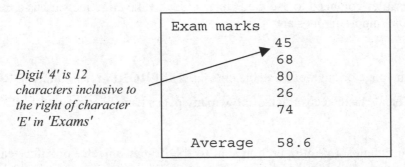

Figure 8.1: Printing from Program 8.1

end of Program 8.1

PROGRAM 8.2   *Printing reports on sales staff*

Specification   For a number of salespeople store their name, the region they work in and the annual value of their sales in one or more arrays. Print this data on the form and to the printer. Two printed reports should be made. One should output the details by salesperson and the other should group these details by region.

The three items of data can be seen printed on the form in Figure 8.2 and as a printed report in Figure 8.3.

1. Declare Open a new project and place three command buttons on it as shown in Figure 8.2. Name them **cmdPrintToForm**, **cmdReportBySalesperson** and **cmdReportByRegion** and set their captions as in the Figure. Set the form's Font to an even spaced font – **Courier New 8 point bold**.

2. We could use three separate arrays or one two-dimensional array to hold the data about the salespeople. We will use the two-dimensional array. You may need to look back at pages 79 – 80 to remind yourself what this type of array is. Recall that all arrays can only hold data of the same data type. So declare it as follows:

```
Dim Salespeople(1 To 20, 1 To 3) As String   'stores details for up to
                                             '20 salespeople
```

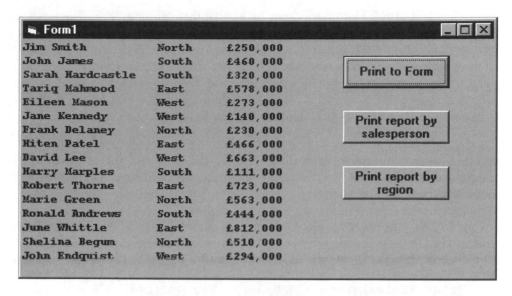

Figure 8.2: Program 8.2 when the Print to Form button has been clicked

3. Write code in the form's Load event to store the details about each salesperson. Note that the sales value is stored in units of a thousand. For example, the sales value for Jim Smith in Figure 8.2 is £250,000, but this is stored as 250.

```
Private Sub Form_Load()
   Salespeople(1, 1) = "Jim Smith"        'store name in column 1 of array
   Salespeople(1, 2) = "North"            'store region in column 2 of array
   Salespeople(1, 3) = "250"              'store sales in column 3 of array
   Salespeople(2, 1) = "John James"       'second salesperson's details
   Salespeople(2, 2) = "South"               'stored in row 2 of array
   Salespeople(2, 3) = "460"
   Salespeople(3, 1) = "Sarah Hardcastle"    'third salesperson's details
   Salespeople(3, 2) = "South"                  'stored in row 3 of array
   Salespeople(3, 3) = "320"
      'and so on up to ........
   Salespeople(16, 1) = "John Endquist"'last salesperson's details
   Salespeople(16, 2) = "West"               'stored in row 16 of array
   Salespeople(16, 3) = "294"
End Sub
```

4. In the code to print the details on the form, Tab(20) displays the sales region in column 20 and Tab(30) displays the sales amount 10 columns further on from the first character of the region. Note that the sales value stored in the array is converted to thousands and formatted to whole pounds.

```
Private Sub cmdPrintToForm_Click()
  Dim Index As Integer
  Form1.Show
  For Index = 1 To 16
    Print Salespeople(Index, 1); Tab(20); Salespeople(Index, 2); _
                Tab(30); Format(Salespeople(Index, 3) * 1000, "£#,##0")
  Next Index
End Sub
```

5. Run the program and check that your output looks like that in Figure 8.2. Then experiment to see how the Tab function works. Change Tab(20) to Tab(14) and run it again. The data for two people, Sarah Hardcastle and Ronald Andrews, is now displayed over two lines, and in six cases the region is displayed after the name with no space between the two items. The reason for the two-line display is because these names are 14 or more characters long and Tab(14) needs to display the sales region in column 14. If the column is "occupied" like this then printing resumes on the next line, in column 14 in this example. Change the 14 back to 20 when you have tried this out.

6. The report we want to produce by clicking the *Print report by salesperson* button is shown in Figure 8.3. The code is essentially the same as for printing to the form except that the Print method of the Printer object is used. The point made in step 5 about setting the Tab positions in unoccupied spaces applies equally to the Printer object.

```
Private Sub cmdReportBySalesperson_Click()
  Dim Index As Integer
  Printer.Print "Report on annual sales made by Salespeople"
  Printer.Print
  Printer.Print "Salesperson"; Tab(20); "Region"; Tab(30); _
                                    "Value of sales"

  Printer.Print
  For Index = 1 To 16
    Printer.Print Salespeople(Index, 1); Tab(20); Salespeople(Index, 2); _
             Tab(30); Format(Salespeople(Index, 3) * 1000, "£#,##0")
  Next Index
  Printer.EndDoc
End Sub
```

```
Report on annual sales made by sales staff

Salesperson          Region      Value of sales

Jim Smith            North       £250,000
John James           South       £460,000
Sarah Hardcastle     South       £320,000
Tariq Mahmood        East        £578,000
Eileen Mason         West        £273,000
Jane Kennedy         West        £140,000
Frank Delaney        North       £230,000
Hiten Patel          East        £466,000
David Lee            West        £663,000
Harry Marples        South       £111,000
Robert Thorne        East        £723,000
Marie Green          North       £563,000
Ronald Andrews       South       £444,000
June Whittle         East        £812,000
Shelina Begum        North       £510,000
John Endquist        West        £294,000
```

Figure 8.3: Report on sales by salesperson

7. Run the program and check that the report is printed correctly.

8. Figure 8.4 shows the report by region. The code below uses Do While…Loop rather than For…Next simply to show you how to loop through an array if you do not know how many items (salespeople) are stored in it. The sales region names make up what is called a **group header**. To process one sales region each row in the array up to the last row with any data in it is looked at to see if its sales region matches the one being processed. So the array must be processed four times in total. The other thing to note here is the **Space** function. The group header name is printed 3 spaces from the left; we could also have written Tab(3).

```vb
Private Sub cmdReportByRegion_Click()
   Dim Index As Integer
   Dim SalesRegion As Integer
   Dim Region As String
   Dim RegionGroup As String
   Dim NumUnderscores As Integer
   Printer.FontSize = 13                'larger point size and
   Printer.FontBold = True              'bold too for report header
   Printer.Print "Report on annual sales made by sales staff"
   Printer.FontSize = 11                'back to normal for rest of report
   Printer.FontBold = False
   For NumUnderscores = 1 To 60         'put line across most of page
      Printer.Print "_";
   Next NumUnderscores
   Printer.Print
   Printer.Print
   For SalesRegion = 1 To 4             'loop 4 times - once per sales region
      Select Case SalesRegion          'find correct group header
         Case 1
            RegionGroup = "East"
         Case 2
            RegionGroup = "North"
         Case 3
            RegionGroup = "South"
         Case 4
            RegionGroup = "West"
      End Select
      Printer.Print Space(3); RegionGroup 'print region 3 columns from left
      Index = 1
      Do While Salespeople(Index, 1) <> ""  'loop while there is data
                                            'in the array to process
         Region = Salespeople(Index, 2)
         If Region = RegionGroup Then        'is region the required one?
            Printer.Print Tab(10); Salespeople(Index, 1); Tab(40); _
                     Format(Salespeople(Index, 3) * 1000, "£#,##0")
         End If
         Index = Index + 1
      Loop
      Printer.Print
   Next SalesRegion
   Printer.EndDoc
End Sub
```

```
Report on annual sales made by sales staff
_____

   East
        Tariq Mahmood              £578,000
        Hiten Patel                £466,000
        Robert Thorne              £723,000
        June Whittle               £812,000

   North
        Jim Smith                  £250,000
        Frank Delaney              £230,000
        Marie Green                £563,000
        Shelina Begum              £510,000

   South
        John James                 £460,000
        Sarah Hardcastle           £320,000
        Harry Marples              £111,000
        Ronald Andrews             £444,000

   West
        Eileen Mason               £273,000
        Jane Kennedy               £140,000
        David Lee                  £663,000
        John Endquist              £294,000
```

Figure 8.4: Report on sales by region

9. Run the program and check that the report is printed correctly.

end of Program 8.2

Summary of key concepts

- Both a form and the printer are objects, and they share the same Print method for displaying output.

- Use the **Tab** and **Space** functions to position output.

Questions on Program 8.1

*1. The role of the EndDoc method will not have been clear from the program as it stands. Comment out Printer.EndDoc in cmdReportBySalesperson, run the program and then click the button to print the report by salesperson. Nothing is printed. Now click to produce the other report. Examine what comes out of the printer. Now remove the commenting and then comment out the same line in cmdReportByRegion, run the program and click both buttons (report by salesperson first). What is printed? Close the program and the other report will be printed. What can you conclude about the way EndDoc works from all this?

**2.   Extend the report by region to include:

- A group footer (i.e. at the end of each sales region) to show the total value of the sales for that region.
- Use the Page property and NewPage method of the Printer object to print the details of each region on a separate page and to print the page number on each page. The report header should now be a page header so that it is repeated on each page. You may wish to make its font smaller.

***3.   Extend the report by salesperson to include:

- The total value of all sales.
- The average value of all sales.
- A 4th column indicating how much the salesperson's value of sales exceeds or is below the average, expressed as a percentage.

End of chapter exercises

*1.   Add a Print command button to Program 4.4 to print a list of the patients in the ward currently selected from the Wards list box. Your code should get the patients' names from the Patients list box. The printed report should have the ward name as a title and state how many patients are in the ward.

**2.   Download the form file Chap08Ex2.frm from the publisher's web site (see the Introduction for the address). Its Load event stores four items of data in four arrays about 16 products sold by a garden centre (product ID, product description, unit price and quantity in stock). Produce the following reports. Write the code in the Click events for the two command buttons on the form.

(a)   The report shown in Figure 8.5 (N.B. this shows only details of the first two products).

(b)   A report displaying the same information as Figure 8.5 but grouped according to the price of the products. Use 3 groups – under £10.00, £10.00 to under £50.00 and £50.00 and over.

```
Report on Garden Centre stock

Product ID  Description            Price      Qty in stock      Stock value

421         garden shears         £12.65         142           £1,796.30
783         wheelbarrow           £34.20          64           £2,188.80
............
                                         Total stock value      £24,445.01
```

Figure 8.5: The report for exercise 2(a)

To use the downloaded form in a project select Project/Add Form, click the Existing tab in the Add Form dialog box and then select Chap08Ex2. To get this form to open when the program runs, select Project/Project1 Properties (or the name of the project instead of Project1 if you have named it by this stage). Then select frmChap08Ex2 from the Startup Object combo box and click OK.

Part Two – Building a Portfolio

Your teacher will set you one or more assignments that will allow you to meet the *Assessment Evidence* for Unit 7 (see Appendix D). Essentially for any assignment you will need to go through the DIDiT (Design, Implementation, Documentation, Testing) stages.

Your teacher is allowed to give you a basic program specification – what an imaginary user of your program requires it to do. Part Two provides a case study like this and has an assignment based on it. It then takes you through the DIDiT stages and shows you how to produce a portfolio of work using the case study.

Chapter 9 introduces the case study. This is called *Gina's Groceries*, based on a small greengrocery run by Gina and her two part-time assistants. An assignment follows with a grid matching the tasks in the assignment to the grade criteria in the Assessment Evidence.

Chapter 10 takes you through the **Design** stage. It shows you how to design the single program form and the receipt that has to be printed. It explains how you can use arrays to store some of the data in the system. A list of **event procedures** and their tasks is drawn up and you are shown how to think about the **processing** requirements of your system.

Chapter 11 takes you through the **Implementation** (coding) stage. It shows you how to build a fully-working program to meet Gina's requirements.

Chapter 12 takes you through the **Documentation** stage. It looks at the two types of documentation you have to produce – **user** documentation for Gina and her assistants and **technical** documentation for fellow-programmers.

Chapter 13 shows you how to do the **Testing** stage. First the principles of how to carry out a test program are reviewed, and then these are applied to two event procedures.

Note that *Gina's Groceries* is provided as a case study to show you how to produce a portfolio of work to meet the Assessment Evidence for Unit 7. You should not use this case study for your own portfolio. Your teacher will provide you with a program specification.

Chapter 9 – The Assignment: Gina's Groceries

The case study

Read the case study below.

Gina's Groceries

Gina's Groceries is a small greengrocery in a parade of shops that sells the usual variety of fruit and vegetables. Customers select what they wish to buy and take it to the till for Gina or one of her two part-time assistants to weigh, price and wrap up the produce. Your task is to write a program that emulates the weighing and pricing, and produces a receipt for each customer.

The program must allow the user to select products and to indicate their weight. Allow weights up to 10 kilograms. You need only deal in fractions to an accuracy of $^1/_{10}$ (0.1) of a kilogram (i.e. 100 gm). The program should display the details of a particular sale when it is made – the product's name, weight, price per kg and cost to the customer. A running total cost of how much the current customer has spent should also be displayed.

You should store two details about each product for sale – its name/type (e.g. Apples – Golden Delicious) and price per kilogram (e.g. £0.90). You need only store details of 8 products as the purpose of the program is to produce a working prototype for Gina, not a full-blown version. However Gina should be able to change the price per kg of any of these products or to change the product itself by inputting a new name/type and its price per kg.

When all the purchases for a particular customer have been processed the program should print a receipt. This should be dated and list the name and cost (but not the weight) of each product bought, and also show the total cost.

Sometimes customers change their mind after they have bought a product and wish to return it. Although this does not happen too often, your program must allow for these returns.

Note the following points from the program specification above:

- How you would design the interface is up to you as long as the listed requirements are met. However, you should aim to reduce the amount of typing Gina and her assistants must do to a minimum since they are busy people when serving their customers.

- In a real system the product details (name and price per kg) would be stored in a file. In this book, file handling is part of Unit 22. This data must therefore be stored in RAM only. The specification could have asked you to get the user to type this in but the great drawback here would be the amount of time it would take you to do this every time you ran the program. Instead hard-code this storage – write code yourself that stores the names and prices of the 8 products when the program runs. Program 8.2 used this technique to store names of sales staff and the value of their sales in an array.

The assignment tasks

Task 1 - Designing the program

To achieve a **grade E** you must:

1.1 Rewrite the program specification given to you in your own words.

1.2 Draw a sketch of the form(s) in your program indicating all the controls. Briefly explain what the more important controls will be used for.

1.3 Design the receipt that Gina will give her customers.

1.4 List the events in your program and briefly state what will happen as each of these occurs.

To achieve a **grade A** you must:

1.5 Do tasks 1.2 and 1.4 to a very good standard. You must allow the user to interact with the program easily and efficiently.

Task 2 – Implementing the program

To achieve a **grade E** you must:

2.1 Write the code for the program. This must be of a reasonable standard and include some commenting (see also task 3.2). Most of Gina's requirements must be met.

To achieve a **grade A** you must:

2.2 Write the code to a very good standard. All of Gina's requirements must be met. Data entry must be clear and easy for the user, and where appropriate data should be validated.

Task 3 – Documenting the program

To achieve a **grade E** you must:

3.1 Write a **user guide** for Gina and her assistants on how to use the program. This must be of a reasonable standard

3.2 Write the **technical documentation** for your program. This should include:

- A printout of your program code, containing a reasonable amount of commenting.
- A program specification, covering input, output and processing.
- The modular structure of the program. List all the event procedures and the tasks they will carry out. This will only extend task 1.4 if you have altered the modular structure since designing it.

To achieve a **grade C** you must:

3.3 Ensure the user guide you have to do for task 3.1 is of a good quality. It must include appropriate graphic images and a sample printed receipt. Any error messages that Gina will get must also be covered.

3.4 Ensure the technical documentation for task 3.2 is of a good standard. In addition you must cover the following:

- Printouts of all the forms and any dialog box in your program. Show the Visual Basic names of all the controls on these forms and explain how these controls and the dialog boxes work.
- A list of all the variables your program uses.
- Any additional explanations of how your program works which are not covered by the code commenting or elsewhere.

Task 4 – Testing the program

To achieve a grade A you must:

4.1 Draw up test plans for each appropriate event procedure to test all major paths and to cover acceptable and unacceptable input.

4.2 Carry out the test plans you have drawn up for task 4.1. Wherever possible provide documentary evidence that the test does what you claim it does. Show clearly how you resolved any problems in your program uncovered by these tests.

In addition to all the tasks above, to achieve at least a grade C you must meet any deadlines your assessor has set and you must not have been given more than a reasonable amount of help.

Meeting the Assessment Evidence

Appendix D lists what you have to do to achieve grades E, C or A. By doing the tasks set above you will be able to meet these criteria. Figure 9.1 matches the assignment tasks to this Assessment Evidence.

Assessment Evidence	Assignment tasks
E1	1.1, 1.3
E2	1.2, 1.4
E3	1.2, 2.1
E4	2.1
E5	1.2, 1.4, 2.1
E6	2.1
E7	2.1
E8	3.1
C1	3.4
C2	3.3
C3	–
A1	1.5, 2.2
A2	2.2
A3	1.5, 2.2
A4	4.1, 4.2

Figure 9.1: Matching the assignment tasks to the Assessment Evidence

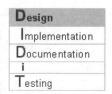

Chapter 10 – Design

What is design?

Design is about preparing the groundwork so that when you come to code your program the only major decisions you have to make are about the coding itself. At the design stage you should have worked out details of the following:

- The layout of the form(s) to be used, to include all the controls.

- The layout of any printed reports

- Data storage

- The event procedures required and the tasks each will carry out

- Processing required

Form design

You should produce paper designs of each form in your project, drawn by hand or by using a software package. For Gina's Groceries we can fit everything onto one form. Figure 10.1 shows the complete design. If you want to see what the form looks like in practice look ahead at figures 11.1 and 11.3. There are three main parts to the form: let us go through them in turn.

Selecting, weighing and selling products. A control to allow the user to select a weight rather than having to type one in is a good way of validating the input. The only control you have met so far that you could use here is the scroll bar, but it is not as good as the control we will use – an UpDown control. This is often known as a spinner or spin button. Clicking the arrow buttons changes the weight.

The product names are displayed in labels and the user selects a product simply by clicking its label. We could use command buttons for this instead; there is little to choose between them. When the user selects a product its name, price per kg, weight and price to pay appear in the list box and the total spent so far appears to the right of the list box. Clicking the *Sell* button saves the name and price paid for the product just sold.

The area of the form for selecting a product and its weight is supposed to look a little like a concept keyboard with a weighing surface above. From now on the term *weighing machine* will refer to this area.

Changing product details. A product is selected from a combo box. The user can replace this product with a new one and enter the new product's price, or leave the new product control blank and change the price of an existing one. Its current price is displayed and there is a text box in which to enter the new price. Clicking the *OK* button saves these changes.

Returning a product. The specification states that customers occasionally change their minds about a purchase after it has been processed. Details of the purchase must be removed from the system. A combo box displays all the purchases made by the current customer. The user selects one of these and then clicks the *Return* button to remove details of this purchase from the system.

There are two other things on the form. The *New Customer* button must be clicked before dealing with a new customer (so that a range of things can be done to the display and data storage, which we will come to later). The *Print Receipt* button prints a receipt for the current customer.

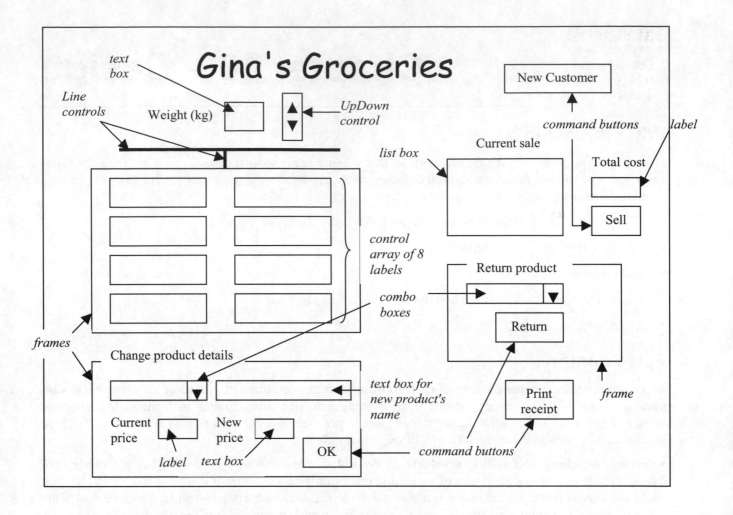

Figure 10.1: Design of the form

Printed report – the receipt

You should design the layout of any printed reports your program will produce. For Gina's Groceries all we need is the receipt, which is shown in Figure 10.2

```
Gina's Groceries        date

Item 1              £2.50
Item 2              £0.80
Item 3              £1.20
Item 4              £0.50


    Total           £5.00

Thank you for your custom
```

Figure 10.2: Design of the receipt

Data storage

If your program needs to use more complex data storage than just a series of single variables then you should plan this now. The only complex type of data structure covered in the Visual Basic chapters for Unit 7 is the array. The other complex structures, records, arrays of records and files, are left until Unit 22. Chapter 9 stated that a real system would store details about Gina's products in a file but, as you have not covered files yet, it told you to store details of the products in temporary storage.

We need to store two things about each of the 8 products the assignment asks us to handle – its name/description and its price per kg. You have two possible solutions:

- Store the product names in one array and the prices in a second array.
- Store both items in a two-dimensional array.

In Chapter 7 you learned that a two-dimensional array can store only items belonging to the same data type. Since the names have to be Strings, the prices would have to be Strings too. This is not a problem but it would require converting from String to Currency when processing the price. We will use two arrays instead, which will let us store the names as String and the prices as Currency.

What about storing details of the products that are sold to a particular customer? The program specification states that the receipt needs to have the name and cost of each product but not the weight. Therefore we need only store two things about each product sold. The solution we will use is to have two more arrays, one each for the product names and costs of the sold products.

You may be finding it difficult to visualise what these arrays look like. Figure 10.3 shows how the product names could be stored in an array called *Products* and the prices in £ per kg stored in an array called *Prices*.

	Products		**Prices**
1	Apples - Granny Smith's	1	0.90
2	Pears - Conference	2	1.10
3	Bananas - Jamaican	3	0.82
4	Grapes - Small seedless	4	1.60
5	Carrots - English	5	0.60
6	Potatoes - Whites	6	0.35
7	Parsnips - French	7	1.05
8	Sprouts - West country	8	0.80

Figure 10.3: Storing the product names and prices in two arrays

Suppose the customer buys 2 kg each of carrots, grapes and potatoes. Figure 10.4(a) shows how these details could be stored in an array *Sold Products* to hold the products sold, and an array *Sold Costs* to hold the prices paid by the customer. Then suppose the customer decides they do not want the grapes after all. The arrays will look like Figure 10.4(b). The only difference between the two sets of arrays is that the element in the *Sold Products* array containing the returned product is now blank. To print the receipt we need to loop through the elements in the *Sold Products* array that have been used for the current customer and print out the contents of those that are *not* blank. Notice that the value in the *Sold Costs* array for the grapes has not been deleted. We could delete it, but there is no point because the code for printing the receipt only needs to look at the data in the *Sold Products* array to see if there is a product to process. For example, in Figure 10.4(b), when processing the 2nd element of *Sold Products,* you do not need to look at the contents of the 2nd element of *Sold Costs*.

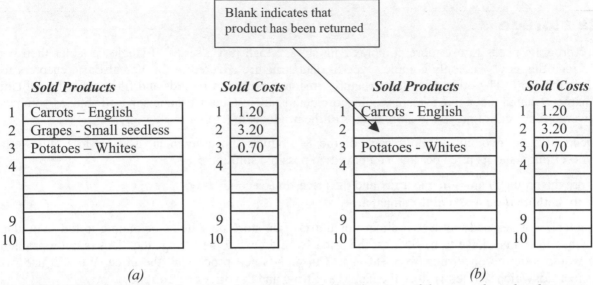

Figure 10.4: (a) storing 3 products that have been sold (b) after one of these products has been returned

Event procedures

At the design stage you should be able to identify all the events that will occur as your program runs and to list most of the tasks they should carry out. You may be able to list all their tasks but sometimes there are small things that crop up when you test event procedures that you simply have not thought about at the design stage. Figure 10.5 lists all the tasks that one might draw up at this stage after a lot of careful thought. Some of these are major tasks. For example, clicking the *Sell* command button stores details of the product just sold into two arrays. Some are minor tasks by comparison. For example, this event procedure also enables the *Print receipt* command button – we do not want the user trying to print a receipt before the customer has bought any products.

There are several points to note about the tasks listed in Figure 10.5.

- The Click event is by far the most common event. The same will probably be true of your own program.

- The UpDown control's event is the Change event. It does not have a Click event even though you click it to change its value.

- Many of the tasks have a visual result – recalculating and displaying the total spent so far by the current customer for example. Some go on behind the scenes – storing details in the arrays is one example. Some of these unseen tasks may not be that obvious at design time. Clicking the *New Customer* command button, for example, involves setting the number of products sold to the current customer and the total amount spent by this customer to 0.

Drawing up a detailed list of tasks like this at design time is not an easy thing for inexperienced programmers. Although assignment task 1.4 asks you to do this as part of the Design stage, you may well improve on your solution as you code the program. One of the technical documentation tasks, task 3.2, asks you to document this modular structure again in the expectation that you will have added to your design solution by this stage. The reason for trying to do it at design time is that it will help you enormously when you start coding. This point cannot be over-emphasised.

Event	*Control*	*Tasks*
Load	Form	• Stores product names in *Products* array • Stores prices of products in *Prices* array • Displays product names in the weighing machine
Selecting, weighing and selling products		
Change	UpDown control	• Displays weight of product
Click	Labels in the weighing machine that display product names	• Calculates cost of sale of selected product • Displays details of sale of selected product in *Current sale* list box – product name, price per kg and cost • Enables *Sell* button
Click	*Sell* command button	• Saves details of the sale (product name and cost to the customer) in the *Sold Products* and *Sold Costs* arrays • Recalculates and displays total spent so far by current customer • Adds the product just sold to the list of products bought by the current customer that are displayed in the *Return product* combo box • Enables the *Print receipt* command button
Returning products		
Click	*Return product* combo box	• Enables *Return* command button (which will be in a disabled state if the product being returned is the first one that the current customer is returning)
Click	*Return* command button	• Removes product sold from *Sold Products* array • Removes returned product from the list of products sold to current customer displayed in *Return product* combo box • If details of the returned product are currently displayed in the *Current sale* list box, removes these details • Recalculates and displays total spent so far by current customer • Disables itself if the product returned is the only product so far sold to current customer (so that user cannot click it to return a product when no products have now been bought)
Changing product details		
Click	*Products* combo box	• Displays price per kg of product selected from *Change product details* combo box
Click	*OK* command button	• Stores details of the new product, or the new price of an existing product, in the *Products* and *Prices* arrays
Other events		
Click	*New Customer* command button	• Clears details of the last product bought by the previous customer from the list box. • Disables the *Save* and *Return* command buttons • Clears the *Return product* combo box • Sets the total amount of money spent by the new customer to 0 and displays this value • Sets number of products sold to the new customer to 0
Click	*Print receipt* command button	• Prints receipt for current customer

Figure 10.5: The tasks of the event procedures

Processing

Processing is about how the data input and stored in a system is manipulated to produce the required output. Output covers both screen and printed output. At the design stage you should decide in principle how all the processing will be carried out. Let us consider three examples of processing in Gina's Groceries.

Display the product names in the weighing machine. These names will have been stored in the *Products* array during the Form's Load event. A loop can be used to go through each product in this array and copy its name to the appropriate label on the weighing machine.

Retrieve the cost per kg in the *Prices* array of the product selected from the *Change product details* combo box, and display this value in the *Current price* label. This process will be done when the user wants to change the price of an existing product. A loop will go through each product in the *Products* array searching for the product selected from the combo box. When the product is found its price can be copied from the *Prices* array (recall that this is stored in the same array element as the product name in the *Products*) to the label and the loop terminated.

Print the receipt. The number of sales made to the current customer will have been calculated, so loop through the *Sold Products* array this number of times. If the content of the array element is blank this means that the product has been returned (see Figure 10.4(b)) so ignore it, otherwise print out the product name and its price from the corresponding element in the *Sold Costs* array. Since the running total cost to the current customer is displayed on the form this can be copied to the receipt.

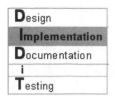

Chapter 11 – Implementation

The Form

It is a fairly simply job to implement the design of the single form in Figure 10.1. Figure 11.1 shows the form in design view and Figure 11.3 shows it when the program is running.

1. Open a new project. You do not need to change the form's default name since we will not reference it in any code. Save it as **GinasGroceries** and then save the project under this name too.

Weighing and selecting products

2. For the upper part of the weighing machine add the label and text box where the weight will be displayed and name the text box **txtWeight**. The two thick lines below it, which are supposed to suggest a weighing surface, are both Line controls (from the toolbox) with a BorderWidth property of **3**.

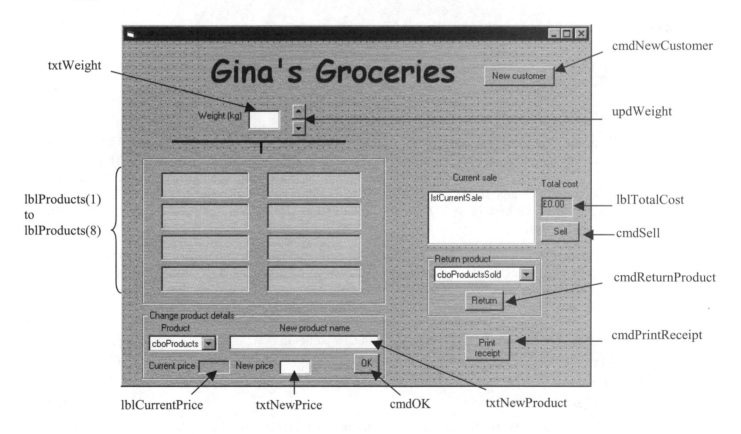

Figure 11.1: The form in design view

3. In our design we decided on an UpDown control to input the weight of a product. This is not part of the standard set of controls and so we need to add it to the toolbox. Select **Project/Components** and in the Components dialog box check the item called **Microsoft Windows Common Controls-2** as in Figure 11.2. The version of Visual Basic you are using will also be part of the name of this item to select. In Figure 11.2 this is **6.0**, and as version 5 is also installed on the computer used for this screen shot, this is listed too. Click **OK** and, depending on which version of Visual Basic you are using, you will get a particular set of controls added to the toolbox. One of these is the UpDown control. Go to step 5 if this control is not available.

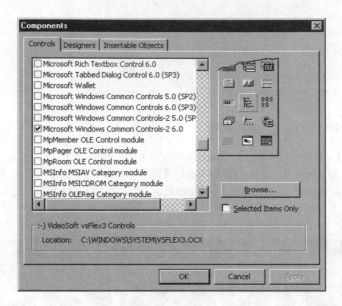

Figure 11.2: The Components dialog box

4. Position an UpDown control on the form. Change its name to **updWeight**. The program specification stated that the weighing machine should handle weights up to 10 kg at 0.1 kg intervals. Its Min property must therefore represent 0.0 kg and its Max property 10.0 kg. As the default Min value is 0 do not change it, but set the Max value to **100**. The default value of its Interval property is 1 so accept this. We now have 101 possible values (0 to 100) which represent 101 possible weights (0.0 kg to 10.0 kg).

5. If the UpDown control in step 4 is not available, or for some reason you cannot use it on the form (on a school or college network, for example, you may get an error message saying that you are not a registered user), use a horizontal scroll bar (HscrollBar) control instead. Give it an appropriate name and set it Max property to **100**. Read the explanation in step 4.

Recall from Chapter 10 that the user selects a product by clicking one of the labels with a product name on the weighing machine. There are two ways we can implement the labels to hold these product names:

- Eight separate labels, each with a different Name property.
- A control array of eight labels.

With the first solution you would need a click event for each label. With the control array you need only one click event for all eight labels. You met this concept in Program 7.3. The other advantage of a control array is that we can use the number of the label that has been clicked as a direct index into the two arrays that store details of the products. For example, if you click the 3rd label (which has an Index property of 3), you can use this fact to process element 3 of the arrays, since this element in the *Products* array stores the product's name and in the *Prices* array stores its price per kg.

Figure 11.3: The form in use

6. Place the first label of the weighing machine (Apples - Granny Smith's in Figure 11.3) on the frame. Change its name to **lblProducts** and set its Index property to **1.** Notice that Visual Basic has changed its name to lblProducts(1). Set its BorderStyle to **Fixed Single**.

7. Place a second label beneath the first one. Change its name to **lblProducts** and set its Index property to **2.** Its name is now lblProducts(2). Set its BorderStyle property as in step 6.

8. Place six more labels on the frame. Name each of them **lblProducts** and set their Index property from **3** to **8** as appropriate. Set their BorderStyle property as in step 6.

9. Select all the labels at once by pressing the **Shift** key down and clicking each of them, and set their Font and BackColor properties to values of your own choice.

Compare the 8 product labels in figures 11.1 and 11.3. The product names appear only at run time, so do not be tempted at this point to set their captions to display the names.

Selling products

10. Place and set the captions of the two labels in Figure 11.1, *Current sale* and *Total cost*. Place the list box and name it **lstCurrentSale**.

11. Place the label to display the total cost and name it **lblTotalCost**. Place a command button, set its caption to **Sell** and name it **cmdSell**.

Returning products

12. Place the frame and change its caption to **Return product**.

13. Put a combo box on this frame and name it **cboProductsSold**. There are three types of combo box and you select the one you need through its Style property. The default is Dropdown Combo, which allows the user to enter an item that is not displayed in the combo box into the upper text part of the control. We do not want this since the only items the user should select are the products they have bought and these will be added to the combo box by our code. The Simple Combo type looks like a text box when the program runs and a drop-down list never appears. The Dropdown List type allows the user only to select an item. This is what we want so change the Style property to **2 - Dropdown List**.

14. Put a command button on the frame. Change its caption to **Return** and name it **cmdReturnProduct**.

Changing products

15. Place the frame and change its caption to **Change product details**.

16. Put a combo box on the frame and name it **cboProducts**. Change its Style property to **2 - Dropdown List** since we want the user to select only from the products displayed.

17. Place the label to display the price of the product selected from the combo box and name it **lblCurrentPrice**

18. Put two text boxes on the frame and name them **txtNewProduct** and **txtNewPrice**. Add their labels as shown in Figure 11.1

19. Place a command button on the frame. Change its caption to **OK** and name it **cmdOK**.

Other controls

20. Place a command button to the right of the title, change its caption to **New customer** and name it **cmdNewCustomer**. Place another command button below the *Return product* frame, change its caption to **Print receipt** and name it **cmdPrintReceipt**.

Form declarations

You must declare global variables to hold all the data that needs to be accessed by more than one event procedure. If an item of data is handled by only one event procedure then you can declare it within that procedure as a local variable. We need global variables to store the following:

Product names and costs per kg and details of the products sold. In Chapter 10 we decided to store all this data in four arrays.

The weight of a product. This must be calculated from the Value property of the UpDown control when the user clicks the control's buttons. It must also be used when one of the product labels is clicked to calculate and display the cost in the *Current sale* list box.

The cost of a sold product. This will be calculated when one of the product labels is clicked and it will be stored when the *Sell* button is clicked.

The total running cost for the current customer. This must be set to 0 when the *New Customer* button is clicked, recalculated when the *Sell* or *Return* buttons are clicked and we will also use it to display the total cost on the printed receipt.

The number of products the current customer has bought. To produce the receipt we need to process only those items in the two arrays that hold details of the products sold to the current customer. If one customer buys 4 products and the next customer buys 3 products, the second customer's products will overwrite the first 3 products bought by the first customer. The 4th product bought by the first customer will still be in the array. If we know how many products a customer buys we can process just this number of items in the array. Its value must be increased by 1 when the *Sell* button is clicked and reset to 0 when the *New Customer* button is clicked. However it must not be reduced by 1 when the *Return* button is clicked. In Chapter 10 we said that the product name in the array will be set to blank if it is returned, so it is still physically in the array. Our code must simply skip any blank entries when printing the receipt.

An index into the products array. When a product is selected from the *Product* combo box (to change its name and/or price) its position in this combo box will be used as an index into the *Products* array. This index will be used when clicking the *OK* button to save the changes.

1.   Declare the global variables at the top of the Code window:

```
Dim Products(1 To 8) As String       'stores product names
Dim Prices(1 To 8) As Currency       'stores product prices per kg
Dim SoldProducts(1 To 10) As String  'stores names of sold products
Dim SoldCosts(1 To 10) As Currency   'stores costs of sold products
Dim Weight As Single                 'weight of product to 0.1 of kg
Dim ProductCost As Currency          'cost of a sold product
Dim TotalCost As Currency            'total cost of products sold
                                       'to current customer
Dim NumberOfSales As Integer         'number of products sold to
                                       'current customer
Dim ProductIndex As Integer          'index into Products when
                                     'changing product name/price
```

Form's Load event

Figure 10.5 lists the three tasks that must be done when the program starts:

- Store the product names in the *Products* array.
- Store the product prices in the *Prices* array.
- Display the product names in the control array of labels

1.   The assignment specification stated that we should store details of the products directly through code rather than asking for the user to input the data (which would be very time-consuming each time you ran the program). There's no short-cut way to code this – it needs 16 lines of code to store the two items of data about each of the eight products. However there is a short-cut way to display the names. A For loop processes each label in turn using its Index property. You set the Index in design view as 1, 2, 3 etc. (steps 6 – 8 above).

```
Private Sub Form_Load()
'Stores product names and prices and displays product names in the control
'array of labels
  Dim Index As Integer
                                      'store product names and prices
  Products(1) = "Apples - Granny Smith's"
  Prices(1) = 0.9
  Products(2) = "Pears - Conference"
  Prices(2) = 1.1
  Products(3) = "Bananas - Jamaican"
  Prices(3) = 0.82
```

```
    Products(4) = "Grapes - Small seedless"
    Prices(4) = 1.6
    Products(5) = "Carrots - English"
    Prices(5) = 0.6
    Products(6) = "Potatoes - Whites"
    Prices(6) = 0.35
    Products(7) = "Parsnips - French"
    Prices(7) = 1.05
    Products(8) = "Sprouts - West country"
    Prices(8) = 0.8
    For Index = 1 To 8  'display product names in control array of labels
      lblProducts(Index).Caption = Products(Index)
      cboProducts.AddItem Products(Index)
    Next Index
    TxtWeight.Text = "0.0"   'could have done this at design time instead
  End Sub
```

2. Run the program and check that the products have been stored and displayed correctly in the weighing machine.

Weighing, selecting and selling products

Weighing – Click event of updWeight

Each click of this control (or one long continuous click) must display a weight 0.1 kg higher or lower in the text box on its left.

1. Although an UpDown control responds to a mouse click it does not actually have a Click event. You need its Change event. Double-click the control to bring up the template, or type in the procedure's first line declaration yourself and then add the code below:

```
Private Sub updWeight_Change()
'adds or subtracts 0.1 to the displayed weight
  Weight = updWeight.Value / 10    'Max property of updWeight is 100 so
                      'divide by 10 to get a weight from 0.0 to 10.0
  If Weight = 0 Then              'if Weight is 0 then text box would
                'display 0 rather than 0.0, so force it to display 0.0
    txtWeight.Text = "0.0"
  Else
    txtWeight.Text = Weight
  End If
End Sub
```

If you used a horizontal scroll bar instead of an UpDown control the code above is fine (except for the name of the control). You can use either the Change or Scroll events. The Change event displays the weight only after moving the scroll box and releasing the mouse; the Scroll event displays a changing weight as the scroll box is moved.

Selecting – Click event of lblProducts control array

Figure 10.5 lists three things that must happen when the user clicks any of the product labels on the weighing machine:

- The cost of the selected product must be calculated (by multiplying its weight by price per kg)

- Details of the sold product – product name, price per kg, weight and cost – must be displayed in the *Current sale* list box.
- The *Sell* button is enabled. The user must not click this until the first product for the current customer has been selected and weighed.

2. Double-click any of the product labels and you will get the template for the click event of the control array of all the labels:

```
Private Sub lblProducts_Click(Index As Integer)

End Sub
```

Index is an item of data sent to the event to identify which label has been clicked. (The technical name for this data is a parameter. Parameters are covered in Chapter 14 as part of Unit 22.) When you placed these labels on the form you set their Index property to 1, 2, 3 etc. and it is this number that is sent to the event procedure. You used this technique of a shared event procedure in Program 7.3.

3. The code uses the Index value to find the appropriate product in the *Products* array and its price per kg in the *Prices* array:

```
'Calculates cost of product and displays details of sold product in list
'box
  ProductCost = Prices(Index) * Weight              'calculate cost
  LstCurrentSale.Clear
  LstCurrentSale.AddItem Products(Index)            'display details
  LstCurrentSale.AddItem "Price per kg: " & Format(Prices(Index), _
          "Currency")
  LstCurrentSale.AddItem Weight & " kg"
  LstCurrentSale.AddItem Format(ProductCost, "Currency")
  cmdSell.Enabled = True                            'enable Sell button
```

Selling – Click event of cmdSell

Figure 10.5 lists four things that must be done when the *Sell* button is clicked:

- Save the name and cost of the sold product in the two arrays, *SoldProducts* and *SoldCosts*.
- Recalculate and display the total amount spent by the current customer.
- Add the product just sold to the list of products bought by the current customer displayed in the *Return product* combo box.
- Enable the *Print receipt* button. This should not be clicked until at least one product has been bought.

4. The procedure must find out which product has been sold and how much it costs. The solution used below is to take this data from the list box. Figure 11.3 shows that the first item displayed in the list box is the name of the sold product and the fourth item is its cost. The List property of the list box is used to access these items.

```
Private Sub cmdSell_Click()
'Processes sale of one product - calculates its cost and stores details
'of the sale
  Dim ProductSold As String                  'name of sold product
  Dim ProductSoldCost As Currency            'cost of sold product
  TotalCost = TotalCost + ProductCost     'calculate total cost so far
  lblTotalCost.Caption = Format(TotalCost, "Currency")
  NumberOfSales = NumberOfSales + 1          'keep count of how many
```

```
                                       'products sold so far to current customer
     ProductSold = lstCurrentSale.List(0)     'name of sold product can
                                       'be taken from first item in list box
     ProductSoldCost = lstCurrentSale.List(3) 'cost of sold product can
                                       'be taken from fourth item in list box
     SoldProducts(NumberOfSales) = ProductSold   'store name of sold product
     SoldCosts(NumberOfSales) = ProductSoldCost 'store cost of sold product
     CboProductsSold.AddItem SoldProducts(NumberOfSales)     'add name of
                                       'product to combo box displaying sold products
     cmdPrintReceipt.Enabled = True
   End Sub
```

5. Run the program and check that you can weigh and sell a few products.

Returning products

Click event of cboProductsSold

The cboProductsSold combo box displays those products bought by the current customer. Clicking the control should do no more than enable the *Return* button, since the user should not be able to click this button until they have selected a product from the combo box.

1. The code is:

```
Private Sub cboProductsSold_Click()
  CmdReturnProduct.Enabled = True
End Sub
```

Click event of cmdReturnProduct

Figure 10.5 lists the five things that should be done when the user clicks the *Return* command button:

- Remove the returned product from the *SoldProducts* array.
- Remove the returned product from the *Return products* combo box which lists the products that the current customer has bought.
- If the returned product is the most recently bought one, its details will be on display in the *Current sale* list box. These should be removed.
- The total amount spent by the customer should be recalculated and displayed.
- If the product returned is the only product the customer has bought so far, then the *Return* button should be disabled as there will be no more products in the combo box to select.

2. The loop to search the *SoldProducts* array for the product selected from cboProductsSold could be either Do While…Loop or Do…Loop Until. The latter is a better choice, though, because the product we are looking for *is* stored somewhere in the array, and so the loop will be executed at least once. The loop uses a standard linear search, processing the items in the array in their physical order, by switching a Boolean value to True when the item has been found and using this to stop the loop.

```
Private Sub cmdReturnProduct_Click()
'Processes a returned product by removing it from SoldProducts array
'and from cboProductsSold, and recalculating total spent so far. Two
'changes to the display of products are also done under certain
'conditions
  Dim SearchProduct As String                'product to return
  Dim Found As Boolean
  Dim Index As Integer  'index into SoldProducts and SoldCosts arrays
```

```
      Index = 1
      Found = False                       'product not found yet
      If cboProductsSold.Text = "" Then  'has product to return been selected?
        MsgBox ("Please select a product to return")
      Else                                'product has been selected
        Do
          SearchProduct = cboProductsSold.Text    'store product selected
          If SoldProducts(Index) = SearchProduct Then    'is product in the
                                     'current element of array the selected one?
            Found = True          'if it is then we've found it
            CboProductsSold.RemoveItem cboProductsSold.ListIndex  'so remove
                                         'it from combo box
            SoldProducts(Index) = ""          'and also from array.
            TotalCost = TotalCost - SoldCosts(Index) 'recalculate how much
                                         'current customer has spent so far
          Else                            'product not yet found in array
            Index = Index + 1             'so move to next product in array
          End If
        Loop Until Found                  'stop searching when product found
        If SearchProduct = lstCurrentSale.List(0) Then   'product to return is
                                          'on display in list box
          lstCurrentSale.Clear            'so remove it.
        End If
        If cboProductsSold.ListCount = 0 Then    'if there are no more products
                                          'in the combo box then
          cmdReturnProduct.Enabled = False      'disable Return button.
        End If
      End If
      lblTotalCost.Caption = Format(TotalCost, "Currency")
End Sub
```

3. Run the program and check that you can return one or more products.

Changing product details

Click event of cboProducts

Selecting a product from this combo box should display its price per kg.

1. We can use a similar loop to the one in the previous event to search the *Products* array for the product selected from the combo box. Then use the index into this array to extract the price from the *Prices* array.

```
Private Sub cboProducts_Click()
'Finds and displays price per kg of product selected
  Dim SearchProduct As String                    'selected product
  Dim Found As Boolean
  ProductIndex = 1
  SearchProduct = cboProducts.Text
  Found = False
  Do
    If Products(ProductIndex) = SearchProduct Then   'if product in array
                                     'is the one we are looking for...
      Found = True
                                     'display its price per kg
      lblCurrentPrice.Caption = Format(Prices(ProductIndex), "Currency")
```

```
      Else
         ProductIndex = ProductIndex + 1     '...but if not move to next one
      End If
   Loop Until Found
End Sub
```

Click event of cmdOK

When the *OK* button is clicked details of the changes to the product name and/or price should be stored in the appropriate arrays.

2.   The code needs to use the form variable *ProductIndex*. In the code for cboProducts_Click above, *ProductIndex* stores the element number of the *Products* array where the product is stored. The code below uses this to store any name change in the same array or any price change in the *Prices* array. Note the example of data validation – that the user has entered a proper number for the price.

```
Private Sub cmdOK_Click()
'Stores changes made to product name and/or price
  Dim NewProduct As String                    'name of new product
  Dim NewPrice As Currency                     'new/changed price per kg
  If Not IsNumeric(txtNewPrice.Text) Then      'has user input a number?
    MsgBox ("You have not entered a valid price")
    txtNewPrice.SetFocus
  Else                                         'numeric value has been input
    If txtNewProduct.Text <> "" Then           'has user input a new product?
      NewProduct = txtNewProduct.Text          'if yes then store its name
      NewPrice = txtNewPrice.Text              'and price
      Products(ProductIndex) = NewProduct      'in appropriate
      Prices(ProductIndex) = NewPrice          'arrays.
      lblCurrentPrice.Caption = ""
      lblProducts(ProductIndex).Caption = NewProduct   'replace product
                                  'name on weighing machine with new name
      cboProducts.RemoveItem cboProducts.ListIndex     'and display it in
      cboProducts.AddItem NewProduct           'combo box
      txtNewProduct.Text = ""
    Else                              'user does not want a new product,
                                      'only to change price of existing one
      NewPrice = txtNewPrice.Text
      Prices(ProductIndex) = NewPrice          'store changed price
      lblCurrentPrice.Caption = ""
    End If
  End If
  txtNewPrice.Text = ""
End Sub
```

3.   Run the program and check that you can change a product's name and its price.

Other events

Click event of cmdNewCustomer

Three things must be done to process a new customer by clicking the *New customer* button (see Figure 10.5):

- If there is a product displayed in the list box this must be removed. Only if the previous customer returned their most recently bought product will it be empty.
- Disable the *Save* and *Return* command buttons.
- Clear the *Return product* combo box.
- Set the total amount spent so far by the current customer to 0 and display this value.
- Set the number of products bought by the current customer to 0.

1. The code is straightforward and needs no selection or looping.

```
Private Sub cmdNewCustomer_Click()
'Sets up the system to process a new customer
  lstCurrentSale.Clear
  cmdSave.Enabled = False
  cmdReturnProduct.Enabled = False
  cboProductsSold.Clear
  NumberOfSales = 0           'number of products sold to current
  TotalCost = 0               'customer and total spent so far must be 0.
  lblTotalCost.Caption = Format(TotalCost, "Currency")
End Sub
```

Click event of cmdPrintReceipt

Clicking the *Print receipt* button produces a printed receipt. We designed the receipt in Figure 10.2.

2. The code uses *NumberOfSales* to loop through the *SoldProducts* array the required number of times. Each execution of the loop could have calculated a running total of the cost, but since the amount spent by the customer is stored in *TotalCost* (which is used by the click events of cmdSave and cmdReturnProduct), we will use this instead.

```
Private Sub cmdPrintReceipt_Click()
'Prints a receipt for the current customer
  Dim Index As Integer
  Printer.Print "Gina's Groceries"; Tab(40); Format(Date, "Long Date")
  Printer.Print
  For Index = 1 To NumberOfSales          'process each product bought
    If SoldProducts(Index) <> "" Then     'this element of array will be
                                          'empty if product has been returned
      Printer.Print SoldProducts(Index); Tab(40); _  'print product if
             Format(SoldCosts(Index), "Currency")     'it is in array
    End If
  Next Index
  Printer.Print
  Printer.Print Tab(30); "Total"; Tab(40); Format(TotalCost, "Currency")
  Printer.Print
  Printer.Print "Thank you for your custom"
  Printer.EndDoc                          'without this method receipt will not
                                          'print until you close the program
End Sub
```

The most difficult line to understand here is

```
    If SoldProducts(Index) <> "" Then
```

Figure 10.4(b) showed that an element of *SoldProducts* will be empty if the product in this element has been returned. This element must be missed out when printing the receipt.

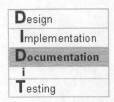

Chapter 12 – Documentation

Types of documentation

Documentation is about explaining your program on paper. There are two types of documentation:

- User documentation
- Technical documentation

The *Assessment Evidence* for Unit 7 states that both of these must be done to achieve a grade E. Two of the three criteria to achieve a grade C are concerned with documenting your program (see Appendix D). Criterion C1 covers user documentation and C2 covers technical documentation. However none of the grade A criteria include documentation.

User documentation

User documentation is written for those who will use your program – Gina and her two assistants who help out in the shop. You should assume that the users have little knowledge of computers, but that they do know how to select and run software. Your user guide should be comprehensive but not use technical language that is unlikely to be understood.

The *What You Need to Learn* section of Unit 7 suggests that your user guide may include the following:

- the hardware and software your program needs
- how to install your program
- how to start your program
- how to use your program
- how to quit your program
- examples of on-screen choices and what they offer
- examples of paths through your program
- screen prints showing the program in action
- information about error messages and what to do about them

For Gina's Groceries the following would be a good way to set out the user guide:

```
1.  Hardware and software needs
2.  How to install the program
3.  How to start the program
4.  How to use the program
    4.1  Selling a product
    4.2  Returning a product
    4.3  Printing a receipt
    4.4  Changing details of a product
5.  Error messages
6.  How to close the program
```

Hardware and software needs

For Gina's Groceries the following are required:

Harware Computer capable of running Windows95 or later
     Keyboard
     Mouse
     Printer. The quality depends on the quality of the receipt Gina wishes to give her customers.

Software Windows95 or later

Note that the software requirement does not include Visual Basic. This is hardly something you could expect Gina to have. Assuming you have named the Visual Basic project file GinasGroceries, you can produce an executable file of your program simply by selecting File/Make GinasGroceries.exe from the main menu. This produces a file you can run from Windows by double-clicking it or by selecting it and pressing Enter. Visual Basic itself is not needed since the file consists only of binary code which the computer can understand.

Installing and starting the program

Assume that you are delivering the program to the user on a floppy disk or CD. Explain how and where they should copy it onto the hard disk of their computer. You might also explain how they could create an icon on the Windows desktop from which to run the program.

Using the program

This is the main section of the user documentation. Here are a few guidelines on how to present your information:

- Write as if you are addressing the user. Use the word *you* from time to time. For example, the phrase '*as you can see in Figure 3*' may be more friendly than '*Figure 3 shows that…*'.

- Use the active voice rather than the passive voice. For example, say '*click the Save button to…*' rather than '*the Save button must be clicked to…*'.

- Use a numbered step-by-step approach to explain those things that require several actions to be done in sequence.

- Use plenty of screen shots to illustrate the points you make.

Depending on the program you have produced, it may be better to include something here on error messages rather than have a separate section on this topic as the list of items from *What You Need to Learn* seems to suggests. Error messages cover everything from friendly messages you have coded yourself when the data entered by the user cannot be accepted, to unfriendly Windows' messages telling you there has been a run-time error (and the program is about to close down). Hopefully your testing will have revealed the unfriendly ones and you will have been able to prevent these happening.

On the next page this section of the user guide for Gina has been written up for you.

Closing the program

In Gina's Groceries we did not provide any means of closing the program other than the usual way of closing any window by clicking the small button with a cross at the top right of the form, or by clicking the icon at the top left and selecting Close from the drop-down menu. (If you wish to use a command button to close a form the only code it needs is the End command.)

User guide example

Below is an example of the sort of thing you might produce for Gina, to explain how to use the program.

---

4. How to use the program

When you run the GinasGroceries file from Windows you'll get the screen shown below. This screen handles everything you need to do.

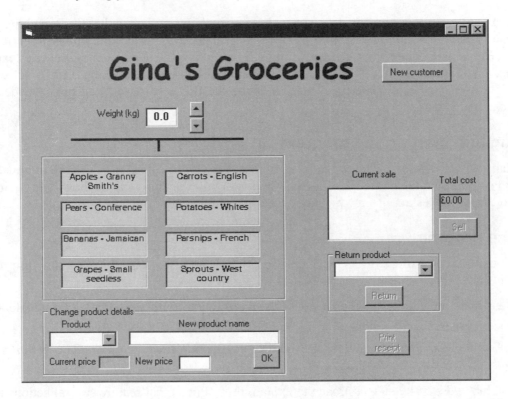

Click the **New customer** button before serving a new customer. You don't need to do this before serving the first customer but it doesn't matter if you do so.

4.1 Selling a product

1. First **weigh the product** by clicking the top arrow button. Each click increases the weight by 0.1 kg (100 gm.). Keep the button clicked to go through the weights quickly. Click the lower arrow button to decrease the weight by 0.1 kg.

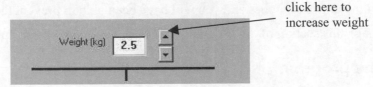

click here to increase weight

---

2. Then click on the product. The product, its price per kg, weight and the cost to the customer will appear below **Current sale**. At this point the program has not recorded that you have sold the product.

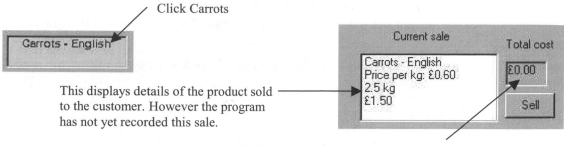

Click Carrots

This displays details of the product sold to the customer. However the program has not yet recorded this sale.

If this is the first product bought by the customer the total cost is £0.00 at this point, which shows that the sale has not yet been recorded

3. To record the sale click the **Sell** button. This will display how much the customer has spent so far.

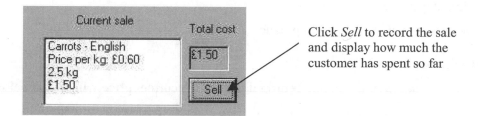

Click *Sell* to record the sale and display how much the customer has spent so far

If you make a mistake by recording the wrong weight or product the program can delete the sale. See the next section.

4.2 Returning a product

This section covers the following situations after a sale has been recorded:

- The customer changes their mind and wishes to return the product.
- The customer wishes to increase or decrease the amount of the product they have bought.
- You selected the wrong weight or product or both.

You must delete the sale and repeat section 4.1 to record a new sale. To delete the sale:

1. Select the product to delete from the drop-down list:

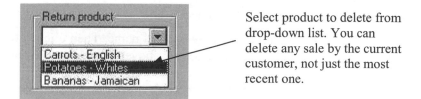

Select product to delete from drop-down list. You can delete any sale by the current customer, not just the most recent one.

2. Click the **Return** button. This does three things:

- Deletes the sale from the system
- Recalculates and displays the total spent so far by the customer
- If the deleted product is the most recently sold it removes its details from the *Current sale* display

If you click Return before you select a product from the drop-down list you'll get the message *Please select a product to return*.

4.3 Printing a receipt

Click the **Print receipt** button to print a receipt for the current customer.

Don't forget to click the **New customer** button before you serve another customer

4.4 Changing details of a product

You can make the following changes to any of the products:

- Its price per kg
- Its name and price per kg

You cannot change just the name of a product

To change the price only:

1. Select the product from the **Product** drop-down list. Its current price will appear below.

2. Enter the new price in £ per kg in the **New price** control. If you enter anything that the program cannot understand as a number you will get the message *You have not entered a valid price*. Examples of acceptable prices are £1.45, 1.45 and 1.4 (the last of these is understood to be £1.40).

3. Click the **OK** button. This stores the new price in the system and clears the current and new price values.

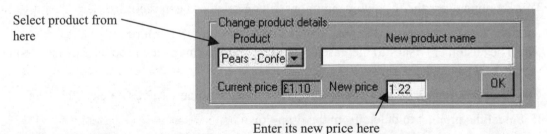

Select product from here

Enter its new price here

To change the product name and the price:

4. Repeat 1 and 2 above and enter the new product name. Then click **OK**. If you forget to enter a new price you'll get the same message as in 2 above – *You have not entered a valid price*.

Technical documentation

Technical documentation is written for fellow programmers and can therefore contain a lot of technical language. In the real world of programming its most important use is to help those who need to understand how the program works because they need to fix things that are going wrong, or add new things to it due to changing user needs. You may need to cover the following:

- A specification of what the program should do
- An outline of the modular structure of your program
- A printed listing of the code. The code should contain comments where appropriate
- A list of all variables and their purpose
- Notes explaining any features not covered by the above points

Tasks 3.2 and 3.4 of the assignment ask you to cover all the above points. The *What you need to learn* section of Unit 7 also states that the results of testing should be included in the technical documentation. However the *Assessment Evidence* for this unit clearly separates the two for assessment purposes and the assignment follows this line by setting separate testing tasks.

Program specification

This is simply a description of what the program should do. If your assessor gives you an assignment along the lines of Gina's Groceries then the specification has been done for you. This is within the spirit of Unit 7. By contrast Unit 22 expects you to be much more active in drawing up the program specification.

A useful way of structuring this section is as follows:

Data output requirements. Describe the data that needs to be output on the screen and at the printer. For Gina's Groceries the receipt is the only printed output needed. The outputs on the screen include:

- display of products on the weighing machine
- details of sold products in the list box
- total cost
- current price and new price
- list of products in the two combo boxes

Data input requirements. List the data that needs to be input in order to produce the output above. For example, the assignment itself states that the product details can be hard-coded (rather than having them all typed by the user when the program runs or read from a file). This is an example of input. Another example is the weight selected on the weighing machine.

Processing. What must be done with the input data to turn it into the output required? There is no need for any technical explanations here. For example, do not discuss *how* the various arrays are used in Gina's Groceries. For printing the receipt you could simply say that the products bought by a particular customer and their cost will be stored by the system and that these items will be printed out. The cost itself is calculated by multiplying the price per kg stored by the system by the weight selected by the user.

Modular structure

The modular structure refers to the way your program is divided into a number of event procedures. In Gina's Groceries we used 10 of these. A good way of covering this is to list the tasks done by each of these events as in Figure 10.5. The modular structure in Figure 10.5 was done at design time and in theory it should not have changed by the time you do the technical documentation. In practice you will almost certainly have changed and improved it as you have done the coding. Task 3.2 in the assignment recognises this.

Code listing

The complete code for Gina's Groceries is about 3 pages when printed from Visual Basic. You have no control over the formatting of the code when printing from Visual Basic but you can make it more presentable, and therefore more readable, by copying it into a word processing package and formatting it there. For example, the convention in this book is that the code is in bold (Courier New, 10 Point) and the comments are in italics and are not bold. This helps distinguish the two parts of the code. A complete listing of the code is given at the end of this chapter.

No matter how readable your code might be because you have formatted it well, there is no substitute for writing it clearly in the first place. Try to ensure that you

- use meaningful names for your variables
- always indent where appropriate and that you use a consistent indent size
- have plenty of comments

List of variables

Although you may have commented in your code what every variable is used for, it is still considered good practice to list the variables separately. In Gina's Groceries we used 10 form variables and 11 local variables. Figure 12.1 shows how you might begin to list these.

Variable name	Data type/comment	Scope	Used for storing...
Products	Array of 8 Strings	Form	names of products for sale
Weight	Single	Form	weight of product in kg
and other form variables			
ProductSold	String	cmdSell_Click	name of sold product
ProductSoldCost	Currency	cmdSell_Click	cost of sold product
and other local variables			

Figure 12.1: List of variables

Additional notes

This is the place to cover anything that you feel helps explain how your program works. Sometimes one or two lines of commenting in the code are not enough. In Gina's Groceries, for example, the use of the two arrays for storing details of the products sold to the current customer is a good example of something that needs an extra bit of explanation. This was covered in Chapter 10 and is certainly an issue that should be resolved at the design stage. However you do not need to document these decisions until you get to the technical documentation stage.

Complete code listing

The complete code for Gina's Groceries is given below.

```
Dim Products(1 To 8) As String      'stores product names
Dim Prices(1 To 8) As Currency      'stores product prices per kg
Dim SoldProducts(1 To 10) As String 'stores names of sold products
Dim SoldCosts(1 To 10) As Currency  'stores costs of sold products
Dim Weight As Single                'weight of product to 0.1 of kg
Dim ProductCost As Currency         'cost of a sold product
Dim TotalCost As Currency           'total cost of products sold
```

```
                                         'to current customer
     Dim NumberOfSales As Integer        'number of products sold to
                                         'current customer
     Dim ProductIndex As Integer         'index into Products when
                                         'changing product name/price
```

```
Private Sub Form_Load()
'Stores product names and prices and displays product names in the control
'array of labels
   Dim Index As Integer
                                         'store product names and prices
   Products(1) = "Apples - Granny Smith's"
   Prices(1) = 0.9
   Products(2) = "Pears - Conference"
   Prices(2) = 1.1
   Products(3) = "Bananas - Jamaican"
   Prices(3) = 0.82
   Products(4) = "Grapes - Small seedless"
   Prices(4) = 1.6
   Products(5) = "Carrots - English"
   Prices(5) = 0.6
   Products(6) = "Potatoes - Whites"
   Prices(6) = 0.35
   Products(7) = "Parsnips - French"
   Prices(7) = 1.05
   Products(8) = "Sprouts - West country"
   Prices(8) = 0.8
   For Index = 1 To 8  'display product names in control array of labels
      lblProducts(Index).Caption = Products(Index)
      cboProducts.AddItem Products(Index)
   Next Index
   txtWeight.Text = "0.0"   'could have done this at design time instead
End Sub
```

```
Private Sub updWeight_Change()
'adds or subtracts 0.1 to the displayed weight
   Weight = updWeight.Value / 10    'Max property of updWeight is 100 so
                           'divide by 10 to get a weight from 0.0 to 10.0
   If Weight = 0 Then              'if Weight is 0 then text box would
                  'display 0 rather than 0.0, so force it to display 0.0
      txtWeight.Text = "0.0"
   Else
      txtWeight.Text = Weight
   End If
End Sub
```

```
Private Sub lblProducts_Click(Index As Integer)
'Calculates cost of product and displays details of sold product in list
'box
   ProductCost = Prices(Index) * Weight         'calculate cost
   lstCurrentSale.Clear
   lstCurrentSale.AddItem Products(Index)        'display details
```

```
    lstCurrentSale.AddItem Weight & " kgs"
    lstCurrentSale.AddItem "Price per kg: " & Format(Prices(Index), _
            "Currency")
    lstCurrentSale.AddItem Format(ProductCost, "Currency")
    cmdSell.Enabled = True                      'enable Sell button
End Sub
```

```
Private Sub cmdSell_Click()
'Processes sale of one product - calculates its cost and stores details
'of the sale
    Dim ProductSold As String                    'name of sold product
    Dim ProductSoldCost As Currency              'cost of sold product
    TotalCost = TotalCost + ProductCost   'calculate total cost so far
    lblTotalCost.Caption = Format(TotalCost, "Currency")
    NumberOfSales = NumberOfSales + 1           'keep count of how many
                                'products sold so far to current customer
    ProductSold = lstCurrentSale.List(0)     'name of sold product can
                                'be taken from first item in list box
    ProductSoldCost = lstCurrentSale.List(3) 'cost of sold product can
                                'be taken from fourth item in list box
    SoldProducts(NumberOfSales) = ProductSold    'store name of sold product
    SoldCosts(NumberOfSales) = ProductSoldCost 'store cost of sold product
    cboProductsSold.AddItem SoldProducts(NumberOfSales)      'add name of
                                'product to combo box displaying sold products
    cmdPrintReceipt.Enabled = True
End Sub
```

```
Private Sub cboProductsSold_Click()
    cmdReturnProduct.Enabled = True
End Sub
```

```
Private Sub cmdReturnProduct_Click()
'Processes a returned product by removing it from SoldProducts array
'and from cboProductsSold, and recalculating total spent so far. Two
'changes to the display of products are also done under certain conditions
    Dim SearchProduct As String              'product to return
    Dim Found As Boolean
    Dim Index As Integer  'index into SoldProducts and SoldCosts arrays
    Index = 1
    Found = False                       'product not found yet
    If cboProductsSold.Text = "" Then  'has product to return been selected?
      MsgBox ("Please select a product to return")
    Else                                 'product has been selected
      Do
        SearchProduct = cboProductsSold.Text    'store product selected
        If SoldProducts(Index) = SearchProduct Then    'is product in the
                                'current element of array the selected one?
          Found = True          'if it is then we've found it
          cboProductsSold.RemoveItem cboProductsSold.ListIndex 'so remove
                                'it from combo box
          SoldProducts(Index) = ""          'and also from array.
          TotalCost = TotalCost - SoldCosts(Index) 'recalculate how much
```

```
                                          'current customer has spent so far
       Else                               'product not yet found in array
          Index = Index + 1               'so move to next product in array
       End If
    Loop Until Found                         'stop searching when product found
    If SearchProduct = lstCurrentSale.List(0) Then   'product to return is
                                             'on display in list box
       lstCurrentSale.Clear                  'so remove it.
    End If
    If cboProductsSold.ListCount = 0 Then   'if there are no more products
                                            'in the combo box then
       cmdReturnProduct.Enabled = False     'disable Return button.
    End If
  End If
  lblTotalCost.Caption = Format(TotalCost, "Currency")
End Sub
```

```
Private Sub cboProducts_Click()
'Finds and displays price per kg of product selected
  Dim SearchProduct As String                 'selected product
  Dim Found As Boolean
  ProductIndex = 1
  SearchProduct = cboProducts.Text
  Found = False
  Do
    If Products(ProductIndex) = SearchProduct Then   'if product in array
                                        'is the one we are looking for...
       Found = True
                                        'display its price per kg
      lblCurrentPrice.Caption = Format(Prices(ProductIndex), "Currency")
    Else
      ProductIndex = ProductIndex + 1      '...but if not move to next one
    End If
  Loop Until Found
End Sub
```

```
Private Sub cmdOK_Click()
'Stores changes made to product name and/or price
  Dim NewProduct As String                      'name of new product
  Dim NewPrice As Currency                       'new/changed price per kg
  If Not IsNumeric(txtNewPrice.Text) Then       'has user input a number?
     MsgBox ("You have not entered a valid price")
     txtNewPrice.SetFocus
  Else                                   'numeric value has been input
     If txtNewProduct.Text <> "" Then    'has user input a new product?
       NewProduct = txtNewProduct.Text   'if yes then store its name
       NewPrice = txtNewPrice.Text       'and price
       Products(ProductIndex) = NewProduct  'in appropriate
       Prices(ProductIndex) = NewPrice      'arrays.
       lblCurrentPrice.Caption = ""
       lblProducts(ProductIndex).Caption = NewProduct   'replace product
                                  'name on weighing machine with new name
       cboProducts.RemoveItem cboProducts.ListIndex     'and display it in
       cboProducts.AddItem NewProduct           'combo box
       txtNewProduct.Text = ""
```

```
      Else                               'user does not want a new product,
                                         'only to change price of existing one
        NewPrice = txtNewPrice.Text
        Prices(ProductIndex) = NewPrice          'store changed price
        lblCurrentPrice.Caption = ""
      End If
    End If
    txtNewPrice.Text = ""
End Sub
```

```
Private Sub cmdNewCustomer_Click()
'Sets up the system to process a new customer
  lstCurrentSale.Clear
  cmdSave.Enabled = False
  cmdReturnProduct.Enabled = False
  cboProductsSold.Clear
  NumberOfSales = 0             'number of products sold to current
  TotalCost = 0                 'customer and total spent so far must be 0.
  lblTotalCost.Caption = Format(TotalCost, "Currency")
End Sub
```

```
Private Sub cmdPrintReceipt_Click()
'Prints a receipt for the current customer
  Dim Index As Integer
  Printer.Print "Gina's Groceries"; Tab(40); Format(Date, "Long Date")
  Printer.Print
  For Index = 1 To NumberOfSales           'process each product bought
    If SoldProducts(Index) <> "" Then     'this element of array will be
                                          'empty if product has been returned
      Printer.Print SoldProducts(Index); Tab(40); _  'print product if
              Format(SoldCosts(Index), "Currency")      'it is in array
    End If
  Next Index
  Printer.Print
  Printer.Print Tab(30); "Total"; Tab(40); Format(TotalCost, "Currency")
  Printer.Print
  Printer.Print "Thank you for your custom"
  Printer.EndDoc                    'without this method receipt will not
                                    'print until you close the program
End Sub
```

Chapter 13 – Testing

What does Unit 7 require?

In my experience most students quite enjoy writing code once they have got the hang of it, and writing up the user documentation is usually enjoyable too. Testing is a different matter; generally students do not like doing it. You will almost certainly have done testing elsewhere on your AVCE course. For Unit 3 on Spreadsheets, for example, testing is a grade E criterion. For Unit 7 it is one of the grade A criteria only (A4). This criterion is as follows:

> Records of thorough module and program testing that check all major paths, acceptable and unacceptable input and all possible events, and show clearly how any identified problems were resolved to produce a good operational program(s).

Let us look at the meaning of the key terms used in this statement.

Module and program testing

The term *module* means event procedure. You should test each event procedure in your program. In Gina's Groceries we had 10 of these. The term *program* refers to your complete program. Sometimes you can test each event procedure separately and be satisfied that they work correctly, but when you test them working *together* in the whole program a few problems may arise.

All possible events

This is saying no more than the point made above, that all modules should be tested individually and working together.

All major paths

Exercise 3 in Chapter 5 asked you to write a program to allow the user to enter as many positive whole numbers as they wish and to display how many of these are odd numbers and how many are even. The numbers had to be input through input boxes and the number 0 indicated that the user had finished. Assuming the variables *Number*, *Even* and *Odd* have been declared as Integers one way to code this is:

```
Even = 0
Odd = 0
Number = InputBox("Enter a number, 0 to quit")
Do While Number <> 0
  If Number Mod 2 = 0 Then
    Even = Even + 1
  Else
    Odd = Odd + 1
  End If
  Number = InputBox("Enter a number, 0 to quit ")
Loop
lblEven.Caption = Even
lblOdd.Caption = Odd
```

How many paths are there through this code? If the user enters 0 the first time they are asked for a number the loop will not be executed at all, but any other number will ensure the loop is entered at least once. There are two paths through the loop; if an even number is entered the If condition is true and if an odd number is entered it is false. Therefore there are three paths through the code in total as shown in Figure 13.1. You could test this code with the following sets of data:

0	to quit the program at once	- tests path 1
4	one even number	- tests path 2
2, 6, 8	even numbers only	- tests path 2
9	one odd number	- tests path 3
5, 35, 23	odd numbers only	- tests path 3
6, 9, 60	mixture of even and odd	- tests paths 2 and 3

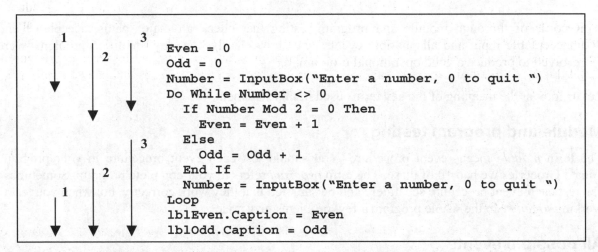

```
      1        3
          2
                   Even = 0
                   Odd = 0
                   Number = InputBox("Enter a number, 0 to quit ")
                   Do While Number <> 0
                     If Number Mod 2 = 0 Then
                       Even = Even + 1
               3     Else
                       Odd = Odd + 1
                     End If
               2     Number = InputBox("Enter a number, 0 to quit ")
      1            Loop
                   lblEven.Caption = Even
                   lblOdd.Caption = Odd
```

Figure 13.1: The three paths through the code

Actually in this example the loop is contrived. The purpose of the example in the Chapter 5 exercises was to test you on loops. You were told to use an input box because this forces you to use a loop. One of the advantages of an event-driven language is that the need for loops is considerably reduced. In the above program the user could have entered their numbers in a text box and you would write the If statement in the click event of a command button. Successive clicks of the button replace the loop. This is good news for testing event-driven programs since fewer loops means fewer paths through the code.

Acceptable and unacceptable data

This is about data validation – only input data that meets specified conditions must be accepted by the program. In the coded example above the acceptable data includes any integer. Unacceptable data would include fractional numbers and characters. You should test it with these three different types of data.

One of the advantages of an event-driven language is that you can often prevent invalid data by the use of the various controls. In Gina's Groceries, for example, the user cannot enter an invalid weight because the UpDown control forces the values to be between 0.0 and 10.0. Another example is when the user indicates which product to return by selecting it from a combo box. The products in the combo box are all valid products. Nevertheless there are many occasions when you need to use a text box and here you must write code to validate the input. (Actually the text box has one or two properties that can aid validation, but these have not been covered in this book.)

When should you test?

Obviously you cannot test your code until you have written it, but at what point after writing it should you test? There are two possible approaches:

- Write the code for an event procedure and then draw up a test plan for this event (see next section). Carry out the test plan. Do this for all the event procedures. When the program is complete carry out these tests again to check that the events work together.

- Complete the coding and then draw up test plans for each event procedure. Carry out the test plans.

If you use the first approach be aware that you cannot always test one procedure in isolation from the others, without perhaps writing some extra code to carry out the test. For example, in Gina's Groceries the first task listed in Figure 10.5 for the *Return* command button's click event is to remove the product sold from the *Sold Products* array. How can we prove that this has happened? If you use the second approach to testing listed above then the printed receipt provides the evidence that the product has been removed. If you use the first approach you will not yet have written the code for printing the receipt. You could get round this by writing extra testing code to loop through the array and print its contents on the form, and then delete this code when you are satisfied with the result.

Although there is a lot to be said for the first method, in practice students usually test when they have finished coding. Of course you will try out each event, or perhaps two or three related events, just after you have coded them to see if things are working. This is not detailed testing though; it might be better to call it checking.

Drawing up a test plan

Figure 13.2 shows the structure of a table you might use in drawing up a test plan for 20 tests. Your code should reveal what the expected result of a test should be, but sometimes it can be tricky working out what should happen until you carry out a test.

Test No.	Event procedure	Purpose	Test data	Expected result	Actual result
1					
2					
20					

Figure 13.2: A table for a test plan

Testing cmdSell_Click

When the user has selected a weight and product these two data items plus cost per kg and cost appear in the list box. To complete and save details of the sale the user has to click the *Sell* button. The code was:

```
TotalCost = TotalCost + ProductCost
lblTotalCost.Caption = Format(TotalCost, "Currency")
NumberOfSales = NumberOfSales + 1
ProductSold = lstCurrentSale.List(0)
ProductSoldCost = lstCurrentSale.List(3)
SoldProducts(NumberOfSales) = ProductSold
SoldCosts(NumberOfSales) = ProductSoldCost
cboProductsSold.AddItem SoldProducts(NumberOfSales)
cmdPrintReceipt.Enabled = True
```

Lines 3 – 7 do some invisible processing that we cannot test in isolation from other procedures. The other lines produce visible results on the form that can be confirmed. Although there is only one path through this code, we should test it when one product only has been sold and also when two or more have been sold to a particular customer. When a second customer begins to be processed the total amount spent should be set to 0. This should have been tested in carrying out a test plan for the click event of cmdNewCustomer, but it would be a good idea to test it here too to confirm that the code above works correctly when a second or subsequent customer is being processed. Figure 13.3 shows a possible test plan for this simple event. The costs in the expected results assume that the price per kg of the products used for the test data have not been changed from those stored during the form's Load event.

Test No.	Event procedure	Purpose	Test data	Expected result	Actual result
1	cmdSave_Click	One product sold to one customer	2 kg apples	Total cost £1.80 Apples only product listed in *Return product* combo box	
2	cmdSave_Click	Two products sold to one customer	1 kg grapes 2 kg pears	Total cost £3.80 Grapes and pears are the 2 products listed in *Return product* combo box	
3	cmdSave_Click	One product only sold to first customer. One product then sold to second customer	3 kg potatoes for first customer. 2 kg carrots for second one.	Total cost £1.05 for first customer. Total cost £1.20 for second customer	

Figure 13.3: Test plan for cmdSave_Click

Testing cmdReturnProduct_Click

This is the most complex event in the program. Its code was as follows:

```
Index = 1
Found = False                       'product not found yet
If cboProductsSold.Text = "" Then   'has product to return been selected?
  MsgBox ("Please select a product to return")
Else                                'product has been selected
  Do
    SearchProduct = cboProductsSold.Text    'store product selected
    If SoldProducts(Index) = SearchProduct Then   'is product in the
                             'current element of array the selected one?
      Found = True               'if it is then we've found it
      cboProductsSold.RemoveItem cboProductsSold.ListIndex  'so remove
                                           'it from combo box
      SoldProducts(Index) = ""                 'and also from array.
      TotalCost = TotalCost - SoldCosts(Index) 'recalculate how much
                                  'current customer has spent so far
    Else                          'product not yet found in array
      Index = Index + 1           'so move to next product in array
    End If
  Loop Until Found                'stop searching when product found
  If SearchProduct = lstCurrentSale.List(0) Then  'product to return is
                                      'on display in list box
    lstCurrentSale.Clear                       'so remove it.
```

```
        End If
        If cboProductsSold.ListCount = 0 Then    'if there are no more products
                                                 'in the combo box then
            cmdReturnProduct.Enabled = False     'disable Return button.
        End If
    End If
    lblTotalCost.Caption = Format(TotalCost, "Currency")
```

The loop searches the *SoldProducts* array for the product selected from the combo box. Since this product *must* be in the array, the two possible paths through the If Then…Else statement inside the loop do not need to be separately tested. The If condition must always become true at some point during the loop. We can therefore reduce the code structure to the following outline:

```
If......Then        If 1 (cboProductsSold.Text = "")
.........
Else
    Do
    .........
    Loop
    If......Then     If 2 (SearchProduct = lstCurrentSale.List(0))
    .........
    EndIf
    If......Then     If 3 (cboProductsSold.ListCount = 0)
    .........
    EndIf
EndIf
```

This gives 7 possible combinations:

	If 1	**If 2**	**If 3**
1	True	True	True
2	True	True	False
3	True	False	True
4	False	False	False
5	False	True	False
6	False	True	True
7	False	False	True

However this does not necessarily mean there are 7 paths through the code. Since If 2 and If 3 are inside the Else part of If 1 they cannot be executed when If 1 is true. Therefore the first 3 combinations reduce to one path. This gives the following paths:

	If 1	**If 2**	**If 3**
1	True	-	-
2	False	False	False
3	False	True	False
4	False	True	True
5	False	False	True

Figure 13.4 shades the lines of code which are executed through four of these paths. The missing path is number 5 since the combination of False, False, True is not possible. This would mean that the selected product is *not* currently displayed in the *Current sale* list box (i.e. it is not the most recently bought one) and it *is* the only one bought so far by the current customer. If a product is the only one so far bought then it will be currently displayed in the list box, so these two situations cannot occur at the same time.

Path 1

A product has not been selected from the *Return product* combo box.

```
Index = 1
Found = False
If cboProductsSold.Text = "" Then
  MsgBox ("Please select a product to return")
Else
  Do
    SearchProduct = cboProductsSold.Text
    If SoldProducts(Index) = SearchProduct Then
      Found = True
      cboProductsSold.RemoveItem cboProductsSold.ListIndex
      SoldProducts(Index) = ""
      TotalCost = TotalCost - SoldCosts(Index)
    Else
      Index = Index + 1
    End If
  Loop Until Found
  If SearchProduct = lstCurrentSale.List(0) Then
    lstCurrentSale.Clear
  End If
  If cboProductsSold.ListCount = 0 Then
    cmdReturnProduct.Enabled = False
  End If
End If
lblTotalCost.Caption = Format(TotalCost, "Currency")
```

Path 2

A product has been selected from the *Return product* combo box.
This product is *not* currently displayed in list box (i.e. is not the most recently bought one)
This product is *not* the only one bought so far by the current customer

```
Index = 1
Found = False
If cboProductsSold.Text = "" Then
  MsgBox ("Please select a product to return")
Else
  Do
    SearchProduct = cboProductsSold.Text
    If SoldProducts(Index) = SearchProduct Then
      Found = True
      cboProductsSold.RemoveItem cboProductsSold.ListIndex
      SoldProducts(Index) = ""
      TotalCost = TotalCost - SoldCosts(Index)
    Else
      Index = Index + 1
    End If
  Loop Until Found
  If SearchProduct = lstCurrentSale.List(0) Then
    lstCurrentSale.Clear
  End If
  If cboProductsSold.ListCount = 0 Then
    cmdReturnProduct.Enabled = False
  End If
End If
lblTotalCost.Caption = Format(TotalCost, "Currency")
```

Path 3

A product has been selected from the *Return product* combo box.
This product *is* currently displayed in list box (i.e. is the most recently bought one)
This product is *not* the only one bought so far by the current customer

```
Index = 1
Found = False
If cboProductsSold.Text = "" Then
  MsgBox ("Please select a product to return")
Else
  Do
    SearchProduct = cboProductsSold.Text
    If SoldProducts(Index) = SearchProduct Then
      Found = True
      cboProductsSold.RemoveItem cboProductsSold.ListIndex
      SoldProducts(Index) = ""
      TotalCost = TotalCost - SoldCosts(Index)
    Else
      Index = Index + 1
    End If
  Loop Until Found
  If SearchProduct = lstCurrentSale.List(0) Then
    lstCurrentSale.Clear
  End If
  If cboProductsSold.ListCount = 0 Then
    cmdReturnProduct.Enabled = False
  End If
End If
lblTotalCost.Caption = Format(TotalCost, "Currency")
```

Path 4

A product has been selected from the *Return product* combo box.
This product *is* currently displayed in list box (i.e. is the most recently bought one)
This product *is* the only one bought so far by the current customer

```
Index = 1
Found = False
If cboProductsSold.Text = "" Then
  MsgBox ("Please select a product to return")
Else
  Do
    SearchProduct = cboProductsSold.Text
    If SoldProducts(Index) = SearchProduct Then
      Found = True
      cboProductsSold.RemoveItem cboProductsSold.ListIndex
      SoldProducts(Index) = ""
      TotalCost = TotalCost - SoldCosts(Index)
    Else
      Index = Index + 1
    End If
  Loop Until Found
  If SearchProduct = lstCurrentSale.List(0) Then
    lstCurrentSale.Clear
  End If
  If cboProductsSold.ListCount = 0 Then
    cmdReturnProduct.Enabled = False
  End If
End If
lblTotalCost.Caption = Format(TotalCost, "Currency")
```

Figure 13.4: The four possible paths through cmdReturnProduct_Click

Figure 13.5 draws up a test plan to test each of the four paths through the code. The brackets indicates the data entered to reach the point where the path itself is finally tested.

Test No.	Event procedure	Purpose	Test data	Expected results	Actual result
1	cmdReturnProduct_ Click	Path 1	(1 kg pears - £1.10 1 kg carrots - £0.60 Return pears) Click *Return* button without selecting carrots	(Total cost £1.10 Total cost £1.70 Total cost £0.60) • Message box asking for a product to be selected • Total cost remains unchanged at £0.60	
2	cmdReturnProduct_ Click	Path 2	(1 kg pears - £1.10 1 kg carrots - £0.60) Return pears	(Total cost £1.10 Total cost £1.70) Total cost £0.60	
3	cmdReturnProduct_ Click	Path 3	(1 kg pears - £1.10 1 kg carrots - £0.60) Return carrots	(Total cost £1.10 Total cost £1.70) • Total cost £1.10 • Details of current sale (of carrots) removed from *Current sale* list box • *Return product* combo box only lists pears	
4	cmdReturnProduct_ Click	Path 4	(1 kg pears - £1.10) Return pears	(Total cost £1.10) • Total cost £0.00 • Details of current sale (of pears) removed from *Current sale* list box • *Return* command button disabled	

Figure 13.5: The test plan for cmdReturnProduct_Click

One of the trickiest things in event-driven programming is making sure the user cannot set off an event when it should not be set off. A common way of doing this is to disable command buttons. If you have overlooked any possible occasions then a thorough test plan ought to reveal this. Do the following practical work to reveal one of these in Gina's Groceries.

1. Carry out the test in Figure 13.5 for path 3.

2. At this point the *Current sale* list box will be empty and only one product, pears, will be listed in the *Return product* combo box. Notice that the *Sell* button is enabled. Although the user should not click it because they have not just sold a product, the important thing is that they *might* do so. Click it and you will get a run-time error – something to avoid at all costs.

Exercise 3 on the next page asks you to correct this problem. Task 4.2 in the assignment asks you *how you resolved any problems in your program uncovered by these tests*. Identifying interface flaws like the enabled *Sell* button is a good example of this.

Exercises on Gina's Groceries

*1. The program handles eight products only but in reality Gina can sometimes stock dozens. The 'concept keyboard' interface used in the program may possibly not be appropriate for a large number of products. How might you redesign the weighing machine part of the interface to handle a lot of products? In broad terms what changes to the code would you need to make to process the new interface?

In the world of software production the user often requires the program to do extra things after they have used it for a while, or perhaps there was something they did not originally wish the program to do but later change their mind. Exercises 2 and 3 ask you to consider examples of this.

**2. In the original program specification the weights of the sold products were not required on the receipt. After using your program for a few weeks Gina now feels that they should be printed on the receipt.

(a) Outline the changes you would have to make to the program to incorporate this change.
(b) Carry out these changes as a practical exercise.

***3. Gina would like to have a printout at the end of the day to show for each different product sold its total weight and cost. It should also show the date, the total cost of all products sold, the number of customers and the average amount each customer spent. Write further code to implement this new requirement.

In Chapter 13 we tested cmdReturnProduct_Click to reveal a flaw in the way the interface for returning a product works. Exercise 4 asks you to correct this and exercise 5 asks you, among other things, to find a similar interface flaw in another Click event.

*4. At the end of Chapter 13 you carried out a test for path 3 for the Click event of the *Return* command button. It revealed that the *Sell* button is enabled when it should not be. Write extra code in either the Click event for cmdSell or for cmdReturnProduct to correct the problem.

**5. Draw up a test plan for cmdOK_Click using the tabular outline in Figure 13.5 and carry out the plan. Testing should reveal a flaw in the interface similar to the one referred to in exercise 3. Identify the flaw and correct it.

Unit 22 – Programs: Specification to Production

Part One – Visual Basic Skills

Part Two – Producing a Portfolio

Part One – Visual Basic Skills

Chapter 14 covers **procedures** and **parameters**. All the events that you have met so far have been coded as event procedures. Visual Basic has another type of procedure – the general procedure – which you should know how to use when building larger programs. Sometimes these procedures need to be passed one or more items of data to do their job. These items of data are known as parameters.

Chapter 15 introduces you to **records**. A record is like a single row in a database table, containing data in a number of fields about an individual student, employee, book or whatever. An **array of records** is like the table itself, consisting perhaps of a great number of records.

Chapter 16 covers **files**. These are essential when you need to permanently store data entered through your program. The two main types of file – **text** files and **random access** files – are discussed. Random access files store their data as records and are generally preferable to text files. The case study in Part Two uses random access files a lot.

Chapter 14 – Procedures

What is a procedure?

A procedure is a separate section of code which performs one or more specific tasks and is identified by having a name.

Types of procedure in Visual Basic

Visual Basic has four types of procedure. These are:

- **Event** procedures
- **Sub** procedures
- **Function** procedures
- **Property** procedures

So far you have used only event procedures where code is executed in response to events such as click, change and so on. The other three types of procedure are not set off directly by events, but are **called** by code within an event procedure or from within another non-event procedure. Property procedures are only used when you adopt an object-oriented approach to programming (not covered by this book). Sub and function procedures are sometimes referred to as **general** procedures and are the subject of this chapter. Figure 14.1 illustrates how the different procedures may be linked. The click event procedure calls two general procedures, and one of these, procedure A, in turn calls another general procedure, function C. Note how control returns to the next line of code after the procedure call when the procedure is finished.

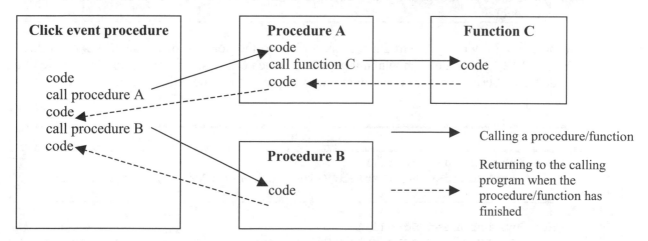

Figure 14.1: An example of how procedures may be linked

Sub and Function procedures

There are two key differences between these types of procedure:

- A function procedure always returns one piece of data to that part of the program which calls it. A sub procedure may return one or more items of data or no data at all. The way in which the two types of procedure return data is different.

- The way in which the procedure is called is different.

You can really understand these only by doing programs 14.1 (sub procedure) and 14.2 and 14.3 (function procedures).

Why use procedures?

Almost all programs you write inevitably use event procedures. You do not *have* to use sub or function procedures, but there are several good reasons why you should:

- **Avoid repeating code**. If you have identical code in two or more event procedures you may be able to write it just once in a procedure instead.

- **Make the code more readable**. An event procedure with many lines of code may be easier to understand if some of the code is put into procedures.

- **Help in debugging a program**. Splitting the program up into small logical units will make it easier to trace any errors in the program when it runs. This is called debugging a program.

- **Use a procedure in other programs**. Suppose you had written some code that validated a date. You could use this procedure in any other program that used a similar date.

- **Pass parameters**. All good programmers ought to pass parameters, where appropriate. Only by having procedures can you do this. Parameters are discussed later in this chapter.

What a procedure does is entirely up to you. There are no hard and fast rules, but as a guide use a procedure to carry out one specific task or a small number of related tasks.

PROGRAM 14.1   *Avoid repeating code*

Specification   Illustrate how procedures can make it unnecessary to repeat code in two or more event procedures.

Look back at program 2.4 which coloured a form according to the position of the scroll boxes in three scroll bars (Figure 2.12). The code is shown in Figure 14.2 – each of the three scroll bars has a single line of identical code for its Scroll event. In this program we will write this code only once, in a procedure.

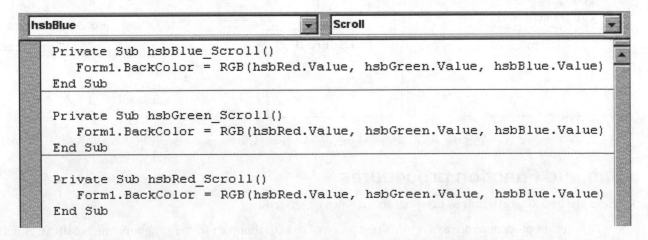

Figure 14.2

1. Open program 2.4 and delete the single line of code in each of the three Scroll event procedures shown in Figure 14.2. (If you did not save this program earlier create it again now, but leave out steps 6 – 8 in program 2.4 as you do not need the event procedure code.)

2. There are two ways of adding a new procedure to the code window. You can write it all from scratch yourself or you can use the menu to provide a template. We'll use the second method in this example. Select **Tools/Add Procedure** and you'll get the Add Procedure dialog box shown in Figure 14.3.

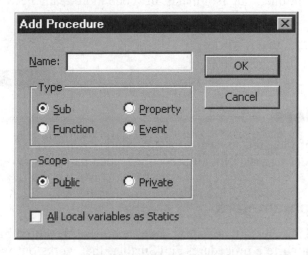

Figure 14.3: The Add Procedure dialog box

3. In the **Name** section, type in the name of the procedure as **ShowFormColour**. As with variable names and names of objects Visual Basic does not allow any spaces in a procedure name.

4. The four types of procedure listed at the start of this chapter are offered in Figure 14.3. The commonest is the **Sub** procedure which is the default. Accept this.

5. Two types of **Scope** are offered. **Public** means that the procedure can be used by all other procedures in a program (and some of these might be on another form). **Private** means that the procedure can be used on only the form on which it is declared. As we are only using one form it doesn't matter which of these we use so accept the default Public.

6. The check box at the bottom of the dialog box allows you to declare all local variables as static. Recall from Chapter 3, and in particular program 3.3, that a static variable retains its value between procedure calls. Normally you do not want variables to be static so again accept the default.

7. Click **OK** and you'll get the template for the new procedure. Write the code to set the form's colour:

```
Public Sub ShowFormColour()
   Form1.BackColor = RGB(hsbRed.Value, hsbGreen.Value, hsbBlue.Value)
End Sub
```

8. Now you have to tell each of the three Scroll event procedures to **call** this sub procedure. Their code should look as follows:

```
Private Sub hsbBlue_Scroll()
   Call ShowFormColour
End Sub
```

```
Private Sub hsbGreen_Scroll()
  Call ShowFormColour
End Sub

Private Sub hsbRed_Scroll()
  Call ShowFormColour
End Sub
```

The keyword **Call** is optional, but as it makes the code more readable we will use it throughout this book.

9. Run the program to check that it works.

end of Program 14.1

Passing parameters

A **parameter** is a piece of data that is sent to a procedure when it is called. The data is used by the procedure to help it carry out its task. Not all procedures need parameters; others may need one or more of them.

Actual and Formal parameters

Suppose the user has typed numbers into two text boxes and these are stored in variables FirstNumber and SecondNumber. You could write a procedure, FindSmaller, that works out which of the two numbers is the smaller, and call it with

```
Call FindSmallerNumber(FirstNumber, SecondNumber)
```

FirstNumber and SecondNumber are two parameters which are passed to the procedure. When you use the keyword Call you must list the parameters inside brackets. (If you don't use Call then the brackets aren't allowed.) Parameters passed to a procedure are called **actual parameters**.

When you declare the procedure FindSmallerNumber you must declare **formal parameters** to match the actual parameters you are sending it. You can use the same identifiers as the actual parameters or different ones. In this book we will always use different identifiers for the actual and formal parameters. When you declare a formal parameter it is optional whether you declare its data type too. However it makes the code a little easier to understand if you do, so we'll adopt the practice in this book. Thus all of the following declarations are correct:

```
Public Sub FindSmaller(NumberOne As Integer, NumberTwo As Integer) 'use
              'different identifiers for actual and formal parameters
Public Sub FindSmaller(NumberOne, NumberTwo) 'data types not declared
Public Sub FindSmaller(FirstNumber As Integer, SecondNumber As Integer)
                                      'use same identifiers
```

Figure 14.4 illustrates the matching of the actual and formal parameters. This example highlights three important rules:

- The number of actual and formal parameters must be the same.
- Parameters are matched according to their position, not according to their names.
- The data types of a matching pair of parameters must be the same.

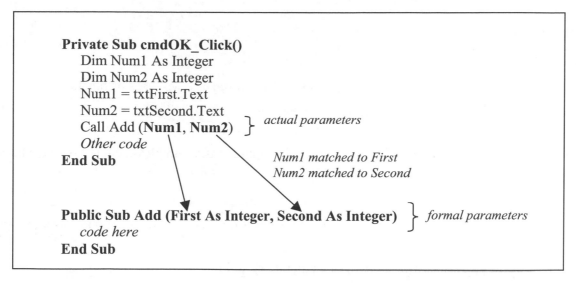

Figure 14.4: Matching actual and formal parameters

Value and Reference parameters

Visual Basic is one of many languages that allow you to declare the parameters passed to a procedure (the actual parameters) as **value** or **reference** parameters. The *What you need to learn* section of Unit 22 does not state that you need to know the difference between these two types of parameter. This book does not declare its parameters as value or reference in any of the chapter programs or the two case studies. The next paragraph briefly explains the difference between the types, and if you would like some practical work on this look at the file *Parameters.doc* that you can download from the web site.

Reference parameters are used when you need to pass data back from a sub procedure to the calling program. The code inside procedure FindSmaller will find out which number is the smaller and since we need to get this information out it must be stored as a reference parameter. The two numbers themselves are not changed in any way, and do not need to be passed out again. Therefore they are **value parameters**. The complete code to call and declare the procedure now becomes:

```
Call FindSmaller(FirstNumber, SecondNumber, SmallerNumber)

Public Sub FindSmaller(ByVal NumberOne As Integer, _
           ByVal NumberTwo As Integer, ByRef Smaller As Integer)
```

Use the keywords **ByVal** and **ByRef** to declare value and reference parameters. When the procedure has found the smaller number it can be passed back to the calling code through Smaller, and this in turn is matched back onto the actual parameter SmallerNumber. Thus two further rules can be drawn up:

- A reference parameter is used when a piece of data needs to be passed out of the procedure.
- A value parameter is a piece of data used by the procedure. Any changes made to it inside the procedure are not passed back again.

If you choose not to declare a parameter as value or reference then Visual Basic treats it as reference by default. This means that any changes you make to the contents of parameter inside the procedure will be passed back to the calling code.

Functions

Types of function

A function is a shorter name for a function procedure. Visual Basic has two types of function:

- **Built-in** functions which are supplied as part of the language
- **User-defined** functions which you write yourself

You have used a number of built-in functions in previous programs. Examples include Format, Mid and Date. Now you need to learn how to write your own.

Calling a function

There are several ways of calling a function. You have already used the two important ones in earlier chapters:

- **Assign its return value to a variable**. For example, the following calls the function Left to store 'S' in the variable Character:

```
Name = "Smith"
Character = Left(Name, 1)
```

- **Display its return value directly**. For example, the letter "S" can be printed directly by calling the function as part of the Print statement:

```
Name = "Smith"
Print Left(Name, 1)
```

PROGRAM 14.2   *Calculating interest*

Specification   Write a function to calculate the amount of interest earned on an investment. The amount invested, the interest rate and the number of years the investment lasts, are to be entered by the user.

If you invested £1000 over 2 years at an interest rate of 10% per year then the interest paid after one year would be £100 (i.e. 10% of £1000). In year 2 you would get 10% of (£1000 + £100), i.e. £110, and so the total interest paid would be £210. In this program a function named **CalculateInterest** will calculate and return this value.

1.   Open a new project and design the form shown in Figure 14.4. Name the controls needed in code as **txtAmountInvested, txtInterestRate, txtYears, lblInterest** and **cmdCalcInterest**.

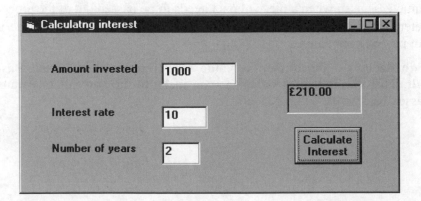

Figure 14.4: Program 14.2

2. Type the following code into the Click event of the command button:

```
Private Sub cmdCalcInterest_Click()
   Dim Interest As Currency
   Dim AmountInvested As Currency
   Dim RateOfInterest As Single
   Dim Years As Integer
   AmountInvested = txtAmountInvested.Text
   RateOfInterest = txtInterestRate.Text
   Years = txtYears.Text
   Interest = CalculateInterest(AmountInvested, RateOfInterest, Years)
   lblInterest.Caption = Format(Interest, "Currency")
End Sub
```

The function CalculateInterest is called as part of an assignment:

```
   Interest = CalculateInterest(AmountInvested, RateOfInterest, Years)
```

Three actual parameters are passed, and the data item returned from the function is stored in the variable Interest.

3. Select **Tools/Add Procedure** and in the dialog box click the **Function** option button and enter its name **CalculateInterest**.

4. Declare the three formal parameters for function CalculateInterest as shown below. The data type of the piece of data that is returned is declared after the last bracket. In this example it is Currency.

```
Public Function CalculateInterest(Principal As Currency, _
                            InterestRate As Single, _
                            NumberYears As Integer) As Currency
```

5. Write the code inside the function to calculate the interest:

```
Dim Interest As Currency
Dim Year As Integer
Interest = 0
For Year = 1 To NumberYears
   Interest = Interest + ((Principal + Interest) * InterestRate / 100)
Next Year
CalculateInterest = Interest
```

The last line is the way to return the calculated interest to the calling part of the program. Assign this data (Interest) to the name of the function (CalculateInterest). Note that Interest is of type Currency because the return data type noted in step 4 is Currency. (However Visual Basic is not always strict about this, which you will discover by doing the extra work on this program at the end of the chapter.)

6. Run the program and check that it works by using the sample data in Figure 14.4 and other data of your choice.

End of Program 14.2

Passing arrays to procedures

Suppose you have declared an array to hold integer numbers as follows:

```
Dim Numbers(1 To 50) As Integer
```

To pass Numbers to a procedure FindMinAndMax, which finds the smallest and largest numbers in the array, you would write:

```
FindMinAndMax(Smallest As Integer, Largest As Integer, Numbers())  'actual
                                          parameters in procedure call
```

Note the empty brackets used for the actual parameter Number. These are optional but it does remind you that an array is being passed. When you declare the array's formal parameter, NameArray, it must not have brackets nor a data type:

```
Public Sub FindMinAndMax(Minimum As Integer, Maximum As Integer, _
                                          NumberArray)
```

PROGRAM 14.3 *Program 7.1 with a function to search the array*

> **Specification**   Identical to program 7.1 but use a general (Function) procedure to search the array for the required number.

In program 7.1 several lines of code in the Click event for cmdFindNumber carried out the search of the array. This task could have been put into a general procedure. If we take the procedure's job as reporting whether or not the number is present (and let the event procedure handle displaying the result of the search) then we can use a function with a Boolean return value.

This program will also show you how to reuse an existing program and save it under another name.

1.   Open a new project and select **Project/Remove Form1** to remove the default form from your program.

2.   Select **Project/Add Form** and in the **Add Form** dialog click the **Existing** tab. Select the form you used in program 7.1 and click **Open**. This form is now added to the program.

3.   Select **File/Save <form name> As** (where <form name> is the name of the form you added in step 2) and rename the form. You can now work on the renamed copy and change it to suit the new program specification.

4.   Try running the program now and you'll get the error message shown in Figure 14.5.

When a program first runs it must either load a named form or execute the code inside a procedure called Main. By default it is set up to load the form you get when you start a new project, i.e. Form1. In step 1 you removed this form and so Visual Basic defaults to the procedure Main. As you haven't written one with this name the program cannot start.

5.   Click **OK** to remove the error message (and if you get a further one saying *Out of memory* simply remove it). Select **Project/Project 1 Properties...** and in the **Startup Object** box change Sub Main to **Form1**. Click **OK**. Now try running the program.

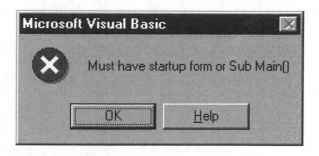

Figure 14.5: The error message

6. Next we need to change the code in the Click event for cmdFindNumber (step 7 of program 7.1). Since its task is now to call the function to search for the required number and to output an appropriate message, any code which contributes to the searching itself can be removed. This means we can remove the variable Element and the loop. The new code should look as follows:

```
Private Sub cmdFindNumber_Click()
  Dim Found As Boolean     'stores function FindNumber's return value
  Dim SearchNumber As Integer
  SearchNumber = txtSearchNumber.Text
  Found = FindNumber(SearchNumber, Numbers()) 'call the function and pass
                                              'it two parameters
  If Found Then
     lblDisplaySearch.Caption = "This number IS in the array"
  Else
     lblDisplaySearch.Caption = "This number is NOT in the array"
  End If
End Sub
```

The return value from the function FindNumber is stored in the Boolean Found and this is used to output the message. Two parameters must be passed to the function – the number to look for (SearchNumber) and the array itself (Numbers).

7. Write the function's declaration directly, or by selecting **Tools/Add Procedure** and clicking the Function option button, as shown below. Since the function must return whether or not the number is present, the return value is declared, outside the parameter brackets, as Boolean.

```
Public Function FindNumber(WantedNumber As Integer, _
                           NumberArray) As Boolean
```

8. Complete the code to carry out the search and return a true or false value as shown below. The search code is the same as that in program 7.1, except that the formal parameter, WantedNumber, is used.

```
  Dim Found As Boolean
  Dim Element As Integer
  Found = False
  Element = 1
  Do While (Found = False) And (Element <= Index)
    If NumberArray(Element) = WantedNumber Then
       Found = True
    Else
       Element = Element + 1
    End If
```

```
   Loop
   If Found Then
      FindNumber = True      'to return a value from the function assign
   Else                      'it to the function's name
      FindNumber = False
   End If
End Function
```

9. Run the program.

end of Program 14.2

Form and Standard modules

So far all our general procedures have been written on the single form belonging to a project. There are two other places you could write them:

- On another form in the same project. This is called another **form module**.
- On a **standard module**, which cannot contain controls, only code.

In program 14.3 you could have put function CalculateInterest on Form2. You would call it with:

```
Interest = Form2.CalculateInterest(AmountInvested, RateOfInterest, Years)
```

You must indicate the form on which the function can be found followed by a '.' before calling it. Note that this call will only work because CalculateInterest was declared as Public. If you had declared it as Private then only code on Form1 could call it.

A standard module must be saved as a separate file to which Visual Basic gives a **bas** extension. You can then use this standard module in any program you write. Procedures in standard modules are often referred to as a **library**. You might write several procedures with a common theme and put them in the same library. An example might be several string-handling routines not provided by the language.

PROGRAM 14.4   *A standard module function*

Specification   Write a function that changes the first letter of a string to upper case. Write it in a standard module and use it in a program.

1.   Open a new project and build the form using the running program shown in Figure 14.6. Name the controls **cmdNewName**, **txtName** and **lblNewName**.

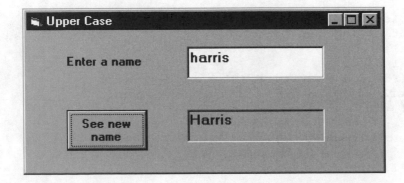

Figure 14.6: Program 14.4

2. Select **Project/Add Module**, make sure the **New** tab is selected in the resulting dialog box, and click **Open**.

3. The new module will be added to the Project Explorer. Save it as **StringLibrary** and Visual Basic will add a **bas** extension (see Figure 14.7).

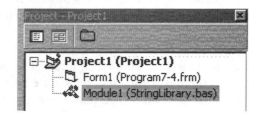

Figure 14.7: The standard module is added to the project

4. Open the Code window for this standard module. As an alternative to getting a template for your function write the template code yourself, and then the code which changes the first letter of the string passed to the function into upper case:

```
Public Function UpperCaseFirstLetter(OldString As String) As String
   Dim FirstLetter As String
   Dim NewString As String
   FirstLetter = UCase(Left(OldString, 1))  'changes the first letter of
   Mid(OldString, 1, 1) = FirstLetter       'OldString to upper case
   NewString = OldString
   UpperCaseFirstLetter = NewString
End Function
```

5. In the Click event for the command button on Form1 enter the code:

```
Private Sub cmdNewName_Click()
   Dim Name As String
   Dim NewName As String
   Name = txtName.Text
   NewName = Module1.UpperCaseFirstLetter(Name)
   lblNewName.Caption = NewName
End Sub
```

Notice that the function call first states which module it is in (Module1).

6. Run the program.

end of Program 14.4

Summary of key concepts

- **General** procedures are non-event procedures. The two main types are **sub** and **function** procedures.

- General procedures are called from within an event procedure or from another general procedure.

- A function may be called in several ways. The commonest is by assigning its return value to a variable. You cannot call sub procedures in this way: call them by using the **Call** statement.

- A function always returns one item of data.

- A **parameter** is a piece of data sent to a procedure when it is called. **Actual** parameters are passed to the procedure and matched to the **formal** parameters which are part of the procedure's declaration. The data type of a matching pair of actual and formal parameters must be the same.

- A **standard module** can contain only code. Its procedures can be used in any programs. Standard modules are sometimes used as **libraries**.

Take it from here...

1. Two methods of calling a function were covered. You could use a third method – call it in the same way as you call a sub procedure using the optional keyword Call. Investigate this method by trying it out in code. What do you think happens to the function's return value? What do you think of this method of calling a function?

2. One of the parameter rules is that the number of actual and formal parameters must be the same. Strictly speaking this is not a rule since Visual Basic does allow optional parameters. Search in Help on the keyword **optional** to find out about these parameters.

Questions on the Programs

Program 14.2

*1. The point was made in step 5 that the variable Interest is declared as Currency because this is the data type declared as the return data type (in step 4). Experiment by changing the data type of Interest, running the program, and then changing the return data type. What can you conclude about how strict Visual Basic is about the data types being the same?

Program 14.4

**1. Change the code in the Click event of cmdNewName so that it changes the first letter of each word in the string you enter into the text box. Your code will need to call the function UpperCaseFirstLetter each time a new word is encountered in the string.

**2. Write a second function in module StringLibrary which changes the first letter of every word in a given string into upper case. Name the function UpperCaseFirstLetters. Test it out by calling it from the Click event of the command button.

End of chapter exercises

*1. When the user clicks a single command button on a form, display the message "This is a procedure call" in a message box. The message should be displayed by calling a sub procedure from the button's Click event.

*2.   Ask the user to type a person's age into a text box and then to click a command button. Validate that the age lies in the range 18 – 40 by calling a function from the button's Click event. If the age is not valid the Click event procedure should display an appropriate message.

**3.   Ask the user to enter two numbers into text boxes as shown in Figure 14.8. Clicking the command button should call a sub procedure to swap the numbers, and the Click event should then display them in the two labels on the right.

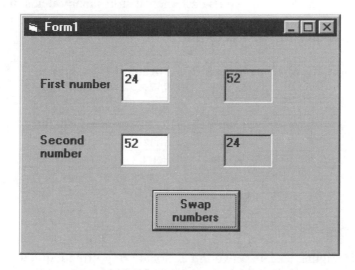

Figure 14.8: Exercise 3

**4.   Write a function that is passed two parameters, a string and a character, and returns the number of times the character is present in the string. Ask the user to enter some text and a search letter in two text boxes, and then to click a command button. The button's event procedure should call the function and then it should output the number of occurrences.

***5.   Write a program that processes invoices for a company selling a variety of products. Ask the user to enter the unit cost of the product, how many were sold and the date the invoice had to be paid by. A check box should be used to indicate if the product is VAT rated. When these details have been entered the user should click a command button. This event should call two general procedures. The first should calculate and return the basic cost of the invoice, including VAT. The second should reduce this basic cost by 10% if the invoice has been paid on time. The final cost should be displayed by the Click event of the command button. Allow the user to process as many invoices as they wish.

Chapter 15 – Records

What is a record?

When a credit card company holds details about its customers it stores many items of data about each one. Four of these items are shown in Figure 15.1. Each item is stored in a column or **field** and all the items for a particular customer are stored in one row or **record**.

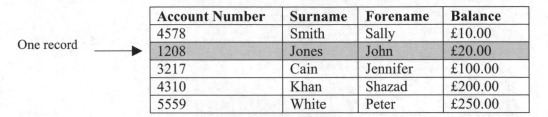

Figure 15.1: Records

An array of records

You could store the data in Figure 15.1 in a two-dimensional array provided that each field is the same data type. This is not always possible and, even if it is, not always desirable. A record allows you to mix data types. If you have many records you can store them in an array; each array element has one record. Figure 15.1 shows an array of records, which is really the same as a table in a database.

How to declare an array of records

There are two stages:

- Declare a single record.
- Declare an array of this single record.

To declare a single record to hold the data for one customer in Figure 15.1 you would write:

```
Public Type CustomerType          'declare data type for one record
    AccountNumber As Integer      'declare the 4 fields
    Surname As String
    Forename As String
    Balance As Currency
End Type
Dim Customer As CustomerType      'declare variable to hold one record
```

Each field is declared separately, sandwiched between the keywords **Type** and **End Type**. The code defines a new data type called CustomerType, similar to the standard data types such as Integer and String. The choice of identifier is yours but it is a good idea to finish it with the word 'Type' so that you can recognise it as a data type in your code. Because you have defined it yourself a Type declaration is often called a **user-defined** data type. The type is declared Public because it must be declared on a standard module (see step 9 of Program 15.1) and made available elsewhere. The last line declares a variable, Customer, of data type CustomerType that is capable of storing four items of data.

To store details of 1000 customers you would extend the declaration as follows:

```
Dim Customers(1 To 1000) As CustomerType
```

Now the variable Customers can store 4 items about 1000 customers, i.e. 4000 items of data.

Processing an array of records

Look carefully at Figure 15.2 which shows how to visualise an array of records. The elements are numbered along the base and one element holds one record, i.e. one customer's details. You can refer to any of the 4000 items of data using the syntax

Customers(Element).Fieldname

The dot between the bracket and the field name is known as the **field separator**. Thus the data item *Jones* is stored in Customers(2).Surname and the item *112.60* stored in Customers(999).Balance.

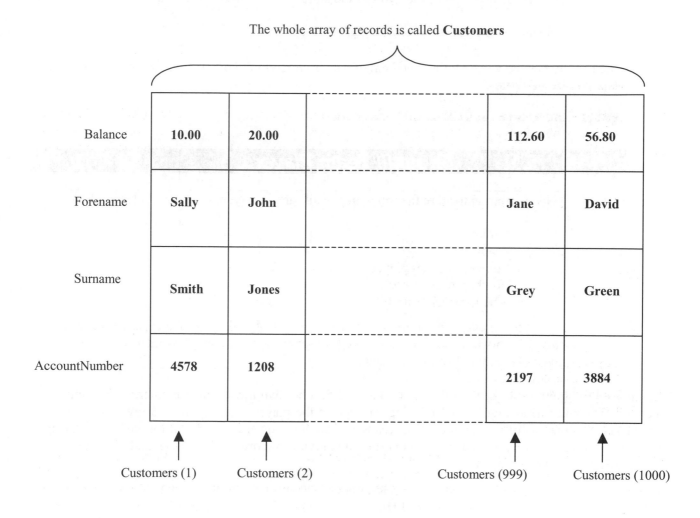

Figure 15.2: An array of records

Think of the syntax as made up of three things that get smaller in size from left to right, as shown in Figure 15.3.

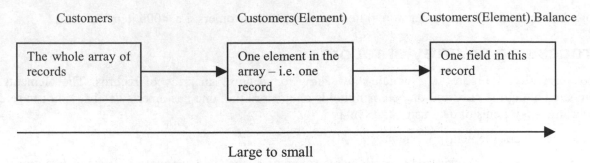

Figure 15.3: *Different sized parts of an array of records*

If you have a text box named txtSurname then you would store what the user types in by writing

```
Customers(Element).Surname = txtSurname.Text
```

If Element currently has the value 60 then the item of data is stored in the 60th record. To output the same piece of data you would write

```
Form1.Print Customers(Element).Surname
```

PROGRAM 15.1   *Football Team Players*

Specification	Write a program to store the following details about players in a football league for one season:

> Name
> Team
> Number of times played
> Number of goals scored
> Whether ever sent off or not

> Store these details in an array of records and display details of one player by using back and forward buttons to navigate through the array. Also allow the user to select a given player and display their details.

The finished program can be seen in figures 15.4 and 15.5. It has two forms, one for entering data and the other for displaying it. In Figure 15.4 clicking Add stores the player's details in an array, and clicking New clears the contents of the input controls ready for the next player's details. In Figure 15.5 clicking Previous displays the previous player's details (i.e. the previous record in the array), and clicking Next displays the next player's details.

Apart from using an array of records the program uses a standard module and a general procedure with parameter passing (both covered in Chapter 14).

Designing the forms

1.   Open a new project and name the form **frmEnterData**.

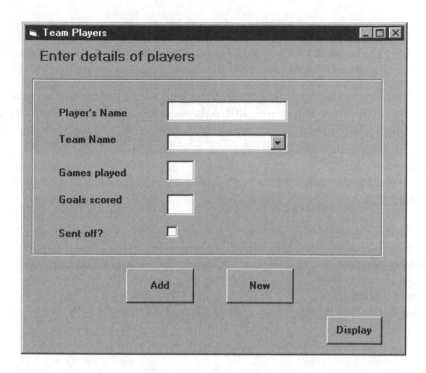

Figure 15.4: Program 15.1 – the opening form

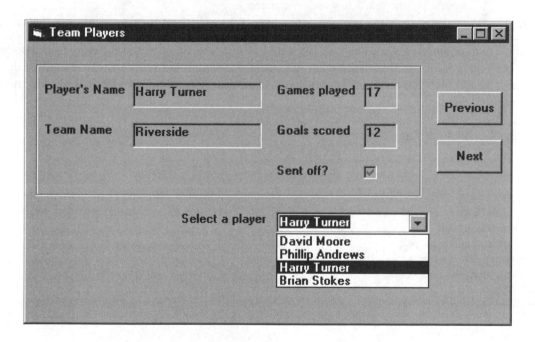

Figure 15.5: Program 15.1 – the second form

2. Design the form using Figure 15.4. The controls for entering data are on a frame. The Team Name control is a combo box and the Sent Off control is a check box. Name the data entry controls **txtPlayer**, **cboTeams**, **txtGames**, **txtGoals** and **chkSentOff**. Set the Text property of the combo box to blank and write several team names of your choice into its List property. You'll need to delete the check box caption and use a separate label.

3. Name the command buttons **cmdAddRecord**, **cmdNewRecord** and **cmdDisplay**.

4. To add the second form select **Project/Add Form**. Make sure the **New** tab is selected and that **Form** is selected in the window. Click **Open**. Name this form **frmDisplayData**.

5. Design the form using Figure 15.5. The controls for displaying data are on a frame. Name the display controls **lblPlayer**, **lblTeam**, **lblGames**, **lblGoals** and **chkSentOff**. Set the Enabled property of the check box to **False** since it is used for display only. Name the command buttons **cmdPrevious** and **cmdNext**. Name the combo box (for selecting a player) **cboPlayers** and set its Text property to blank.

Declaring variables

6. In the General section of frmEnterData declare two global variables. Since we will need to use Number on both forms we must declare it in a different way. Omit Dim and declare it with the Public keyword:

```
Dim Element As Integer        'current element of the array
Public Number As Integer      'number of players' details in array
```

7. In the General section of frmDisplayData declare:

```
Dim Element As Integer        'current element of the array
```

Although this variable has the same name as one of those in frmEnterData, it is a *different* variable.

8. In step 6 you declared a variable to be used by both forms. The array of records must also be used by both but you cannot use this method for declaring a user-defined type. Instead you must declare it on a standard module (covered in program 14.4). Select **Project/Add Module**. With the **New** tab selected and **Module** highlighted, click **Open** and you'll get a standard module. A standard module cannot have any controls, only code. You have to save it as a separate file and Visual Basic will give it a '.bas' extension. Save it now.

9. In this standard module declare a type, and a variable of this type using the keyword Public:

```
Public Type PlayerType      'data type for one record. Public IS optional
  PlayerName As String                    'declare the 5 fields
  TeamName As String
  Games As Integer
  Goals As Integer
  SentOff As Boolean
End Type
Public Players(1 To 20) As PlayerType       'stores details of 20 players
                                        'Public keyword is not optional
```

Entering data

10. In the Load event of frmEnterData initialise the two global variables:

```
Element = 0
Number = 0
```

11. When details of one player are stored in the array we need to increment these two global variables. The complete code for the Click event of cmdAddRecord is:

```
Private Sub cmdAddRecord_Click()
   Element = Element + 1
   Number = Number + 1
   Players(Element).PlayerName = txtPlayer.Text
   Players(Element).TeamName = cboTeams.Text
   Players(Element).Games = txtGames.Text
   Players(Element).Goals = txtGoals.Text
   If chkSentOff.Value = 0 Then      '0 means check box is NOT checked
      Players(Element).SentOff = False
   Else                              'holds 1 - check box IS checked
      Players(Element).SentOff = True
   End If
End Sub
```

An **If** statement is needed to convert the Value property of the check box to the Boolean value needed for the SentOff field of the record.

12. The Click event of cmdNewRecord sets all the fields to blank and positions the cursor in the text box ready for the next player's name. The check box can be set to unchecked by default since a player is more likely never to have been sent off (hopefully!).

```
Private Sub cmdNewRecord_Click()
   txtPlayer.Text = ""
   cboTeams.Text = ""
   txtGames.Text = ""
   txtGoals.Text = ""
   chkSentOff.Value = 0                'set check box to unchecked
   txtPlayer.SetFocus
End Sub
```

13. The cmdDisplay button simply opens frmDisplay.

```
Private Sub cmdDisplay_Click()
   frmDisplayData.Show
End Sub
```

Displaying data

When frmDisplayData loads there are several things that must happen:

- The combo box must show the players' names;
- Details of the first player in the array should be displayed;
- The Previous button should be disabled because the current record is the first one;
- The Next button should be disabled if the user hasn't entered any data or has entered only one player's details.

14. The code to handle this is:

```
Private Sub Form_Load()
  Dim Index As Integer
  Element = 1
  cmdPrevious.Enabled = False
  If frmEnterData.Number = 0 Then            'no data yet entered
    cmdNext.Enabled = False
  ElseIf frmEnterData.Number = 1 Then 'details of only 1 player entered
    cmdNext.Enabled = False
    Call DisplayPlayer(Element) 'procedure call with 1 parameter
  Else                              'details of 2 or more players entered
    cmdNext.Enabled = True
    Call DisplayPlayer(Element)  'procedure call with 1 parameter
  End If
  For Index = 1 To frmEnterData.Number  'populate combo box with names
    cboPlayers.AddItem Players(Index).PlayerName
  Next Index
End Sub
```

Note:

- There is a call to procedure DisplayPlayer, but we haven't written it yet.
- When the variable Number is used, it is prefixed by the name of the form on which it is declared and a dot separator is placed between the two (frmEnterData.Number).

15. When the Previous or Next button is clicked the current element of the array must be changed, and the previous or next player's details displayed by calling procedure DisplayPlayer. If the Previous button is in a disabled state when you click Next, it must be enabled to be able to go back one record.

```
Private Sub cmdNext_Click()
  Element = Element + 1
  Call DisplayPlayer(Element)
  cmdPrevious.Enabled = True      'ensure user can go back one record
End Sub

Private Sub cmdPrevious_Click()
  Element = Element - 1
  Call DisplayPlayer(Element)
End Sub
```

Note that there is more that can be done on enabling and disabling the Previous and Next buttons, but this is left for you to do in question 4 on the program later.

16. When the user selects a player's name from the combo box their details should be displayed. Recall that the ListIndex property of list and combo boxes holds the index of the selected item, and that indexing starts at 0. For example, the third name in the combo box has a ListIndex value of 2, but this name in our array of records is in element 3 (because we numbered the array from 1). Therefore you must add 1 to the ListIndex value.

```
Private Sub cboPlayers_Click()
  Dim RecordNumber As Integer
  RecordNumber = cboPlayers.ListIndex + 1
  Call DisplayPlayer(RecordNumber)
End Sub
```

17. The procedure DisplayPlayer has been called in five places in the code above. One parameter is passed to it – the current element in the array. Since this parameter is only used and not changed by the procedure, it can be passed by value rather than by reference.

```
Public Sub DisplayPlayer(Index As Integer)
   With Players(Index)
      lblPlayer.Caption = .PlayerName
      lblTeam.Caption = .TeamName
      lblGames.Caption = .Games
      lblGoals.Caption = .Goals
      If .SentOff = True Then
         chkSentOff.Value = 1          'set check box to checked
      Else
         chkSentOff.Value = 0          'set check box to unchecked
      End If
   End With
End Sub
```

The new thing in the code above is the use of **With...End With**. You can use this with a user-defined type simply to cut down on code. Instead we could have written

```
lblPlayer.Caption = Players(Index).PlayerName
lblTeam.Caption = Players(Index).TeamName
'etc
```

which requires writing *Players(Index)* on each line.

18. Run the program and check that everything works. Recall that the Previous and Next buttons have intentionally not been made to work fully. Question 4 on this program asks you to take this further.

end of Program 15.1

Reflections on program 15.1

If you run program 15.1 a few times you will realise that one drawback is having to enter all the players' details each time. In real-world programs this data would be kept as records on file and read from the file as appropriate. If only one player's details have to be read then a single record variable could be used. If several players' details, or perhaps the whole file, have to be read and copied into RAM then an array of records would be used. Files are studied in the next chapter.

Summary of key concepts

- A **record** is a data structure in which you can mix data types. It is made up of one or more **fields**.

- To declare a record use **Type...End Type**. You build a **user-defined** data type and then declare a variable of this type.

- To use a variable on all the forms in a program declare it in the General section as **Public** and omit the keyword Dim, e.g. Public Number As Integer. When the variable is used on a form other than the one on which it is declared, it must be prefixed by the name of the form and a dot separator used, e.g. frmEnterData.Number.

- To use a **user-defined type** on more than one form in a program, declare it in a standard module.

- **With…End With** can be used when assigning or reading data to a given record. It saves having to write out part of the syntax when processing individual fields.

Questions on the Program

*1. Rewrite the code in the Click event for cmdAddRecord using **With…End With**.

*2. Set the Sorted property of the combo box on frmDisplayData to True. Enter several players' names not in alphabetical order. Make a note of the order you entered the names. Try selecting these players from the combo box on frmDisplayData. Can you explain why the wrong player's details are usually displayed? (Change the Sorted property back to False when you've finished.)

*3. Run the program and enter three records. Then click the Next button on the second form three times or more. Nothing appears in the Player's Name, Team Name or Sent Off controls, but the other two controls show 0 values. Explain why. Then keep clicking the Previous button until you get an error message. Can you explain what it is saying?

**4. There is some enabling/disabling of the Previous and Next buttons in the code but it doesn't cover all situations. Extend the code so that the buttons are enabled only when necessary. For example, if the array is full the Next button should be disabled, (though in a real program you would either make sure the array is large enough or use a dynamic array).

***5. Extend the program to do the following:

- allow the user to select a team and scroll through only details of players in this team;

- in a list box display the name and team of all players who have been sent off;

- in a list box display the name and team of all players who have scored at least a given number of goals. Allow the user to input the number of goals to search on.

End of chapter exercises

**1. Store the following details of a member of a health club in a record – name, weight (in kilograms), height (in metres and centimetres, e.g. 1.86) and age. Have two command buttons on the form. Clicking one of them should ask the user for these details by using a series of input boxes. Clicking the other should print details of the member on the form.

***2. Students on a two-semester course take an exam at the end of each semester. Allow the user to enter student names and their mark (out of 100) in each exam. Store all the data in an array of records. Display:

- the average mark in each exam;
- the name of the student with the highest mark in each exam;
- the names of those students who passed the course. At least 50 marks in both exams are needed for a pass.

Design the form appropriately. Use a general procedure to validate the mark (i.e. to accept only a value from 0 to 100).

Chapter 16 – Files

What is a file?

In all the programs covered so far, any stored data is lost when the program closes, and would have to be entered again when the program next runs. For a program like 15.1, where a lot of data might be stored in an array of records, this is clearly a waste of time. The solution is to store the data permanently – in a file.

Types of file in Visual Basic

Visual Basic supports three types of file. You are likely to use only two of these:

- Text files
- Random access files

There are several key differences between these files:

- A text file stores all its data as characters, represented by their ASCII codes. For example, it would store the number 25 as character 2 (ASCII code 50) and character 5 (ASCII code 53). In binary these two ASCII codes are 0110010 (50) and 0110101 (53). A random access file would store this number differently. Assuming it is stored as a 2-byte integer it would be stored as 0000000000011001.

- A random access file stores only records. In a text file there is no naturally built-in structure to the data since it is simply stored as a sequence of characters.

- You cannot open a text file to be both read from and written to, but you can with a random access file.

- With a random access file you can read and write to any position within the file. For example, you can read the 5th record or overwrite the 8th record. This is also called **direct access**. You cannot directly change the data in a text file. To change some data you would have to read all the data before the data you wish to change and write this to a new file; then write the changed data to the new file. Finally read all the data after the changed data and write this to the new file too.

Opening/closing a file

You must always open a file before you can use it. To open a **text** file use one of the following;

```
Open Filename For Input As #1      'to read from the file
Open Filename For Output As #1     'to write to the file
Open Filename For Append As #1     'to write to the end of the file
```

- The **Open** statement opens a file if it exists. If it doesn't exist, Open first creates it and then opens it.

- Filename is a String variable that holds the name of the file. You need to tell Visual Basic the full path to the file too, e.g. "c:\My VB Work\Programs\Students.txt".

- The **Input**, **Append** and **Output** statements indicate how you wish to read/write. If you open a file for Output, Visual Basic deletes the contents of the file (even if you don't write anything to it). To add data to an existing file you must use Append, which adds the data after the existing data.

- **As #1** assigns the file the number 1. All files are identified by a number, not by their name. If you have two or more files open at the same time they must have different numbers.

To open a **random access** file you must tell Visual Basic the length (in bytes) of the records it stores. This means that you must state the length of any String fields in your defined data type. For example, if you were storing records from program 16.1 on file, the PlayerName and TeamName fields (step 9 in program 16.1) must have defined lengths. If these were 20 and 14 bytes then the total length of a record would be 40 bytes since the other three fields need only 6 bytes. Assuming a variable, OnePlayer, has been declared to hold one record, you could write either of the following to open the file:

```
Open Filename For Random As #1 Len = 40
Open Filename For Random As #1 Len = Len(OnePlayer)
```

The second method is more convenient as it uses the **Len** function to find the length of the record for you. Note that the first use of the word 'Len' is just part of the syntax and not a function call.

When you have finished using a file always close it. To close either a text or random access file is very easy:

```
Close #1
```

Reading from a file

Visual Basic keeps an imaginary file pointer as it reads through a file. When the file is opened it points to the first line of a text file or the first record of a random access file. Suppose a text file holds a series of whole numbers, one on each line in the file. Assuming Number has been declared as an Integer, the following code would display these on a form:

```
Do While Not EOF(1)          'EOF means End Of File. NB pass it just the
   Input #1, Number          'number of the file, not # sign too
   Form1.Print Number
Loop
```

The **EOF** function returns True when the end of a file has been reached. The While condition uses the **Not** logical operator and is saying *continue until the end of the file is reached*. The **Input** statement reads the item of data on the current line in the file and stores it in Number. After reading the single item of data on the line, the file pointer points to the next line.

With a random access file you can read (and write) only one record at a time. You cannot read or write individual fields within a record. To read and display the whole of a random access file you would write:

```
Do While Not EOF(1)
   Get #1, , OneTeam          'OneTeam is a record variable
   'code to display the contents of the record goes here
Loop
```

The middle argument for the **Get** statement above is missing, indicated by the pair of commas. Visual Basic numbers the records in a random access file from 1 onwards, and the missing argument here is this record number. In the code above the file pointer is automatically moved to the next record each time round the loop, so there is no need to state the record number.

When you wish to go directly to a particular record you *do* need to state the record number. The next example reads a record from the file at record position *RecordNumber*. It uses the **Seek** statement, whose second argument is the record number where the file pointer should be positioned.

```
        Seek #1, RecordNumber
        Get #1, , OneTeam
```

Seek is not always needed before Get. In the example above you could read the record directly with Get if you provide the record number:

```
        Get #1, RecordNumber, OneTeam
```

Writing to a file

For text files use the **Write** or **Print** statements. (Program 16.1 illustrates the slight difference between these.) So

```
        Write #1, Number
```

writes the contents of Number to the current file pointer position.

With a random access file use the **Put** statement. This works in the same way as the Get statement to read from a file. It may need to know the record number and must be passed one whole record to write to the file:

```
        Put #1, , OneTeam                    'write to current file pointer position
        'or
        Put #1, RecordNumber, OneTeam        'write to RecordNumber record number
```

Getting the file name

When you open an existing file you must supply its name. There are three ways of doing this:

- Hardcode the full path and file name
- Use App.Path
- Use the CommonDialog control

Hardcode the full path and file name

Assuming Filename has been declared as a String you might write:

```
        Filename = "c:\My Visual Basic Work\Members.dat"
```

The disadvantage of this method is that the file must be in the folder specified by the path. If you move the file to another folder you have to change the code.

Use App.Path

App is a Visual Basic object that gives information about your application or program. The **Path** property stores the application's path. The example below adds the file name to the path.

```
        Filename = App.Path & "\Members.dat"
```

The file must be in the same folder as your program, but this method is more flexible than hardcoding the full path and file name since you can move the program and file into any folder and the code will work.

Use the CommonDialog control

The CommonDialog control can be added to the toolbox. Let's have a practical demonstration of how it works.

1. Open a new project. Select **Project/Components** and in the Components dialog box check the item called **Microsoft Common Dialog Control** as shown in Figure 16.1. Click **OK**.

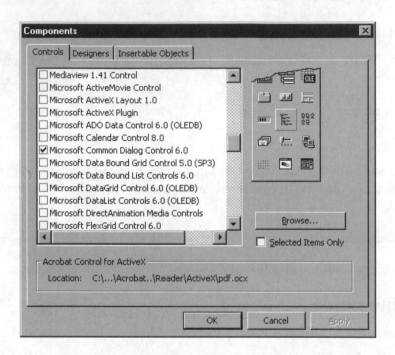

Figure 16.1: Selecting the CommonDialog control

2. The control will be added to the toolbox. Like the Timer control it is invisible at run time and can be placed anywhere on the form. Place this control and a command button on the form, and keep their default names CommonDialog1 and Command1.

3. Code the Click event of the command button as follows:

```
Private Sub Command1_Click()
    CommonDialog1.ShowOpen
    Form1.Show
    Print CommonDialog1.FileName
End Sub
```

The ShowOpen method will display the same dialog box (window) you get when you select File/Open from a Windows application. The FileName property stores the full path and name of the file you select from this dialog box.

4. Run the program. Click the button and you'll get the very familiar Open dialog box. Select any file you want, or even type in a file that isn't listed, click **Open** and you'll see the path and file name printed on the form.

It is important to realise that all the ShowOpen method of this control has done is to get a path and the file name. It has not opened the file. You still need to use the Open statement to do this.

PROGRAM 16.1 *Text file to hold names and ages*

Specification Allow the user to enter people's names and ages and store these in a text file. Allow the user to display the contents of the file at any time.

Figure 16.2 shows the program after two sets of names and ages have been stored in the file.

1. Open a new project. Place the controls and set the captions as shown in Figure 16.2.

2. Name the controls **txtName**, **txtAge**, **cmdAddToFileWrite**, **cmdAddToFilePrint**, **cmdDisplayFile** and **lstDisplayFile**.

3. Declare a global variable to hold the name of the file:

```
Dim Filename As String
```

4. In this program we will use App.Path for getting a file name. Text files normally have a '.txt' extension, so our file will be called NamesAndAges.txt.

```
Private Sub Form_Load()
    Filename = App.Path & "\NamesAndAges.txt"
End Sub
```

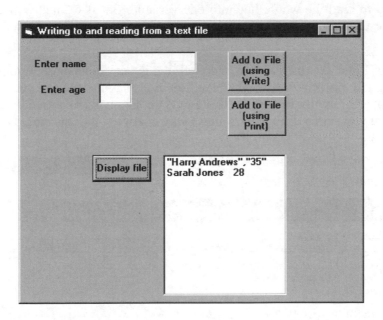

Figure 16.2: Program 16.1 after two names and ages have been stored

5. The code for the Click event of the upper Add command button is:

```
Private Sub cmdAddToFileWrite_Click()
    Dim Name As String
    Dim Age As String
    Name = txtName.Text
    Age = txtAge.Text
```

```
      Open Filename For Append As #1    'open the file,
      Write #1, Name, Age               'write two items of data to it, then
      Close #1                          'close it
      txtName.Text = ""
      txtAge.Text = ""
      txtName.SetFocus
   End Sub
```

6. The code for the lower Add command button is the same but uses Print rather than Write. Type the code in now.

7. In the Click event to display the file, write:

```
Private Sub cmdDisplayFile_Click()
   Dim DataToDisplay As String
   Open Filename For Input As #1
   lstDisplayFile.Clear
   Do While Not EOF(1)
     Line Input #1, DataToDisplay
     lstDisplayFile.AddItem DataToDisplay
   Loop
   Close #1
End Sub
```

Rather than reading the two items of data on each line in the file into two variables, the **Line Input** statement is used to read the whole line into one variable. But if we had wanted to display people aged over 20, for example, we would need to read in the items separately, in order to test the age data.

8. Run the program. Enter a name and age and click the upper command button. Enter another name and age and click the lower button. Click the button to display the file and you'll see how Write and Print store the data differently in the file. Write puts quotation marks around each piece of data and separates them with a comma. Print simply puts spaces between the two pieces of data.

end of Program 16.1

PROGRAM 16.2   *Random access file of Garden Centre products*

Specification   A garden centre stores the following details about each of its 800 products:

- ID
- Description
- Price
- Quantity in stock
- Reorder level (i.e. number to which stock has to fall before it is reordered)

Write a program which stores details of products in a random access file. The number of products in the file should always be displayed. The program should allow the user to search for a product both by record number and by product ID. It should also display the entire contents of the file in a list box in product ID order. Use the CommonDialog control to retrieve the name of the file.

You can see the program in Figure 16.3 though in a real program you would not display the file name; it is displayed here simply to demonstrate that the CommonDialog control has worked. Since the products were not entered into the file in product ID order, the display in the list box does not reflect their physical order in the file. The details at the bottom left are of record number 3. In a real application you are unlikely to search for a given record number (unless the key field contains values which are the same as the record number values, e.g. membership numbers from 1 upwards). It is included here to illustrate direct access to a given record.

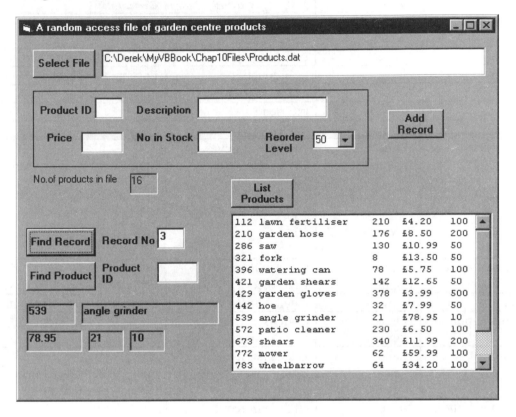

Figure 16.3: Program 16.2

1. Open a new project and design the form using figures 16.3 and 16.4. As usual the Text property of all the text boxes should be set to blank. The 5 input text boxes are enclosed by a Shape control whose Shape property is set to **0 – Rectangle**. The 5 labels in the bottom left of the form should have their Border Style property set to **1 – Fixed Single**.

2. Place a CommonDialog control anywhere on the form.

3. Declare the following in the General section:

```
Private Type OneProduct
    ProductID As Integer          '2 bytes storage needed
    Description As String * 18    '18 bytes
    Price As Currency             '8 bytes
    QuantityInStock As Integer    '2 bytes
    ReorderLevel As Integer       '2 bytes
End Type                          'total 32 bytes to store 1 record
Dim Filename As String
Dim NumberOfRecords As Integer    'no. records currently stored in file
```

Since random access files store records and we must read and write whole records to the file, we need to declare a type to hold details of one product. A variable of type OneProduct has *not* been declared here. Since several event procedures will need to use this variable it is much safer to declare it locally when needed. Note that the length of the Description field is declared. **You must always state the length of String fields when using random access files**.

Control	Property	Property setting	Comment
Command button	Name Caption	cmdSelectFile Select File	
Text box	Name	txtFilename	Holds path + name of file
Text box	Name	txtProductID	For input of product ID
Text box	Name	txtDescription	For input of description
Text box	Name	txtPrice	For input of price
Text box	Name	txtQuantityInStock	For input of no. in stock
Combo box	Name List Text	cboReorderLevel 10 50 100 200 50	There are 4 reorder levels 50 is commonest reorder level, so set as default
Command button	Name Caption	cmdAddRecord Add Record	
Label	Name	NumberOfRecords	Displays no. of records in file
Command button	Name Caption	cmdDisplayFile List Products	
List box	Name Font Sorted	lstDisplayFile Courier New size 8 True	 Font to keep output in columns Display products in ID order
Command button	Name Caption	cmdFindRecord Find Record	
Text box	Name	txtFindRecord	To enter record number to search for
Command button	Name Caption	cmdFindProduct Find Product	
Text box	Name	txtFindProduct	To enter product ID to search for
Label	Name	lblProductID	At bottom left of form
Label	Name	lblDescripton	At bottom left of form
Label	Name	lblPrice	At bottom left of form
Label	Name	lblQuantityInStock	At bottom left of form
Label	Name	lblReorderLevel	At bottom left of form

Figure 16.4: Properties of the controls in program 16.2

4. In the Click event for cmdSelectFile we'll use the CommonDialog control to get the file name, then open the file and display how many products it holds. To calculate the number of products (records), divide the total size of the file in bytes by the size of one record. The LOF (**L**ength **O**f **F**ile) function is used to get the size of an open file.

```
Private Sub cmdSelectFile_Click()
  Dim Product As OneProduct          'one record
  CommonDialog1.ShowOpen             'display the Open (file) dialog box
  txtFilename.Text = CommonDialog1.Filename 'display selected file name
  Filename = txtFilename.Text
  Open Filename For Random As #1 Len = Len(Product)    'open file
  NumberOfRecords = LOF(1) / Len(Product) 'calculate no. records in it
  lblNumberOfRecords.Caption = NumberOfRecords
  Close #1
End Sub
```

5. Clicking the Add Record button writes the record to the file, updates the number of products in the file, and clears the text boxes ready for the next product:

```
Private Sub cmdAddRecord_Click()
  Dim Product As OneProduct                   'one record
  Filename = txtFilename.Text
  Product.ProductID = txtProductID.Text 'store input data into one record
  Product.Description = txtDescription.Text
  Product.Price = txtPrice.Text
  Product.QuantityInStock = txtQuantityInStock.Text
  Product.ReorderLevel = cboReorderLevel.Text
  Open Filename For Random As #1 Len = Len(Product)    'open file
  Put #1, NumberOfRecords + 1, Product  'write record after current record
  Close #1
  NumberOfRecords = NumberOfRecords + 1
  lblNumberOfRecords.Caption = NumberOfRecords 'update no.products in file
  txtProductID.Text = ""                      'clear input for next product
  txtDescription.Text = ""
  txtPrice.Text = ""
  txtQuantityInStock.Text = ""
  txtProductID.SetFocus
  cboReorderLevel.Text = "50"        'set reorder level to default value
End Sub
```

6. To display the contents of the file in the list box use a **For...Next** loop. Each execution of the loop processes one record. Although you earlier set the font of the list box to Courier New to display the output in columns, this only works properly for strings of a specified length. Three of the fields are Integers and only by storing them as Strings can we make them occupy a given amount of space.

```
Private Sub cmdDisplayFile_Click()
  Dim Index As Integer
  Dim DataToDisplay As String        'details of one product
  Dim Quantity As String * 4         '3 fields to store as fixed-length
  Dim Price As String * 6            'Strings
  Dim ReorderLevel As String * 3
  Dim Product As OneProduct          'one record
  Filename = txtFilename.Text
  lstDisplayFile.Clear
  Open Filename For Random As #1 Len = Len(Product)
  For Index = 1 To NumberOfRecords   'loop through all records in file
    Get #1, , Product       'read one record. Note no parameter between the
        '2 commas - Geting a record positions file pointer for next read
    Quantity = Product.QuantityInStock
    Price = Format(Product.Price, "currency")
```

```
            ReorderLevel = Product.ReorderLevel
            DataToDisplay = Product.ProductID & " " & Product.Description _
                    & " " & Quantity & " £" & Price & " " & ReorderLevel
        lstDisplayFile.AddItem DataToDisplay
    Next Index
    Close #1
End Sub
```

7. Use Get to display the contents of a record from the file using its record number. The code checks that the record number entered by the user is a valid one.

```
Private Sub cmdFindRecord_Click()
    Dim RecordNumber As Integer
    Dim Product As OneProduct          'one record
    Filename = txtFilename.Text
    RecordNumber = txtFindRecord.Text
    If (RecordNumber > 0) And (RecordNumber <= NumberOfRecords) Then
        Open Filename For Random As #1 Len = Len(Product)
        Get #1, RecordNumber, Product                'read required record
        lblProductID.Caption = Product.ProductID     'and display its fields
        lblDescription.Caption = Product.Description
        lblPrice.Caption = Product.Price
        lblQuantityInStock.Caption = Product.QuantityInStock
        lblReorderLevel.Caption = Product.ReorderLevel
        Close #1
    Else
        MsgBox "Invalid record number"
    End If
End Sub
```

8. Finding a product with a given product ID involves a linear search through the file from the first record using **Do While…Loop**. A Boolean value is switched to True if the record is found and the loop stops.

```
Private Sub cmdFindProductID_Click()
    Dim RecordNumber As Integer
    Dim Found As Boolean
    Dim ProductID As String
    Dim Product As OneProduct
    ProductID = txtFindProduct.Text
    RecordNumber = 0
    Found = False
    Filename = txtFilename.Text
    Open Filename For Random As #1 Len = Len(Product)
    Do While (Not EOF(1)) And (Found = False) 'loop until no more records
                                              'or record is found
        RecordNumber = RecordNumber + 1
        Get #1, RecordNumber, Product
        If Product.ProductID = ProductID Then          'record found?
            Found = True
            lblProductID.Caption = ProductID
            lblDescription.Caption = Product.Description
            lblPrice.Caption = Product.Price
            lblQuantityInStock.Caption = Product.QuantityInStock
            lblReorderLevel.Caption = Product.ReorderLevel
```

```
        End If
    Loop
    Close #1
    If Not Found Then
        MsgBox ("Product ID " & ProductID & " is not in the file")
    End If
End Sub
```

9. Run the program. Click Select File and enter a file name of your choice, e.g. Products.dat. Enter details of several products, display them and then try looking for a given product by record number and by ID. Enter valid and invalid record numbers.

end of Program 16.2

Summary of key concepts

- The two main types of file are **text** files and **random access** files (**direct access** files). Data in text files is stored as a sequence of characters but in random access files it is stored as records.

- In code, files are referenced by an integer number, e.g. #1.

- The **Open** and **Close** statements open and close a file. A text file can be opened for input or output, but not both at the same time. A random access file *can* be opened for both.

- Use the **Input** statement to read from a text file and the **Get** statement to read from a random access file.

- Use the **Write** or **Print** statements to write to a text file and the **Put** statement to write to a random access file.

- Use the **Seek** statement to position the file pointer at a particular record in a random access file. Get and Put can also do this.

Take it from here...

1. Only the ShowOpen method of the CommonDialog control was used in this chapter. Experiment with the **ShowSave**, **ShowPrinter** and **ShowColor** methods.

2. When using the CommonDialog control to get a file name you can state which folder or directory you wish the Open dialog box to display by setting one of the control's properties. Try this out.

3. In program 16.2 the LOF function is used to find the size of an open file in bytes. Find the name of the function that is used to do the same for a file that is not open.

4. The number that identifies a file has been coded as '#' followed by an integer number (e.g. #1) in the programs. Visual Basic provides an alternative way by using the **FreeFile** function. Find out how this works.

Questions on the Programs

Program 16.1

*1. Delete the word **Line** from the line of code
```
Line Input #1, DataToDisplay
```

and run the program. How is the data displayed in the list box? What can you conclude about what Visual Basic stores in DataToDisplay when Line is omitted?

**2. Add a command button which calculates and displays the average age of the people stored in NamesAndAges.txt. You will have to read the name and age for each person into two separate variables and then process the age variable. (Note: write the data to the file with Write not Print.)

Program 16.2

**1. Add three option buttons to display in the list box details of those products:

- which cost more than a given price – the user enters the search price in a text box;
- whose number in stock exceeds a given value – the user enters this stock value in a text box;
- whose reorder level is the same as or greater than a given level – user selects level from combo box.

End of chapter exercises

**1. Write a program which displays the names of students on a selected GNVQ/AVCE course by reading from a text file, as shown in Figure 16.5. The text file, Students.txt, has the names and course codes for 125 students and can be found on the web site. The names are unsorted in the file but should be displayed alphabetically in a list box. The course codes are:

HC-F	Foundation Health & Social Care	HC-N	Intermediate Health & Social Care
IT-N	Intermediate ICT	IT-V	Advanced ICT Year 1
IT-VU	Advanced ICT Year 2		

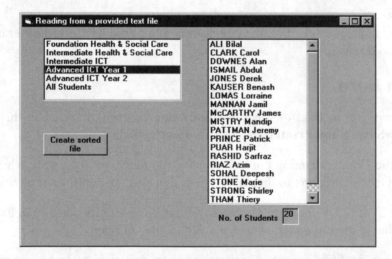

Figure 16.5: Exercise 1

When you have this working, add a command button to create a second file with the names in alphabetical order. Do this by copying the contents of the list box to the new file.

**2. Programmers working on new business applications sometimes have to convert text files into random access files. Write a program which does this for the file in exercise 1, Students.txt. Include a list box to display the contents of the new file. If you allow strings of 20 and 5 for the student name and course code fields the total size of the random access file should be 3125 bytes (125 records x 25 bytes).

**3. Write a program that generates a random number from 0 to 100 every second and stores it in a text file as shown in Figure 16.6. (Search Help for the Rnd function to find out about producing random numbers.) Use the CommonDialog control for getting the file name. The contents of the file are displayed in Figure 16.6 both in a text box and in a list box. To display the contents of a text file in a text box you should read the entire contents into a single String variable and simply display the contents of this variable at one go. If the variable is *FileContents* then you would write:

```
FileContents = Input(LOF(1), #1)
TxtRandomNumbers.Text = FileContents
```

This uses the Input function which is different from the Input statement you use when opening a file. This function returns a string of characters and its first parameter states how many to return. This parameter is the LOF (**L**ength **O**f **F**ile) function, which in turn returns the size of the file in bytes. To display the numbers on separate lines in the text box you must set its MultiLine property to True.

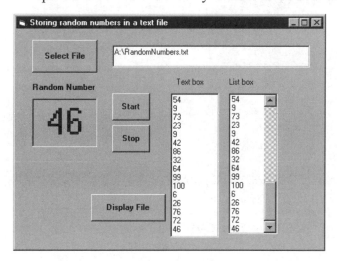

Figure 16.6: Exercise 3

***4. Write a program to store the following details about second-hand cars for sale:

- registration number
- make (e.g. Ford)
- model
- year of manufacture
- price

Store the details in a random access file and display them in a list box. Do not allow duplicate registration numbers. Allow the user to search for the following (and display the results in the list box):

- a particular car using the registration number to search on – the user should select the registration number from a combo box;
- all cars of a given make and model entered by the user;
- all cars less than a given number of years old – allow the user to enter the number of years.

Part Two – Building a Portfolio

Your teacher will set you one or more assignments that will allow you to meet the *Assessment Evidence* for Unit 22 (see Appendix E). Essentially for any assignment you will need to go through the DIDiT (Design, Implementation, Documentation, Testing) stages.

Unlike Unit 7 your teacher is not allowed to give you a basic program specification (the full user requirements). Ideally you are expected to find a real user and, through your discussions with them, draw up their requirements yourself. If you cannot find a real user the unit allows your teacher to act their part. Your job would then be to question the teacher and find out what they want the program to do.

The case study used in Part Two assumes that you have been through the discussion stage with your user and have drawn up a list of requirements. Then an assignment is given which could be used for any Unit 22 programming project. The rest of Part Two takes you through the DIDiT stages and shows you how to produce a portfolio of work using the case study.

Chapter 17 introduces the case study. This is called *TJ's Tennis*, and is about running a league for junior members of a tennis club. The assignment follows with a grid matching its tasks to the grade criteria in the unit's Assessment Evidence.

Chapter 18 starts by showing you how to draw up a **program specification** to meet the requirements of Unit 22. It then takes you through part of the **Design** stage. It shows you how to design the forms, printed reports and files needed by the TJ's Tennis program. A method of documenting file structures is explained.

Chapter 19 takes you through the rest of the **Design** stage. As with the case study in Unit 7, a list of events and their tasks is first drawn up. The chapter then goes further by showing you how to develop a fuller modular structure through using general procedures for some of the tasks identified in the events. It uses two documentation methods – the **modular structure chart** for showing how general procedures are called from event procedures, and a tabular method for documenting general procedures.

Chapters 20, 21 and **22** cover the **Implementation** (coding) stage. They show you how to build a fully-working program using the design worked out in Chapters 18 and 19.

Chapter 23 covers the **Documentation** and **Testing** stages. Only technical documentation is required by Unit 22. The principles of how to test a program were explained in Chapter 13 and so are not repeated here.

Chapter 24 discusses what you might cover in **evaluating** your finished program.

Chapter 17 – The Assignment: TJ's Tennis

The case study

In Unit 7 a program specification for Gina's Groceries was given to you. There was nothing for you to find out about what the user required. For Unit 22 you are expected to play a major part in drawing up the basic program specification. Ideally you should find a real user who has a problem that you can write a program for. Failing this your assessor can give you a problem and they will act the part of the user. You are expected to question your teacher/user to find out more about their requirements.

To show you how to carry through a project from design to testing to meet the Assessment Evidence for Unit 22, we will have to assume that the process of finding out the user's requirements has been done. The case study at the end of this chapter, *TJ's Tennis,* summarises what is needed.

Assignment tasks

Task 1 – Program specification

To achieve a **grade E** you must:

1.1 Clearly describe what your user wishes the program to do.

1.2 Clearly describe the program specification. You should briefly cover the input, output and processing needed to meet the user requirements in 1.1.

Task 2 – Designing the program

To achieve a **grade E** you must:

2.1 Draw a sketch of the form(s) in your program indicating all their controls. Briefly explain what the more important controls will be used for.

2.2 Design the layout of any printed output from your program.

2.3 List the events in your program and briefly state what will happen as each of these takes place.

2.4 Describe and explain how data will be stored in your program (arrays, records, files).

To achieve a **grade C** you must:

2.5 Do tasks 2.1 to 2.4 well.

Task 3 – Implementing the program

To achieve a **grade E** you must:

3.1 Write the code for the program. This must be of a reasonable standard and demonstrate the use of suitable event procedures. Some of the user's requirements should be met.

To achieve a **grade C** you must:

3.2 Ensure that the code is of a good standard. You should demonstrate the appropriate use of general procedures. All or nearly all the user's requirements should be met.

Task 4 – Documenting the program

To achieve a **grade E** you must:

4.1 Write the **technical documentation** for your program. This should include:

- A printout of your program code, containing a reasonable amount of commenting.
- The modular structure of your program. List all the event procedures and the tasks they will carry out.

To achieve a **grade C** you must:

4.2 Ensure task 4.1 is done well. In addition the technical documentation should include screen prints of your forms in use, including any error messages, and examples of any printed output. You must annotate all of these.

To achieve a **grade A** you must:

4.3 Explain clearly all the calculation and manipulation of data in your program

4.4 Draw modular structure charts of your program.

4.5 Document any general procedures you have used.

4.6 Draw diagrams to show how you designed the finished forms and printed output.

Task 5 – Testing the program

To achieve a **grade C** you must:

5.1 Draw up test plans for each appropriate event and general procedure to test all major paths and to cover acceptable and unacceptable input.

5.2 Carry out the test plans you have drawn up for task 5.1. Wherever possible provide documentary evidence that the test does what you claim it does. Show clearly how you resolved any problems in your program uncovered by these tests.

Task 6 – Other tasks

To achieve a **grade A** you must:

6.1 Write a detailed evaluation of your program. This should include the following:

- A review of how far it meets the user's requirements.
- A review of its good and bad features.
- Possible improvements.

6.2 Your writing throughout this assignment must use technical language well and have few spelling and grammatical errors.

Notes on the assignment:

1. To achieve a grade C you must also meet any deadlines set by your assessor and you must not have been given more than a reasonable amount of help to solve the tasks.

2. Tasks 2.3 and the second bullet point in task 4.1 look the same, but because 2.3 is done at design time (before coding) and 4.1 is done when the coding is finished, there are differences. These are discussed at the beginning of Chapter 23.

3. Task 4.6 seems to cover tasks 2.1 and 2.2. If you do not change your original designs in task 2 then task 4.6 is just about the same, except that for technical documentation you should use the Visual Basic names for all form controls that are referred to in code. If you do make changes to the original designs these will be incorporated into task 4.6.

Meeting the Assessment Evidence

Appendix E lists what you have to do to achieve grades E, C or A. By doing the tasks in this assignment you will be able to meet these criteria. Figure 17.1 matches these tasks to the Assessment Evidence.

Assessment Evidence	Assignment tasks
E1	1.1
E2	1.2
E3	2.1, 2.2, 2.3, 2.4
E4	3.1
E5	*see note below*
E6	4.1
C1	2.5, 3.2
C2	5.1, 5.2
C3	4.2
C4	-
A1	4.3, 4.4, 4.5, 4.6
A2	6.1
A3	6.2

Figure 17.1: Matching the assignment tasks to the Assessment Evidence

Note: E5 expects 'a clear progression towards your solution.' This is not a separate task. Your assessor will be looking to see if you have made a reasonable attempt at finding out the user's requirements before design and had a good attempt at design before coding.

TJ's Tennis

TJ's Tennis is a large complex with many indoor and outdoor tennis courts. It has more than 300 members including a junior membership of over 100. About 40 of the junior members are part of a regular coaching programme, with usually 8 – 10 members to one coach. Each coach has players with a range of abilities. Three or four times each year these junior members are divided into small leagues of about six players. Each player plays the others in the league and league tables are produced when the matches are complete. For example, a league with six players will have a maximum of 15 matches (see Figure 18.8, for example). One or two players are promoted and demoted after each league round and this builds up a lot of healthy competition. All the recording and listing of match results and final league tables is done on paper and TJ's wants it all 'put on the computer.'

The league tennis matches are scored as follows. Each match is the best of three sets, so that the winner can win 2-0 or 2-1 in sets. The first player to win 6 games in a set wins the set but they must win by at least two clear games. For example a player can win 6-0 or 6-4 but not 6-5. If the score reaches 6-6 in a set a tiebreaker game is played and the winner takes the set 7-6. The tiebreaker can be used in all three sets (unlike in professional tennis where it is not used in the deciding set). The match winner scores 2 points. If the score is 2-0 in sets the loser gets 0 points, but if it is 2-1 in sets the loser gets 1 point.

TJ's wants the computerised system to do the following:

- For each new league round, store the players' names, which league they are in and the initials of their coach. Leagues are numbered 1, 2, 3 etc. TJ's thinks that for the foreseeable future 8 leagues will be adequate.

- Store the results of each match. This must include the names of the two players, who won and lost, and the score for each set.

- TJ's requires a printout of the players (and their coaches' initials) in each league. This is to be pinned up on the club's junior notice board before each league round.

- At the end of each league round TJ's also wants a printout of each league showing the results of each match (the two players and the score for each set) and a list of the players in order of total points scored, ranked from 1 onwards. TJ's would like the option of printing the results for any particular league or for all the leagues together.

TJ's does not require the system to work out who is promoted and demoted after each league round. This will be decided by the club and fed into the next round when new data is entered into the computerised system.

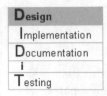

Chapter 18 – Program Specification and Design

Program specification

A good starting point is a paragraph in the *What you need to learn* section of Unit 22:

> A good specification states the user's needs in such a way that there is no doubt about the scope of the problem and what you need to do to resolve it. You and the user must agree on the specification before you begin work on program design.

To draw up an acceptable program specification you need to discuss the following with your user:

- What information they want output and how it should be presented.
- What data needs to be input in order to produce this output.
- Where this data to input will come from (data capture) and how it will be input.
- What data processing must be done to turn the inputted data into the required output.

Output

There are three types of output to be considered:

- Printed reports
- Screen output/reports
- Files

TJ's Tennis has asked for the following printed output:

1. For each league a list of the players' names and their coaches' initials. This will be pinned up on the club's junior notice board before each league round starts.

2. At the end of a league round a separate printout for each league showing the results of all the matches and a list of the players in order of total points scored. For each match the two players and the score for each set should be listed.

3. The same as for 2 above but for any particular league.

TJ's does not require any screen reports, or at least they cannot think of anything in their early discussions with you that they need output on the screen. When printed output 2 and 3 above has been produced at the end of a league round TJ's says there is no need to store this information permanently on the computerised system (i.e. in files). The printed reports themselves will do as a permanent record.

Input – data needs

You have agreed with TJ's to store the following about each player:

- Their first name and surname.
- Their coach's initials. All coaches can be identified by two-character upper case initials, e.g. HG, DT.
- The league they are currently playing in. Leagues are numbered from 1 onwards.

TJ's thinks that for the foreseeable future 8 leagues will be adequate. At this early stage you have of course not decided how to cater for a particular number of leagues in your code. It might turn out that increasing the number of leagues at a future date would mean more work on your (or another programmer's) part. You need to be sure that TJ's is quite happy with 8.

For each tennis match between two players in the same league you agree with TJ's to store:

- The first name and surname of both players.
- Who won and who lost.
- The score for each set.

You have confirmed that the date of the match does not need to be stored and you have cleared up a problem that had been on your mind – how to store details of an unfinished match. TJ's wishes to store details only of those matches played to the finish. Both players of an unfinished match score no points, and as TJ's does not want these matches to be on the printed reports there is no need to store anything about them.

Input – data capture and input method

TJ's keeps a list of its junior members on paper. It has each member's personal details, including whether or not they are part of the coaching scheme and so an automatic player in the leagues, and their coach's name. This will be the main data source for the players' details in your program, though your user, who organises the league, knows the players' names and coaches and probably will not need to consult the written records much. Match results are recorded on paper as they are played (Figure 18.1). All data input will of course be done through the keyboard.

League	Winner	Loser	Score		
2	Carol Guthrie	Harry Hillman	6 2	2 4	6 4
1	Steve Wilson	Ben Green	6 4	6 0	
1	Joe White	Ben Greend	6 2	2 6	7 6

Figure 18.1: Keeping a record of matches played

Processing

Processing mainly involves turning stored data into output. The decisions about how to implement this in code are yours as the programmer and do not involve the user. The user does have a role, however, in that you need to be clear about any facts or user requirements that may affect the processing. The main example in this project is the points scoring system. A match winner scores 2 points. A match loser scores 1 point if the match goes to three sets but 0 points if it needs only two sets. However you have confirmed with TJ's that the system does not need to work out who is promoted and demoted after each league round. This will be done on paper and fed into the next round when new data is entered.

Design

Chapter 10 listed the main stages in the design of an event-driven program like Visual Basic. We will go through the same sequence of tasks again for TJ's Tennis. These tasks are:

- form design
- design of printed reports
- data storage
- design of overall modular structure
- processing required

In this chapter we will cover all of these except the modular structure.

Designing the forms

You should produce paper designs of all the forms in your project, drawn by hand or by using a software package. For TJ's Tennis we will have four forms as outlined in Figure 18.2.

General name	Purpose
Main form	A 'switchboard' into the rest of the project. Contains buttons to open each of the other forms
Players form	Enter details of players in the leagues. Display these details. Allow user to change details of any player. Allow user to delete details of any player.
Matches form	Enter details of all matches. Display these details. Allow user to change details of any match. Allow user to delete details of any match
Reports form	Print 3 reports: For each league a list of players and their coach. For a selected league all match results and a final league table. Match results and final league tables for all leagues.

Figure 18.2: Summary of the program's four forms

Main form

Figure 18.3 shows a sketch of the design of the main form.

Players form

Figure 18.4 shows a sketch of this form. It has four events:

Form's Load event. This should display details of all players currently stored in the system in the list box.

***Save* command button's Click event**. This will write the three items of data about a player entered into the text boxes to a file and display these details in the list box.

***Change* command button's Click event**. The user should have first selected a player from the list box and have selected one or more of the three check boxes. Input boxes will be used to get the amended data from the user. Any changes will be immediately updated in the list box.

***Delete* command button's Click event**. The user should have first selected a player from the list box. Details of this player will be deleted from the system and be removed from the list box display.

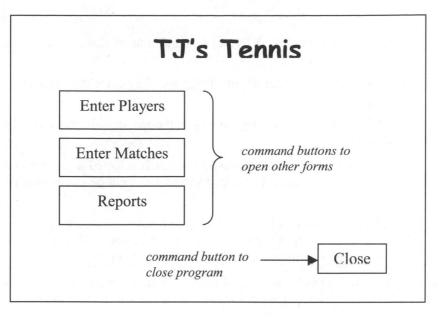

Figure 18.3: Main form

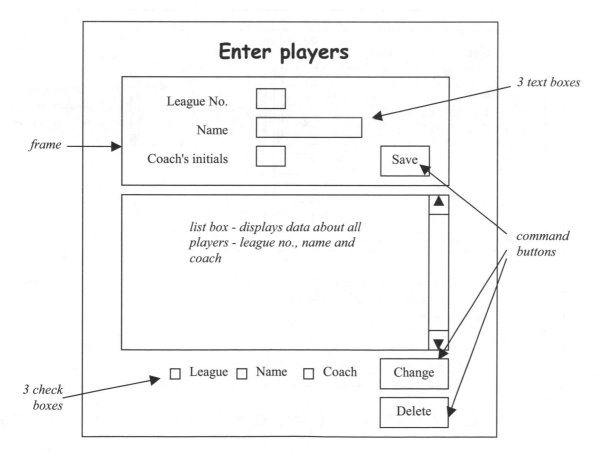

Figure 18.4: Players form

Matches form

Figure 18.5 shows a sketch of this form. It has five events and four of these behave in a similar way to those events that occur on the Players form.

Form's Load event. This should display details of all the matches currently held in the system in the large list box.

Combo box's Click event. This will display the players in the league selected from the combo box in both the Winner and Loser list boxes.

***Save* command button's Click event**. The user should have first selected a winner and loser from the two smaller list boxes and have entered the set scores. These details will be stored in a file and displayed in the list box.

***Change* command button's Click event**. The user should first have selected a match from the large list box and have selected one or more of the six check boxes. Input boxes will be used to get the amended data from the user. Any changes will be immediately updated in the list box.

***Delete* command button's Click event**. The user should have first selected a match from the large list box. Details of this match will be deleted from the system and be removed from the list box display.

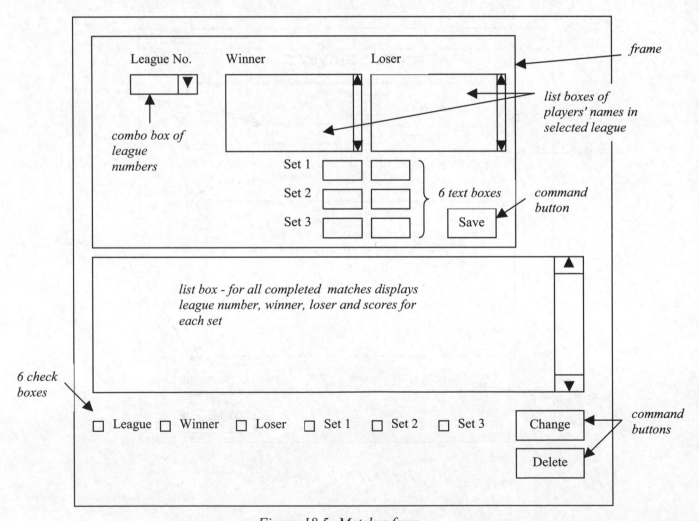

Figure 18.5: Matches form

Reports form

Figure 18.6 shows a sketch of this form. It has only one event – The *Print* command button's Click event. This prints the report selected through the three option buttons.

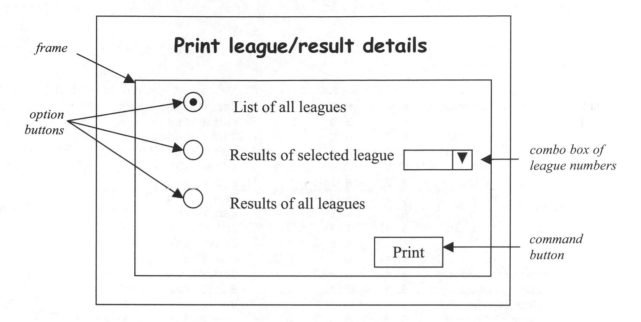

Figure 18.6: Reports form

Printed reports

The two printed reports that TJ's has asked for were described in the section on Output earlier in this chapter. You should produce sample reports (using a word processor, spreadsheet or whatever) to show TJ's for their approval. Figures 18.7 and 18.8 show what the reports look like.

```
TJ's Tennis Junior League

League 1              Coach

Steve Wilson          DS
Jane Diamond          WM
Sue Smith             DS
Joe White             WM
Sam Bates             TD
Ben Green             TD


League 2

Carol Guthrie         WM
Harry Hillman         DS
Wendy Williams        WM
Nasser Hussain        MD
Sean Gray             DS
John Jackson          WM
...and so on
```

Figure 18.7: List of leagues, players and coaches

```
TJ's Tennis Junior League

League 1

1. Steve Wilson      8
2. Jane Diamond      7
3. Sue Smith         6
4. Joe White         5
5. Sam Bates         5
6. Ben Green         3


Steve Wilson    6 4    6 0             Ben Green
Steve Wilson    6 2    3 6    6 3      Sam Bates
Steve Wilson    6 2    6 1             Jane Diamond
Steve Wilson    6 2    6 4             Joe White
Ben Green       6 2    4 6    6 3      Jane Diamond
Sue Smith       6 2    6 1             Ben Green
Joe White       6 2    6 1             Sam Bates
Joe White       6 2    2 6    7 6      Ben Green
Jane Diamond    6 2    6 4             Joe White
Sue Smith       6 4    6 2             Steve Wilson
Sue Smith       6 4    6 7    7 6      Joe White
Jane Diamond    6 4    6 0             Sam Bates
Sam Bates       6 4    6 4             Ben Green
Sam Bates       6 4    6 1             Sue Smith
Jane Diamond    6 3    6 1             Sue Smith
```

Figure 18.8: Results for a selected league

In Figure 18.8 two players scored 5 points but their rankings are different. Whether this is acceptable or whether TJ's would want such players ranked equally must be cleared up. It may be, for example, that the result of the match between the two players who have the same points should determine the final league ranking. This is really a processing issue, which was covered earlier, but it may be that only by sketching out what the report may look like, that the issue comes to light at all. For this project let us assume that TJ's is happy with the different rankings and does not require any extra processing on your part. Remember that TJ's does not require the system to identify the promoted and demoted players after a league round. If there are two or more players tied for a single promotion place, for example, TJ's will decide on the worthy player without the help of your program!

Data storage

The main new things you learned in the Visual Basic chapters in Unit 22 were records and files. All the players' and match details will be stored on file. Although we will need to use a record data structure to read and write from the files, our program will not need an array of records to store all the file details in memory. We can just process the file directly as required.

For each of the files your program uses you should state:

- its name
- its record structure
- the likely size of the file when in use
- how the file is processed – how data is added, deleted and changed (assuming all 3 must be done)
- what it is used for

Two files are needed for TJ's Tennis. Because they store data we will give a '.dat' extension to their name.

Players.dat file

This stores details of each player in the junior league. Figure 18.9 shows a useful way of documenting the details of the file. Note that the League field has been declared as String. It could have been Integer, but as much of the processing of this field will be working with strings, the String type has been used. Note, though, that as it is declared to be one byte in size, meaning that it can only hold one numeric digit, only 9 league numbers can be used. If TJ's ever needed 10 or more leagues the field length would have to be changed. However you may recall that TJ's were sure 8 leagues would be enough for the foreseeable future.

A question that should be resolved at this stage is how do we delete a record from the file? You can delete a record *logically* by keeping it in the file and having a field that stores information about whether or not the record should be treated as deleted. On the other hand you can delete a record *physically* so that the file becomes smaller. For TJ's Tennis there is nothing to choose between the two methods but in some business applications the choice may be a crucial one. If a file consists of a very large number of records, and quite a lot of these are logically deleted, it may make processing of the file too slow. For TJ's we will physically delete records from the file.

External file name	Players.dat		General name	Players	
Description	Stores details of each player in the junior leagues				
Used for	Displaying players' details in the list box on the Main form				
	Displaying players' names in the Winner and Loser list boxes on the Matches form				
	Printing the list of leagues from the Reports form				
Processing	New records are appended. Amended records remain in the same place in the file. Deleted records are physically deleted.				
Record structure					
Field name	**Field description**		**Data type (and length)**		**No. bytes**
League	League number (1, 2 etc,)		String		1
Name	Name of player		String		19
Coach	Initials of player's coach (2 characters)		String		2
Record size	22 bytes				
Typical size of file	22 x number of players in the junior league. With 40 players this is 880 bytes.				

Figure 18.9: Details of Players.dat file

Matches.dat file

This stores details of all the completed matches. The file's details are shown in Figure 18.10. There are several ways we could store the scores. The method used here is to have an array that holds up to six one-character strings. So if the score is 6-4, 1-6, 6-0 the winner's number of games in set 1 (6 games) would be stored in Scores(1), the loser's games in set 1 (4 games) stored in Scores(2), the winner's games in set 2 (1 game) stored in Scores(3) and so on. If the match is won in two sets Scores(5) and Scores(6) would not store anything. As with the Members file we will physically delete any records.

Now that we have looked at the files in detail let us return to the question about whether or not any arrays of records might be needed for data storage. We concluded earlier that this data structure is not needed for storing all the records from the files in memory, but what about calculating and storing how many points each player has scored at the end of a league round? The Players file does not store a running total of points scored by each player and the Matches file does not store the points scored for each match. Since these figures can be calculated from the data that *is* stored (in the Matches file), there is no need to store the data permanently.

However we will use an array of records to temporarily store the players' names and their total points, and loop through the records in this array to print out the league tables.

External file name	Matches.dat	General name	Matches
Description	Stores details of each match completed in one junior league round		
Used for	Displaying match details in the list box on the Matches form Printing league positions and match results from the Reports form		
Processing	New records are appended. Amended records remain in the same place in the file. Deleted records are physically deleted.		
Record structure			
Field name	**Field description**	**Data type (and length)**	**No. bytes**
MatchID	Each match is numbered from 1 onwards	Integer	2
League	League number	String	1
Winner	Name of winner	String	19
Loser	Name of loser	String	19
Scores	Scores for each set	String array	6
Record size	47 bytes		
Typical size of file	47 x number of matches in the junior league. For example, with 7 leagues of 6 players there could be 105 matches = 4935 bytes		

Figure 18.10: Details of Matches.dat file

Deleting records from files

Although there are only two files the choice of physically deleting records, rather than logically deleting them, also requires two other files. For example, in Figure 18.11 suppose we want to delete the match between Steve Wilson and Joe White (record 4). You would copy all the records before the one to delete (records 1 to 3) to another file, skip the one to delete, and then copy the rest to the other file (record 5 only). Assuming the other file is in the same folder as Matches.dat, it must have a different name. So the trick is now to delete Matches.dat and then rename the other file as Matches.dat.

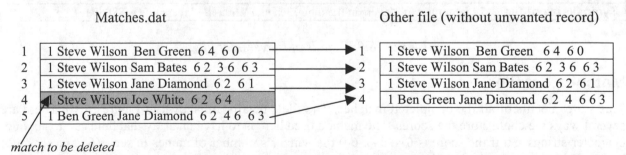

Figure 18.11: Deleting a record from a file

Processing

You might look back at the end of Chapter 10 to see what was said about processing in Gina's Groceries. Processing is about how the data input and stored in a system is manipulated to produce the required output. Let us consider two examples from TJ's Tennis.

Print the leagues which will be pinned up on the junior notice board. Figure 18.7 showed the design of this report. We need a loop to process each league in turn. Each execution of the loop runs through all the records in the Players file looking for those players in the league currently being processed. There are two ways of resetting the file pointer to the first record at the start of the loop. You can close the file and then open it again, or keep it open and use Get with a parameter value of 1. We will use the close/open method.

Calculate the number of points each player has won in a particular league. Copy all the players' names in the league being processed into the array of records identified in Figure 18.10 for this purpose. Initialise the total points they have scored, which are also stored in the array, to 0. Then loop through all the records in the Matches file. If the current match read from the file belongs to the league being processed check to see if the match was won in 2 or 3 sets. If it was won in 2 sets the winner gets 2 points and the loser 0 points. So search for the winner's name in the array of records and add 2 points to their total points also stored in this array. If the match was won in 3 sets do the same thing with the winner, and also search for the loser's name in the array and add 1 point to their total.

Design
Implementation
Documentation
i
Testing

Chapter 19 – Design: Modular Structure

Modular structure

The term 'modular structure' refers to the way in which the whole program is broken up into procedures. Compared to a non-visual language, Visual Basic makes things easier by having event procedures. You have no choice but to structure your program using these event procedures. However you do have the choice about writing your own general procedures. One of the differences between Units 7 and 22, in this book at least, is that Unit 22 expects you to use general procedures where appropriate.

Deciding on the general procedures you need at the design stage is not easy. You need to carefully work out what you want to happen when an event is triggered. If a particular task must happen that is not directly related to the event itself, then you should probably put it into a general procedure. If it needs particular items of data to do this task pass these as parameters.

Chapter 14 listed several reasons for using general procedures. The first one was to avoid repeating code – if the same task is done in two or more event procedures put the code into a general procedure and call it when needed. In the last chapter we identified four events which, among other things, should display details of players stored in the system in the list box on the Players form. These were the form's Load event and the Click events of the form's three command buttons – to save details of a new player, to change a player's details and to delete a player. All four events should call the same general procedure.

Event procedures

It is useful first to identify all the event procedures in your program, as shown in Figure 19.1. Notice the dominance of the Click event. **The asterisked tasks will be assigned to general procedures**.

General procedures

It is important to realise two things about the general procedures at this point in the design process:

- A single asterisk in Figure 19.1 does not necessarily mean the task is done by a single procedure. For example, you will see later that the task of printing a list of leagues and their players from the Reports form involves calling a general procedure, which itself calls another general procedure. At this stage we have not thought about how to carry out the processing and so all we can do is state that a general procedure will be used.

- Two or more tasks may be expressed differently, but in the end require the same code and therefore the same general procedure. For example, it was pointed out above that four events on the Players form need to display details of all players in the list box. Figure 19.1 tells us that Click event of the *Change* button on this form *updates changed details in list box*, whilst the same event for the *Delete* button *removes deleted player's details from list box*. Both tasks actually do the same thing – loop through the Players file and copy each record to the list box.

Ideally at design time you should be able to state the following for each general procedure that you intend to write:

- Its name
- The type of general procedure – a sub procedure or a function procedure

- Exactly what it does
- List its parameters (if any)
- If it is a function procedure, what its return value is
- Where it is called from

This is a tall order for inexperienced programmers, and it is very likely that you will decide much of this as you code. You may not have understood parameter passing and will therefore have to miss this part out. Your program can work perfectly without parameters, but the overhead is more global variables and the likelihood of more errors. The *What you need to learn* section of Unit 22 states that you should know about parameter passing, so use parameters where appropriate. Fortunately if you find them difficult, they are not essential for a program to work.

Event	Control	Processing
Main form – command buttons		
Click	*Close*	Closes program
Click	*Enter Players*	Displays/loads Players form
Click	*Enter Matches*	Displays/loads Matches form
Click	*Reports*	Displays/loads Reports form
Players form		
Load	Form	Assigns Players file *Displays all players' details in list box
Click	*Save* command button	Appends one player's details to Players file *Adds new player's details to list box
Click	*Change* command button	Changes any details of player selected in list box and writes changes to Players file *Updates changed details in list box
Click	*Delete* command button	Deletes details of player selected in list box from Players file *Removes deleted player's details from list box
Matches form		
Load	Form	Assigns Players and Matches files *Displays details of all completed matches in list box
Click	*Leagues* combo box	Displays names of players in the selected league in the Winner and Loser list boxes
Click	*Save* command button	Appends details of one match to Matches file *Adds new match details to list box
Click	*Change* command button	Changes any details of match selected in list box and writes changes to Players file *Updates changed details in list box
Click	*Delete* command button	Deletes details of match selected in list from Matches file *Removes deleted match's details from list box
Reports form		
Load	Form	Assigns Players and Matches files
Click	*Print* command button	Identifies which option button is selected *Prints list of leagues *Prints results of selected league *Prints results of all leagues

Figure 19.1: The tasks of the event procedures

Modular structure of Main form

Figure 19.2 shows a **modular structure chart** for the Main form. A line with an arrow indicates a call to a general procedure. In this example the procedure *DisplayPlayers* has the task of copying the records in the Players file to the list box.

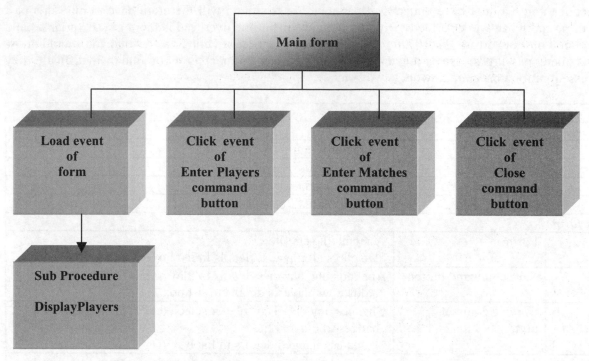

Figure 19.2: Modular structure chart of the Main form

Modular structure of Players form

There are four event procedures on this form – the form's Load event and the Click event of the three command buttons. Figure 19.1 indicates that each of these has to display players' details in the list box. The processing required to do this from the form's Load event is clear – loop through the Players file and copy each record to the list box. When you save details of a new player you could add the details directly to the list box, and when you delete a player you could remove the selected player directly. You cannot *change* details of a player in a list box directly though. The simplest solution for all these tasks is to clear the list box and loop through the file since any additions, changes or deletions will have just been saved. Therefore we can use the sub procedure *DisplayPlayers* each time. Figure 19.3 shows the modular structure of the Players form.

Documenting general procedures

DisplayPlayers is the first general procedure we have designed so far, so at this point you ought to learn a method for documenting the design of this type of procedure. Figure 19.4 shows a method of documenting *DisplayPlayers*. Use this method for all the general procedures in your program.

Modular structure of Matches form

This is shown in Figure 19.5. The form has the same four events as the Players form plus the Click event of the leagues combo box. As with the Players form we can have a common sub procedure that loops through the (Matches) file and displays all its records. This is called *DisplayMatches*. There are two more general procedures. One of these, function *ValidMatch*, is straightforward, but the purpose of the other, *RenumberMatchIDs*, will be clear only when we have thought carefully about how to identify which match to change or delete from the file.

If the system stores details of a match that has already been stored, the final league table will be wrong. We ought to check for this. Function *ValidMatch* returns True if the match has not been saved before and False if it has. At this stage in the design we are not concerned with *how* the function does this, although we can and should identify any data it needs to do the task. Obviously it needs to know the names of the two players. These are passed as parameters and are indicated in the modular structure chart next to the arrow going to the function. The arrow going *from* the function indicates a return value.

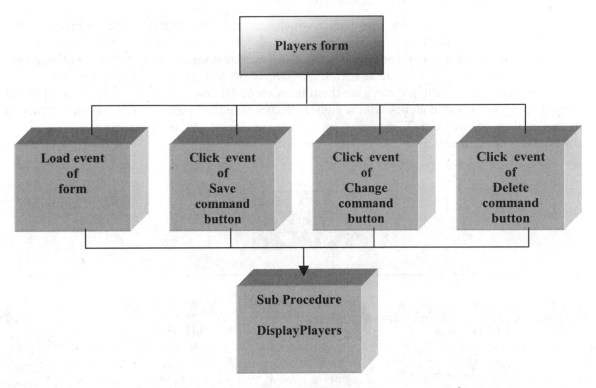

Figure 19.3: Modular structure chart of the Players form

Name	DisplayPlayers
Type	Sub Procedure
Parameters	None
Called from	Load event of Players form Click event of each command button on Players form
Purpose	Copies all records from Players file to list box on Players form

Figure 19.4: Documenting the general procedure DisplayPlayers

Now consider how we know which record in the *Matches* file to process if the user clicks the *Change* or *Delete* buttons. TJ's will input players' details in league order but enter the match details in the order in which they are played (i.e. probably no particular order). What this means is that we do not need to sort the list box on the Players form but that we probably should sort the one on the Matches form. Even if TJ's entered the players in no particular order it would be easy to find the player in the list box to change or delete. It would be more difficult to do this with the match details in the matches list box if they were unsorted. If the first part of the match details in the list box is the league number we could use this to sort the matches, by setting the list box's Sorted property to True. If we did set it to True there would be a problem. On the Players form we could use the list box's ListIndex property to identify which player has been selected from it (because the items are displayed in the list box in file order), but we could not use this method to identify which match has been selected.

We therefore need another method for identifying which record in the Matches file to process. The solution is to give each match an ID, e.g. number each match from 1 onwards as it is saved. So if the user selects match 16 then record number 16 in the file needs to be processed. Note that the match numbers will need to be in the list box (look ahead at Figure 21.1 where the last column contains the match IDs), but as TJ's has no interest in them, we can hide them from view. The next problem is that if we delete a match we must renumber those matches with a higher number than the deleted one. If you delete match 26, for example, then those from 27 onwards must be renumbered. A sub procedure can do this – *RenumberMatchIDs* in Figure 19.5.

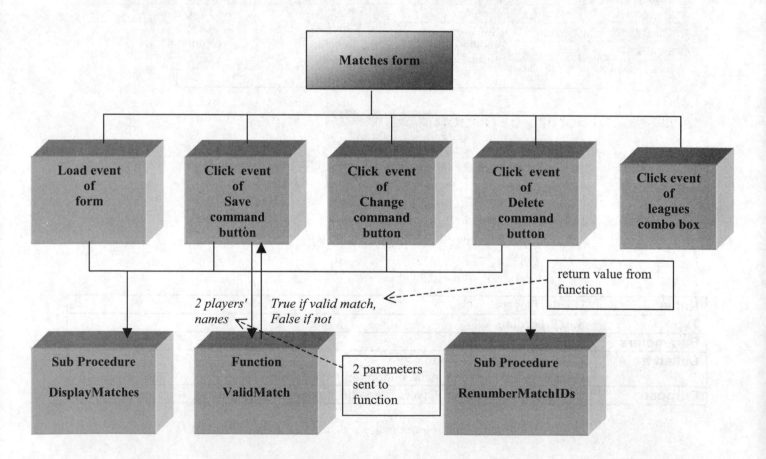

Figure 19.5: Modular structure chart of the Matches form

The three general procedures shown in the modular structure of the Matches form are documented below in Figure 19.6

Name	DisplayMatches
Type	Sub Procedure
Parameters/ReturnValue	None
Called from	Load event of Matches form Click event of each command button on Matches form
Purpose	Copies all records from Matches file to list box on Matches form

Name	ValidMatch
Type	Function
Parameters/ ReturnValue	Names of two players in one match Returns True if match details of these two players have not been entered before, i.e. a valid match. Otherwise returns False
Called from	Click event of Delete command button on Matches form
Purpose	Checks if match details to be saved are already saved

Name	RenumberMatchIDs
Type	Sub Procedure
Parameters	None
Called from	Click event of Delete command button on Matches form
Purpose	When a match has been deleted renumbers match Ids

Figure 19.6: Documenting the general procedures on the Matches form.

Modular structure of Reports form

Figure 19.7 shows the modular structure for the Reports form. Each of the three sub procedures called from the Click event of the *Print* button handles one of the three print options on the form. Let us look at each in turn.

Sub Procedure PrintLeagues

This prints the list of leagues, players and their coaches shown in Figure 18.7. The question is how many leagues are there to print? Function *NumberOfLeagues* returns this value, but as usual at this stage of the design, we do not need to be concerned with the detail of *how* it does this (other than being confident that we can code a solution!).

Sub Procedure PrintSelectedLeagueResults

This procedure produces the points league table and match results for the league selected from the combo box. It calls *PrintPointsResults* to handle the league positions (see Figure 19.8). This procedure is passed the league number selected from the combo box. You can see from Figure 19.7 that this procedure in turn calls a function *PlayersInLeague*. This is sent the league number currently being processed and it returns the number of players in that league. *PrintPointsResults* needs to know this in order to process the required number of positions in the league table.

PrintSelectedLeagueResults then calls sub procedure *PrintMatchResults* to handle the results of all the matches in the selected league (see Figure 19.8). This procedure needs to know which league to process and so this is passed as a parameter.

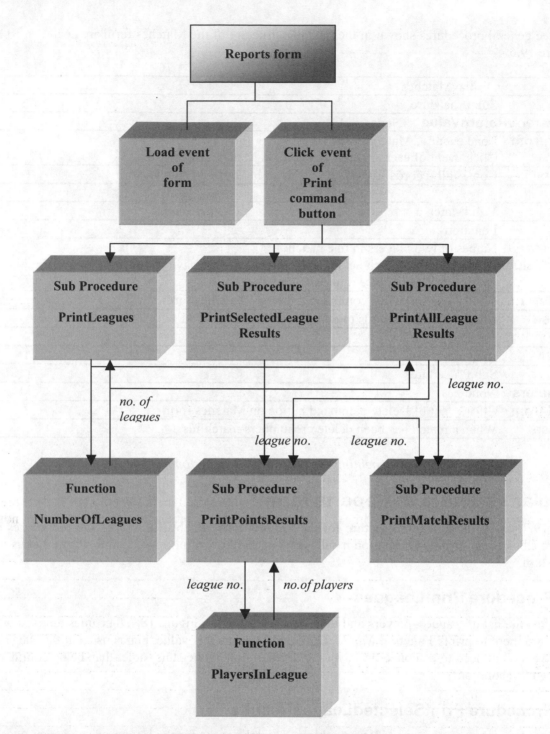

Figure 19.7: Modular structure chart of the Reports form

Sub Procedure PrintAllLeagueResults

This procedure is similar to *PrintSelectedLeagueResults* except that it prints the results not of one league but of all the leagues. It needs to call function *NumberOfLeagues* to find out how many leagues there are, and then it is simply a case of calling the same two procedures called from *PrintSelectedLeagueResults*. It calls them each time it processes one of the leagues.

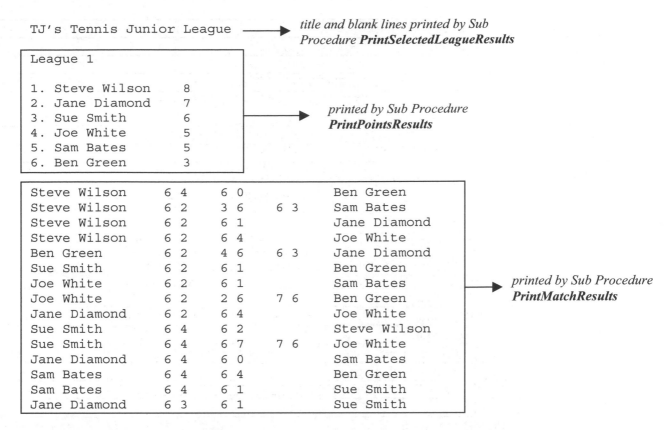

Figure 19.8: How the results of a selected league are printed using three procedures

Documenting the general procedures

Figure 19.9 contains documentation for the 7 general procedures used on the Reports form. Note the extra item of information in some of these procedures about which other procedures they call. We did not have this degree of procedure calling on the other forms.

Name	PrintLeagues
Type	Sub Procedure
Parameters	None
Called from	Click event of Print command button on Reports form
Calls	Function NumberOfLeagues
Purpose	Prints list of leagues with players' names and their coaches' initials

Name	PrintSelectedLeagueResults
Type	Sub Procedure
Parameters	None
Called from	Click event of Print command button on Reports form
Calls	Sub Procedure PrintPointsResults, Sub Procedure PrintMatchResults
Purpose	Prints report title and league number on printed report of league results

Figure 19.9: Documentation of general procedures on the Reports form

Name	PrintAllLeagueResults
Type	Sub Procedure
Parameters	None
Called from	Click event of Print command button on Reports form
Calls	Function NumberOfLeagues, Sub Procedure PrintPointsResults, Sub Procedure PrintMatchResults
Purpose	Prints report title and league number on printed report of league results

Name	NumberOfLeagues
Type	Function
Parameters ReturnValue	None Number of leagues
Called from	Sub Procedure PrintLeagues, Sub Procedure PrintAllLeagueResults
Purpose	Finds out how many current leagues there are in the system

Name	PrintPointsResults
Type	Sub Procedure
Parameters	A league number
Called from	Sub Procedure PrintSelectedLeagueResults, Sub Procedure PrintAllLeagueResults
Calls	Function PlayersInLeague
Purpose	Prints league table for league number passed to it

Name	PrintMatchResults
Type	Sub Procedure
Parameters	A league number
Called from	Sub Procedure PrintSelectedLeagueResults, Sub Procedure PrintAllLeagueResults
Purpose	Prints results of all matches for league number passed to it

Name	PlayersInLeague
Type	Function
Parameters ReturnValue	A league number Number of players in the league passed to it
Called from	Sub Procedure PrintPointsResults
Purpose	Finds how many players are in a particular league

Figure 19.9 (continued)

Chapter 20 – Implementation: Main and Players Forms

Standard module

You might recall from step 8 in Program 15.1 that a record is an example of a user-defined type, and that you must declare user-defined types on a standard module. The Players form stores details of a player input by the user in a record and writes this to the Players file. Standard modules cannot contain any controls, only code. When you save a standard module Visual Basic gives it a **.bas** file name extension.

1. Select **Project/Add Module**. You do not need to change its default name of Module1 but save it as **Tennis**, so that its full name is Tennis.bas.

2. To declare a record to hold a player's league number, name and coach's initials write the following in the module. Step 3 in Program 16.2 stated that when writing records to a file you must declare the length of any String fields.

```
Public Type PlayerType      'data type for a record to store one player
    League As String * 1     '1 byte
    Name As String * 19      '19 bytes
    Coach As String * 2      '2 bytes
End Type                     '22 bytes in total
```

There are two ways of declaring a variable that must be used by two or more forms. Declare it on one form as Public and use it on another one by prefixing it with the name of the form it is declared on. The other way is to declare it in a standard module and use it in the normal way on any form. We will use this method.

3. Declare the single variable that will be used by the Players form and at least one other form:

```
Public PlayersFile As String      'Players file
```

The Forms

The design of the four forms in Chapter 18 can be used directly in building them in Visual Basic. The only thing we did not decide on at design time was the names of the controls that will be used in our coding. First we will get the four forms, although you will not use two of these until the next chapter.

1. Open a new project and name the form **frmMain**. Delete its caption.

2. Select **Project/New Form**. Make sure the **New** tab is selected and that the **Form** icon is highlighted, and click **Open**. Name the new form **frmPlayers** and set its caption to **Players**.

3. Get two more forms. Name them **frmMatches** and **frmReports** and set their captions to **Matches** and **Reports**.

The Main form

Figure 20.1 shows the form in use. It is based on Figure 18.3.

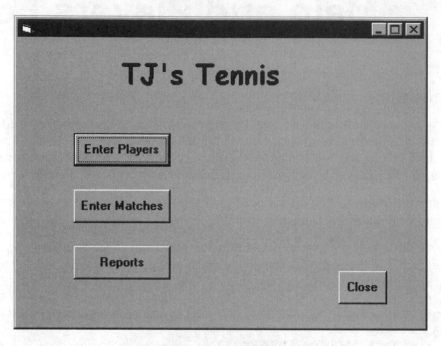

Figure 20.1: The Main form

1. On frmMain place a label and enter the title **TJ's Tennis**. The font in Figure 20.1 is **30 pt bold Comic Sans MS**.

2. Place the four command buttons and change their captions to those in Figure 20.1. Name them **cmdPlayers**, **cmdMatches**, **cmdReports** and **cmdClose** as appropriate.

3. When one of the group of three command buttons is clicked we want the appropriate form to appear. Use the Show method of the form you want to open and the End command to close your program.

```
Private Sub cmdMatches_Click()
   frmMatches.Show
End Sub

Private Sub cmdPlayers_Click()
   frmPlayers.Show
End Sub

Private Sub cmdReports_Click()
   frmReports.Show
End Sub

Private Sub cmdClose_Click()
   End
End Sub
```

4. Try out the form by running the program. (You may feel that you would like a command button on each of the three forms to be able to return to the Main form. Put these on and code their Click events if you would like them.) When you are satisfied the navigation works save the forms as **Products**, **Matches** and **Reports** and save the project as **TJsTennis**.

The Players form

Figure 20.2 shows the finished form in use. It is based on the sketch in Figure 18.4.

1. Place a label and set its caption to **Enter Players**. The font in Figure 20.2 is **14 pt bold Comic Sans MS**.

2. Place the frame and remove its caption. Place the three labels and text boxes on the frame. Set the labels' captions and name the text boxes **txtLeague**, **txtName** and **txtCoach** as appropriate.

3. Place the command button on the frame, set its caption and name it **cmdSave**.

4. Place the list box and name it **lstPlayers**. Set its Sorted property to **True** so that the players will be displayed in league order.

5. Place the three check boxes below the list box. Change their captions to those shown in Figure 20.2 and name them **chkLeague**, **chkName** and **chkCoach**.

6. Place the two command buttons at the bottom right of the form. Set their captions to **Change** and **Delete** and name them **cmdChange** and **cmdDelete**.

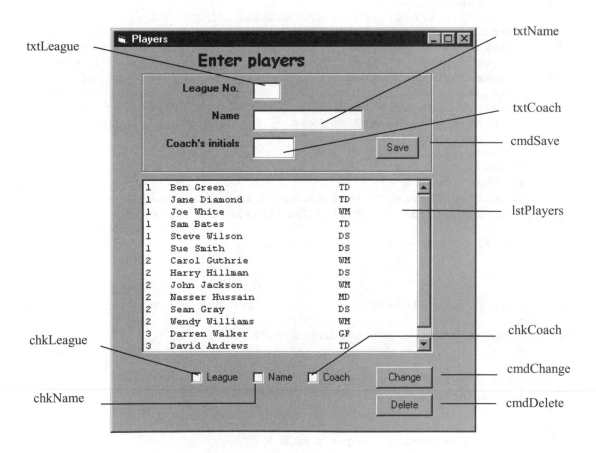

Figure 20.2: The Players form

Our modular structure chart for the Players form (Figure 19.3) showed that it needs four event procedures and one sub procedure. Let us code each of these in turn.

The Form's Load event

Figure 19.1 lists two things that must be done – assign the Players file and display all its details in the list box. A sub procedure, *DisplayPlayers*, will display the data so all we need to do here is call it.

1.   Write the code for the Form's Load event.

```
Private Sub Form_Load()
  PlayersFile = App.Path & "\Players.dat" 'assign Players file
  Call DisplayPlayers        'display details of players in list box
End Sub
```

Click event of cmdSave

Clicking the *Save* button writes the player's details to the Players file. We ought to check that each text box has some data in it before attempting to store any data. We will not validate the league number because we do not know how many leagues a particular league round will have.

2.   Write the code for the event procedure.

```
Private Sub cmdSave_Click()
'Writes details of one player to the Players file
  Dim NumberOfRecords As Integer 'number of records in Players file
  Dim OnePlayer As PlayerType  'a record holding details of one player
  If txtLeague.Text <> "" Then          'league number entered?
    If txtName.Text <> "" Then          'player name entered?
      If txtCoach.Text <> "" Then          'coach's initials entered?
        OnePlayer.League = txtLeague.Text 'if all 3 entered store
        OnePlayer.Name = txtName.Text     'details in record
        OnePlayer.Coach = txtCoach.Text
        txtName.Text = ""
        txtName.SetFocus
        txtCoach.Text = ""
        Open PlayersFile For Random As #1 Len = Len(OnePlayer)
        NumberOfRecords = LOF(1) / Len(OnePlayer) 'how many records
                                            'in the file?
        Put #1, NumberOfRecords + 1, OnePlayer    'write new record
                                          'after the last one in the file
        Close #1

        Call DisplayPlayers               'add the new player to list box
      Else
        MsgBox ("Enter coach's initials")
      End If
    Else
      MsgBox ("Enter player's name")
      txtName.SetFocus
    End If
  Else
    MsgBox ("Please enter league number")
    txtLeague.SetFocus
  End If
End Sub
```

Note here how to position the file pointer just past the last record in the file in order to append the new record. This was covered in step 4 of Program 16.2, but as we will be doing this often in TJ's Tennis it is worth going over again. The line

```
NumberOfRecords = LOF(1) / Len(OnePlayer)
```

calculates the number of records in the file by dividing the total number of bytes in the file (returned from the function LOF) by the number of bytes in one record (returned from Len(OnePlayer)). The next line

```
Put #1, NumberOfRecords + 1, OnePlayer
```

positions the file pointer just past the last record and writes the new record to this position.

Sub procedure DisplayPlayers

This procedure displays all the data from the Players file in the list box.

3. The code uses *With...End With*. Recall from Chapter 15 that this saves you having to prefix each field (.League, .Name and .Coach) with the record variable (OnePlayer).

```
Private Sub DisplayPlayers()
'Displays details of all players in list box
  Dim Index As Integer
  Dim NumberOfRecords As Integer     'number of records in Players file
  Dim OnePlayer As PlayerType
  Dim OnePlayerDetails As String     'stores league number, player's name
                          'and coach's initials as a concatenated string
  lstPlayers.Clear
  Open PlayersFile For Random As #1 Len = Len(OnePlayer)
  NumberOfRecords = LOF(1) / Len(OnePlayer)   'how many records in file?
  For Index = 1 To NumberOfRecords            'loop through each record
    Get #1, , OnePlayer                       'read one record
    With OnePlayer                            'process this record
      OnePlayerDetails = .League & "   " & .Name & "          " & .Coach
    End With
    lstPlayers.AddItem OnePlayerDetails        'display details in list box
  Next Index
  Close #1
End Sub
```

The use of the two commas in the line of code

```
Get #1, , OnePlayer
```

was covered in step 6 of Program 16.2. The missing parameter between these commas is the record number in the file of the record that is to be read. Since the loop processes the records in their order in the file, the file pointer will be positioned at the next record after a read operation. You could put *Index* between the commas but this would have the same effect as leaving the parameter out.

Click event of cmdChange

If the user has made a mistake over the league number, name or coach of any player they can put this right by selecting one or more of the three check boxes and then clicking the *Change* button. The

ListIndex property of the list box can be used to retrieve the record in the Players file that needs to be changed. For example, suppose Joe White's name in Figure 20.2 should be Joe Whitely. When you select this name the ListIndex property will contain the value 2 (since this is the 3rd item in the list). Add 1 to this to position the file pointer at the start of the 3rd record in the file. (There is a hidden flaw in this technique which careful testing should uncover. This is considered shortly.)

4. In the code that follows, when the record is read from the file the file pointer moves to the start of the next record. So when you write the changed record back to the file you must use the old record position value. The variable *RecordNumber* is used above for both these actions. Note that input boxes are used to get the changed data from the user.

```
Private Sub cmdChange_Click()
'Allows user to change details of a stored player
  Dim OnePlayer As PlayerType
  Dim RecordNumber As Integer
  If lstPlayers.Text <> "" Then     'user HAS selected player in list box
    RecordNumber = lstPlayers.ListIndex + 1
    Open PlayersFile For Random As #1 Len = Len(OnePlayer)
    Get #1, RecordNumber, OnePlayer
          'check which details of selected player need to be changed
    If chkLeague.Value = 1 Then
      OnePlayer.League = InputBox("Enter league number")
    End If
    If chkName.Value = 1 Then
      OnePlayer.Name = InputBox("Enter player's name")
    End If
    If chkCoach.Value = 1 Then
      OnePlayer.Coach = InputBox("Enter coach's initials")
    End If
    Put #1, RecordNumber, OnePlayer     'write changed record back to file
    Close #1
    Call DisplayPlayers
  Else                                       'nothing selected from list box
    MsgBox ("You must select a player first")
  End If
End Sub
```

Task 5.2 of the assignment asks you to explain how you resolved any problems in your program uncovered by testing. Careful testing of this click event should uncover a crucial problem. Step 5 tests it with data that will not uncover the problem and step 6 uses data that will reveal it.

5. If you have any details stored in the Players file delete the file from Windows and enter details of the first three players exactly as in Figure 20.2. Select Jane Diamond from the list box, click the *Coach* check box and then click the *Change* button. Change her coach to WM. The change should correctly appear in the list box.

6. Add details of a 4th player: **1   David Shore   TD**

7. Now change David Shore coach to DS. Jane Diamond's coach has been changed instead!

The problem is because we set the Sorted property of the list box to True (step 4 of designing the Players form). In step 5 above the three players were added in alphabetical order (of first name). Since they were all in league 1 they appeared in the list box in the order they were added to the file. Therefore there is a match between the ListIndex property and the file record number. In step 6 above the new record is displayed as the 2nd item in the list box (ListIndex is 1) but it is in the 4th record position in the file.

The solution is simply to change the list box's Sorted property to False. Provided TJ's inputs the players in league order then they will be displayed in order. But you would need to check that they are happy with a display that will not be in league order if they enter the players out of league order. As there are unlikely to be more than 40 or 50 players the club may not be concerned with the order, especially as they are unlikely to make more than the odd mistake when inputting the data.

However, if TJ's insists on a league order display, you would have to rethink your implementation. A possible solution is to make your code give each player an ID, from say 1 onwards, as the players are added to the file. You will use this technique in the next chapter to allow the user to change details of matches.

8.   Change the Sorted property of the list box to **False**. Now try changing David Shore's coach to WM.

Click event of cmdDelete

Clicking the *Delete* button deletes the player selected in the list box from the Players file. The principle of physically deleting a record from a file was explained in Figure 18.11.

9.   To physically delete a record from a file you must copy all the records except the one to delete to a new file, delete the old file, and then rename the new file the same as the old one. Use the **Kill** statement to delete a file, and note that this deletes it completely; it does not go to the Recycle Bin.

```
Private Sub cmdDelete_Click()
'Deletes details of a player from Players file
  Dim Index As Integer
  Dim NumberOfRecords As Integer
  Dim RecordNumberToDelete As Integer
  Dim NewFilename As String          '(temporary) new file name
  Dim OnePlayer As PlayerType
  If lstPlayers.Text <> "" Then      'user HAS selected player in list box
    RecordNumberToDelete = lstPlayers.ListIndex + 1
    NewFilename = App.Path & "\PlayersNew.dat"
    Open PlayersFile For Random As #1 Len = Len(OnePlayer)
    Open NewFilename For Random As #2 Len = Len(OnePlayer)
    NumberOfRecords = LOF(1) / Len(OnePlayer)
    For Index = 1 To NumberOfRecords        'loop through all records in
                                            'Players file
      Get #1, , OnePlayer                   'read one record from file
      If Index <> RecordNumberToDelete Then 'if current record is not
                                            'the one to delete then
        Put #2, , OnePlayer                 'write it to the new file
      End If
    Next Index
    Close #1
    Close #2
    Kill PlayersFile                        'delete Players file
    Name NewFilename As PlayersFile         'and give its name to the
              'temporary file - this is now the new Players file minus
              'the unwanted record
    Call DisplayPlayers        'remove deleted player from list box
  Else                         'user has not selected a player from list box
    MsgBox ("You must select a player first")
  End If
End Sub
```

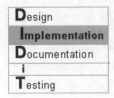

Chapter 21 – Implementation: Matches

Standard module

The first thing we did in the last chapter was to make some declarations on a standard module. We can now add to these declarations.

1. In the code window of the standard module (Module1) declare a data type to hold details of one match. On page 183 we decided that the field, *Scores*, to hold the number of games won by each player in each set would be an array of six strings. Scores(1) will hold the number of games won by the match winner in set 1, Scores(2) the number won by the match loser in set 1, Scores(3) the number won by the match winner in set 2 and so on.

```
Public Type MatchType          'data type for a record to store one match
  MatchID As Integer           '2 bytes
  League As String * 1         '1 byte. Could be String or Integer
  Winner As String * 19        '19 bytes
  Loser As String * 19         '19 bytes
  Scores(1 To 6) As String * 1 '6 bytes
End Type                       '47 bytes in total
```

2. Declare the single variable that will be used by the Matches and Reports forms:

```
Public MatchesFile As String    'Matches file
```

The Matches form

We designed the Matches form in Figure 18.5. Figure 21.1 shows the form in use. The list box displays match details in league order, unlike the solution we eventually used for displaying player details in the previous chapter. The last column of values in the list box shows the match IDs. An ID of 1 indicates the first match stored in the file and so on. The IDs are needed to search for the selected match when the user wishes to change any match details or to delete the match. With 8 leagues of 6 players there could be 120 matches, so it is unlikely TJ's would want to scroll through looking for a given match if they were not in league order. Match results will not be input in any league order if they are added soon after the matches have been played, so sorting is a sensible thing to do. When you give the finished product to TJ's you would reduce the width of the list box to hide the IDs since they are of no interest to the user.

1. On frmMatches place the frame and remove its caption.

2. Place the combo box and name it **cboLeagues**. Add a label. Recall that TJ's said 8 leagues would be more than enough, so enter the numbers **1** to **8** in its List property. Set its Style property to **2 - Dropdown List** so that only these numbers can be selected (see step 13 on page 107).

3. Place the two list boxes. Name the left one **lstWinner** and the right one **lstLoser** and add their labels. As each one will only display the six or so players in a given league there is no need to change their Sorted property.

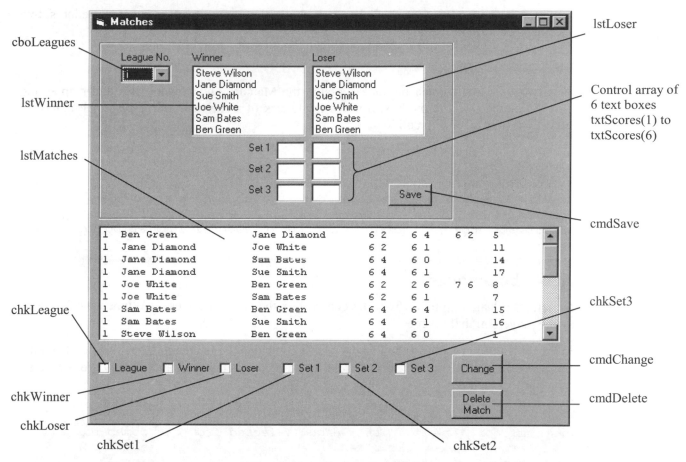

Figure 21.1: The Matches form

4. The six text boxes to input the results of each set will be a control array of text boxes. You covered control arrays in Chapter 7, and if you did the Gina's Groceries project in Unit 7, you used a control array of labels as a kind of concept keyboard for the shop's products. Place the first text box in the upper left position so that it holds the match winner's score for set 1. Name it **txtScores** and set its Index property to **1**. You can see in its Properties window that Visual Basic knows this control as txtScores(1).

5. Copy this text box and then paste it. Visual Basic asks you if you wish to create a control array. Click **Yes**. Position the text box to the right of the first one. Note that its Index property has the value 2 and the control is known as txtScores(2).

6. Paste and place four more text boxes. Check that their Index property is from 3 to 6. Add the labels for the 6 text boxes – **Set 1**, **Set 2**, **Set 3**.

7. Place a command button on the frame, change its caption to **Save** and name it **cmdSave**.

8. Place the list box. Name it **lstMatches** and set its Sorted property to **True**.

9. There is no advantage having the six check boxes as a control array. So place six independent check boxes below the list box. Set their captions and name them **chkLeague**, **chkWinner**, **chkLoser**, **chkSet1**, **chkSet2**, **chkSet3** as in Figure 21.1.

10. Finally add the two command buttons to the bottom right of the form. Their captions should be **Change** and **Delete Match** and their names **cmdChange** and **cmdDelete**.

The modular structure chart for this form in Figure 19.5 shows that it requires five event procedures, two sub procedures and a function procedure.

The Form's Load event

Figure 19.1 lists two things that must be done – assign the Matches and Players files and display the details of any saved matches in the list box. Since it is the task of a sub procedure, *DisplayMatches*, to display the details, we simply have to call it.

1. Write the code for the Form's Load event.

```
Private Sub Form_Load()
  MatchesFile = App.Path & "\Matches.dat"      'assign Matches file
  PlayersFile = App.Path & "\Players.dat"      'assign Players file
  Call DisplayMatches        'display details of matches in list box
End Sub
```

Click event of cboLeagues

When the user selects a league number from the combo box the two list boxes, lstWinner and lstLoser, should display the players in that league.

2. The code processes each record in the Players file. It compares the league number selected from the combo box with the content of the *League* field in the record being read and, if they are the same, displays the player's name.

```
Private Sub cboLeagues_Click()
'Displays names of players in the league selected from the combo box in
'in the winner and loser list boxes
  Dim LeagueNumber As Integer
  Dim OnePlayer As PlayerType
  LeagueNumber = cboLeagues.Text
  lstWinner.Clear
  lstLoser.Clear
  Open PlayersFile For Random As #1 Len = Len(OnePlayer)
  Do While Not EOF(1)
    Get #1, , OnePlayer
    If LeagueNumber = OnePlayer.League Then   'if league selected from
            'combo box is same as league in current record from file then
      lstWinner.AddItem OnePlayer.Name    'add player's name to list boxes
      lstLoser.AddItem OnePlayer.Name
    End If
  Loop
  Close #1
End Sub
```

3. Try out the combo box. You will need to have entered a few players, preferably in more than one league, to see it working fully.

Click event of cmdSave

Clicking the *Save* button stores details of a match in the Matches file. The user should first have selected two different players.

4. The code contains three validation checks, handled by three nested Ifs. First it checks that two players have been selected, then that they are not the same players, and finally that no match details for these two players are already on file. However there is no checking that any set scores have been entered. If a match is won 2-0 in sets then a minimum of four scores are needed (e.g. 6-4, 6-2), so there *could* be a check that the first four text boxes of the control array have numeric digits in them. This is a point you could discuss with TJ's.

```
Private Sub cmdSave_Click()
'Saves details of a match in the Matches file
  Dim Index As Integer
  Dim LeagueNumber As String
  Dim NumberOfRecords As Integer
  Dim Winner As String          'player selected from winner list box
  Dim Loser As String           'player selected from loser list box
  Dim OneMatch As MatchType     'a record to store details of one match
  LeagueNumber = cboLeagues.Text
  If (lstWinner.Text <> "") And (lstLoser.Text <> "") Then 'user must
                               'select players from both list boxes
    Winner = lstWinner.Text
    Loser = lstLoser.Text
    If Winner <> Loser Then    'two selected players must be different
      If ValidMatch(Winner, Loser) Then 'calls function to find out if
      'details of this match have already been stored. If not then store them
        NumberOfRecords = FileLen(MatchesFile) / Len(OneMatch)
        OneMatch.MatchID = NumberOfRecords + 1
        OneMatch.League = LeagueNumber
        OneMatch.Winner = Winner
        OneMatch.Loser = Loser
        For Index = 1 To 6           'store the scores for each set
          OneMatch.Scores(Index) = txtScores(Index).Text
        Next Index
        Open MatchesFile For Random As #1 Len = Len(OneMatch)
        Put #1, NumberOfRecords + 1, OneMatch
        Close #1
        Call DisplayMatches        'display details of match in list box
        For Index = 1 To 6         'set the scores to blank ready for
          txtScores(Index).Text = ""           'next match scores
        Next Index
      Else                         'function ValidMatch returns False - details
                                   'of this match have already been stored
        MsgBox ("You have already entered details of this match")
      End If
    Else                     'user has selected the same two players
      MsgBox ("Winner and loser must not be the same person")
    End If
    Else                     'user has not selected two players
      MsgBox ("You must select a winner and a loser")
  End
End Sub
```

There are four points to note in the code above:

- The code to find the number of records in a file is a little different to the code we have used before. Compare the two:

```
NumberOfRecords = FileLen(MatchesFile) / Len(OneMatch) 'used above
NumberOfRecords = LOF(1) / Len(OneMatch)              'used in Chapter 20
```

You can only use the LOF function when the is file is open. The FileLen function can be used on open or unopened files. In the code for cmdSave_Click the Matches file is not yet open when we need to calculate how many records it contains.

- The function *ValidMatch* is called to check if match details of the two selected players have already been stored. The two players are passed as parameters to the function, which returns True if the match has not been stored and False if it has.

- The control array of text boxes that has the set scores is processed by a For…Next loop. If we had not created a control array but had 'individual' text boxes instead, we would need to write code to process each one.

- Since the field *Scores* is an array it can be processed using a For…Next loop.

You cannot check that the event procedure works because you have not yet written the two general procedures that it calls.

Sub procedure DisplayMatches

This does a similar job to sub procedure *DisplayPlayers* on the Players form – it displays all the data from the Matches file in a list box.

5. Like *DisplayPlayers* the code builds up a concatenated string of all the details for one match. Note that although the match ID is the first field declared in the *MatchType* data type on the standard module, it is concatenated last. We need it to be at the right of the list box so we can hide it from the user. The match ID is of no interest to TJ's but, as discussed earlier, we need it to process any changes or deletions the user may wish to make. If we had it as the first item in the list box and hid it from the user in this position, we would not be able to sort the matches in the list box on league number; they would be sorted on match ID which is what we do not want.

```
Private Sub DisplayMatches()
'Displays details of all stored matches in the list box
  Dim Index As Integer
  Dim NumberOfRecords
  Dim OneMatch As MatchType
  Dim OneMatchDetails As String   'stores league number, names of both
           'players, match scores and match ID as a concatenated string
  lstMatches.Clear
  Open MatchesFile For Random As #1 Len = Len(OneMatch)
  NumberOfRecords = LOF(1) / Len(OneMatch)
  For Index = 1 To NumberOfRecords
    Get #1, , OneMatch
    With OneMatch   'build up the concatenated string of match details
      OneMatchDetails = .League & "   " & .Winner & "   " & .Loser & _
          .Scores(1) & " " & .Scores(2) & "    " & .Scores(3) & " " & _
          .Scores(4) & "    " & .Scores(5) & " " & .Scores(6) & "    " & _
          .MatchID
    End With
    lstMatches.AddItem OneMatchDetails   'display details in list box
  Next Index
  Close #1
End Sub
```

Function ValidMatch

This function's task is to check whether or not details of the match the user is trying to save have already been stored. If the same match is stored more than once the league tables will clearly be wrong.

6. The return value from the function is initially set to True, and this is switched to False if the If condition is true. This condition checks the two players' names in the current record against those selected from the list boxes. The latter are sent to the function as parameters.

```
Private Function ValidMatch(Winner As String, Loser As String) As Boolean
'Returns True if match details have not already been stored in Matches
'file and False if they have
  Dim OneMatch As MatchType
  ValidMatch = True          'assume match details are not already stored
  Open MatchesFile For Random As #1 Len = Len(OneMatch)
  Do
    Get #1, , OneMatch
    With OneMatch
      If ((.Winner = Winner) And (.Loser = Loser)) _
                 Or ((.Winner = Loser) And (.Loser = Winner)) Then
        ValidMatch = False
      End If
    End With
  Loop Until EOF(1)
  Close #1
End Function
```

7. You are now ready to try out the cmdSave click event procedure. Use data to check each of the three If statements – i.e. select only one player, select the same two players, select two different players and attempt to store their match details twice.

Click event of cmdChange

If the user has made a mistake over the league number, name of the winner or loser, or of any of the match scores, they can put this right by selecting one or more of the six check boxes and then clicking the *Change* button. The match ID of the selected game, which is listed in but not physically displayed in the list box (we want to hide it from the user, remember), is used to find the appropriate record in the Matches file. The amended data is collected through input boxes. The code is quite long so let us split it into two parts.

8. The first part goes through the records in the Matches file and compares the match ID of the current record in the file with the ID of the match selected from the list box. Note carefully how the match ID is extracted from the concatenated string that makes up the selected item in the list box. The Right function (covered early in Chapter 6) is used to extract the last three characters of the string. As there could be as many as 150 matches displayed in the list box three characters are needed. Visual Basic can extract a string and store it in the Integer variable, *SearchMatchID*, provided the string is made up of numeric digits only. Note that when reading a record from the file inside the loop we need to use *RecordNumber* as the parameter to indicate which record to read, rather than have the 'empty' pair of commas we have used before. The code in step 9 needs to use the value of *RecordNumber* to write the changed record back to its correct position in the file.

```
   Private Sub cmdChange_Click()
   'Allows user to change any match details (stored in Matches file)
     Dim RecordNumber As Integer
     Dim OneMatch As MatchType
     Dim Found As Boolean          'True when required match located in file
     Dim SearchMatchID As Integer       'ID of match selected from list box
     If lstMatches.Text <> "" Then      'has user selected a match?
       Found = False
       RecordNumber = 0
       SearchMatchID = Right(lstMatches.Text, 3)    'extract match ID from
                                                     'selected item in list box
       Open MatchesFile For Random As #1 Len = Len(OneMatch)
       Do
         RecordNumber = RecordNumber + 1
         Get #1, RecordNumber, OneMatch
         If SearchMatchID = OneMatch.MatchID Then   'required match found?
           Found = True
         End If
       Loop Until Found               'quit loop when required match found
       'code in step 9 below goes here ................
     Else                             'item not selected from list box
       MsgBox ("You must select a match first")
     End If
   End Sub
```

9. The second part processes each of the six check boxes. It stores the amended data in the current record, writes this back to the file in the correct position and then displays the amended data in the list box by calling *DisplayMatches*. Type the following between *Loop Until Found* and *Else* in the code in step 8. Figure 21.2 shows the first of the two input boxes when you wish to change the score of set 1. Ben Green is the match winner.

```
       If chkLeague.Value = 1 Then            'change league number?
         OneMatch.League = InputBox("Enter new league number")
       End If
       If chkWinner.Value = 1 Then            'change winner?
         OneMatch.Winner = InputBox("Enter new winner")
       End If
       If chkLoser.Value = 1 Then             'change loser?
         OneMatch.Loser = InputBox("Enter new loser")
       End If
       If chkSet1.Value = 1 Then              'change result of first set?
         OneMatch.Scores(1) = InputBox(OneMatch.Winner & _
                                       ": number of games won in set 1")
         OneMatch.Scores(2) = InputBox(OneMatch.Loser & _
                                       ": number of games won in set 1")
       End If
       If chkSet2.Value = 1 Then              'change result of second set?
         OneMatch.Scores(3) = InputBox(OneMatch.Winner & _
                                       ": number of games won in set 2")
         OneMatch.Scores(4) = InputBox(OneMatch.Loser & _
                                       ": number of games won in set 2")
       End If
       If chkSet3.Value = 1 Then              'change result of third set?
         OneMatch.Scores(5) = InputBox(OneMatch.Winner & _
                                       ": number of games won in set 3")
         OneMatch.Scores(6) = InputBox(OneMatch.Loser & _
```

```
                                        ": number of games won in set 3")
     End If
     Put #1, RecordNumber, OneMatch
     Close #1
     Call DisplayMatches              'now show changes in the list box
```

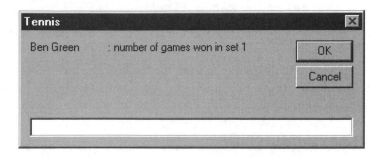

Figure 21.2

10. Try out the event procedure. Change details of three or four matches, making sure you try out all the check boxes.

Click event of cmdDelete

Clicking the *Delete* button deletes the match selected in the list box from the Matches file.

11. Most of the code is similar to that in the click event of cmdDelete on the Players form. It copies all the records, except the one that is to be deleted, from the Matches file to a new file, then deletes the old file and renames the new one after the old file. There is one difference between the code of the two delete click events. This procedure uses the match ID to find the record to delete from the file; the other one used the position of the selected player in the list box through the control's ListIndex property. The reason for the difference is that the items in the list box on this form are sorted, as explained on page 190.

```
Private Sub cmdDelete_Click()
'Allows user to delete match selected in list box from Matches file
  Dim Index As Integer
  Dim NumberOfRecords As Integer
  Dim OneMatch As MatchType
  Dim NewFilename As String        'new file name
  Dim SearchMatchID As String      'ID of match selected from list box
  If lstMatches.Text <> "" Then    'has user selected a match?
    SearchMatchID = Right(lstMatches.Text, 3)
    NewFilename = App.Path & "\MatchesNew.dat"
    Open NewFilename For Random As #2 Len = Len(OneMatch)
    Open MatchesFile For Random As #1 Len = Len(OneMatch)
    NumberOfRecords = LOF(1) / Len(OneMatch)
    For Index = 1 To NumberOfRecords
      Get #1, , OneMatch
      If Index <> SearchMatchID Then  'if current record is not the
                                      'one to delete then
        Put #2, , OneMatch            'copy it to new file
      End If
    Next Index
```

```
      Close #1
      Close #2
      Kill MatchesFile                    'delete Matches file
      Name NewFilename As MatchesFile     'and give its name to new file
      Call RenumberMatchIDs               'renumber the match IDs
      Call DisplayMatches                 'remove deleted match from list box
    Else                      'user has not selected a match from list box
      MsgBox ("You must select a match first")
    End If
  End Sub
```

Note that before the deleted match is removed from the list box sub procedure *RenumberMatchIDs* is called. If you delete match ID 26, for example, then those matches from 27 onwards must be given new IDs if the match ID is to be used as a direct pointer to the match's record in the file.

Sub procedure RenumberMatchIDs

12. The code loops through all the records and renumbers the match ID of each one. Strictly only those matches with IDs higher than the deleted match ID need to be renumbered. This is something you could discuss in doing task 6.1 of the assignment (Chapter 17). This asks you to identify good and bad features and to suggest possible improvements. Although renumbering all the matches is hardly a *bad* feature it is an inefficient one. To improve it you might pass the match ID of the deleted record as a parameter to *RenumberMatchIDs* and use this in the starting point of the loop.

```
Private Sub RenumberMatchIDs()
'Renumbers the IDs of the matches in the Matches file
  Dim Index As Integer
  Dim RecordNumber As Integer
  Dim NumberOfRecords As Integer
  Dim OneMatch As MatchType
  RecordNumber = 1
  Open MatchesFile For Random As #1 Len = Len(OneMatch)
  NumberOfRecords = LOF(1) / Len(OneMatch)
  For Index = 1 To NumberOfRecords
    Get #1, RecordNumber, OneMatch
    OneMatch.MatchID = RecordNumber     'renumber the ID and
    Put #1, RecordNumber, OneMatch      'write the new record back to file
    RecordNumber = RecordNumber + 1
  Next Index
  Close #1
End Sub
```

When reading from the file the variable *RecordNumber* is needed here, rather than using an 'empty' pair of commas. Remember that we have to write the changed record back to its old position, and this position is stored in *RecordNumber*. After writing the changed record we must add 1 to *RecordNumber* to position the file pointer just past this changed record ready for the next read.

Chapter 22 – Implementation: Reports

Standard module

Later in this chapter the code to calculate the number of league points for each player will use an array of records as a temporary store of names and points (see the end of Chapter 18). We must define the data type for these records in a standard module.

1. In the standard module (Module1) declare the following:

```
Public Type PlayersAndPointsType  'data type for record to store players'
                                  'names and total points
   Name As String * 19            '19 bytes
   Points As Integer              '2 bytes
End Type                          '21 bytes in total
```

The Reports form.

We designed the Reports form in Figure 18.6. Figure 22.1 shows the finished version.

Figure 22.1: The Reports form

1. On frmReports place the frame and remove its caption.

2. Place the three option buttons. They should not be stored as a control array but as 'separate' controls. Change their captions to those in Figure 22.1 and name them **opt1**, **opt2**, and **opt3**. As you will see they are only used in the code once and there is really no reason to use more meaningful names.

3. Place the combo box. Name it **cboLeagues** and, as with the combo box on the Matches form, enter the numbers **1** to **8** in its List property. Change its Style property to **2 - Dropdown List**.

4. Place the command button. Set its caption to **Print** and name it **cmdPrint**.

The Form's Load event

Figure 19.1 lists what must be done – assign the Matches and Players files.

1. Write the code for the Form's Load event.

```
Private Sub Form_Load()
  MatchesFile = App.Path & "\Matches.dat"      'assign Matches file
  PlayersFile = App.Path & "\Players.dat"      'assign Players file
End Sub
```

Click event of cmdPrint

Clicking the Print button must first find which of the three option buttons has been selected. Figure 19.7 shows that this Click event calls three sub procedures; each of these handles one of the options. So our code at this point simply needs to call each one.

2. Write the code for cmdPrint's click event:

```
Private Sub cmdPrint_Click()
'Checks which option is selected and processes it (by calling the
'the relevant procedure
  Dim Choice As Integer            'option selected (1, 2 or 3)
  If opt1.Value = True Then
    Choice = 1
  ElseIf opt2.Value = True Then
    Choice = 2
  Else
    Choice = 3
  End If
  Select Case Choice
    Case 1                               'option 1 selected
      Call PrintLeagues
    Case 2                               'option 2 selected
      If cboLeagues.Text = "" Then
        MsgBox ("You must select a league first")
      Else
        Call PrintSelectedLeagueResults
      End If
    Case 3                               'option 3 selected
      Call PrintAllLeagueResults
  End Select
End Sub
```

3. If you wish to try this out you will have to comment out the three procedure calls and put appropriate message boxes inside each Case. Alternatively you could write declarations for the three procedures and add the message boxes as single lines of code in each.

Printing the leagues

From Figure 19.7 you can see that selecting the first option, to print out all the leagues, calls sub *PrintLeagues* which in turn calls function *NumberOfLeagues*.

Sub procedure PrintLeagues

We designed the printed output to show the players in each league in Figure 18.7. It simply lists the players and their coaches in each league.

1. An outer loop processes one league and the inner loop goes through all the records in the Players file. The method used here to get the file pointer back to the start of the file to process each league is to open and close the file at the start and finish of each league (see page 185). The outer loop needs to know how many leagues to process. Function *NumberOfLeagues* returns this information.

```
Public Sub PrintLeagues()
'Prints list of leagues with players' names and coaches' initials
  Dim Index As Integer
  Dim Record As Integer
  Dim NumberOfRecords As Integer
  Dim Leagues As Integer          'number of leagues
  Dim OnePlayer As PlayerType
  Leagues = NumberOfLeagues       'call to function NumberOfLeagues
  Printer.Print "TJ's Tennis Leagues "      'print report header
  Printer.Print
  Printer.Print "Player"; Tab(25); "Coach"
  Printer.Print
  For Index = 1 To Leagues                  'print each league
    Printer.Print "League " & Index
    Printer.Print
    Open PlayersFile For Random As #1 Len = Len(OnePlayer)
    NumberOfRecords = LOF(1) / Len(OnePlayer)
    For Record = 1 To NumberOfRecords        'go through whole file
      Get #1, , OnePlayer
      If Index = OnePlayer.League Then      'is current player in the
                                     'league which is being printed?
        Printer.Print OnePlayer.Name; Tab(25); OnePlayer.Coach  'if yes
                                     'then print details
      End If
    Next Record
    Close #1
    Printer.Print
  Next Index
  Printer.EndDoc
End Sub
```

Function NumberOfLeagues

This returns the number of leagues in the current league round. It processes each record in the Players file and finds the highest value stored in the *League* field.

2. The code uses a standard method of finding the highest number in a series of numbers. It initialises the highest value to 0 and then looks at all the numbers in turn. If a number exceeds the current highest value then it is assigned to the highest value.

```
Public Function NumberOfLeagues() As Integer
'Returns the number of leagues stored in the system
  Dim Leagues As Integer              'number of leagues
  Dim Index As Integer
  Dim NumberOfRecords As Integer
  Dim OnePlayer As PlayerType
```

```
      Open PlayersFile For Random As #1 Len = Len(OnePlayer)
      NumberOfRecords = LOF(1) / Len(OnePlayer)
      Leagues = 0
      For Index = 1 To NumberOfRecords          'process all records in file
        Get #1, , OnePlayer
        If OnePlayer.League > Leagues Then       'does current league number
                                'exceed highest league number so far found?
          Leagues = OnePlayer.League    'if yes then this becomes highest no.
        End If
      Next Index
      Close #1
      NumberOfLeagues = Leagues              'return value from function
    End Function
```

3. Now you can try printing out the leagues. You will need players in at least two leagues to see it working properly.

Printing selected league results

From Figure 19.7 you can work out that selecting the second option, to print out the results of the league selected from the combo box, calls sub *PrintSelectedLeagueResults* which in turn calls sub *PrintPointsResults* and sub *PrintMatchResults*. Sub *PrintPointsResults* calls function *PlayersInLeague*.

Sub procedure PrintSelectedLeagueResults

Figure 22.2 is nearly the same as Figure 19.8 and shows what the report should look like. This sub procedure prints only the title and the league number; it calls the two sub procedures to print the details.

1. The code is as follows:

```
Public Sub PrintSelectedLeagueResults()
'Prints results of league selected from combo box. Calls two procedures -
'one to print the points and one to print the individual match results
  Dim League As String
  League = cboLeagues.Text
  Printer.Print "Results of League " & League
  Printer.Print
  PrintPointsResults (League)  'procedure call to print league positions
  Printer.Print
  Printer.Print
  PrintMatchResults (League)   'procedure call to print match results
  Printer.EndDoc
End Sub
```

Sub procedure PrintPointsResults

It was explained at the end of Chapter 18, at design level, how to calculate the total number of points scored by each player in a particular league. The code is fairly long and can be broken into three parts. These are:

- Copy the names of the players in the selected league into an array and initialise their points to 0
- Calculate the points for each player
- Print the league table

2. There are several local variables to declare. The variable *PlayersAndPoints* is of type PlayersAndPointsType which we declared in the standard module at the start of this chapter. It is an array that stores 10 sets of players and their points. The assumption here is that there will never be more than 10 players in a league.

```
Public Sub PrintPointsResults(League As String)
   Dim Winner As String
   Dim Loser As String
   Dim NumberOfRecords As Integer
   Dim NumberOfPlayers As Integer  'number of players in selected league
   Dim PlayersAndPoints(1 To 10) As PlayersAndPointsType  'the data type
                'PlayersAndPointsType is declared on the standard module
   Dim Index As Integer
   Dim Record As Integer           'index into array PlayersAndPoints
   Dim Points As Integer           'number of points a player has
   Dim Element As Integer          'index into array PlayersAndPoints
   Dim Position As Integer         'one player's position in league table
   Dim OnePlayer As PlayerType
   Dim OneMatch As MatchType
```

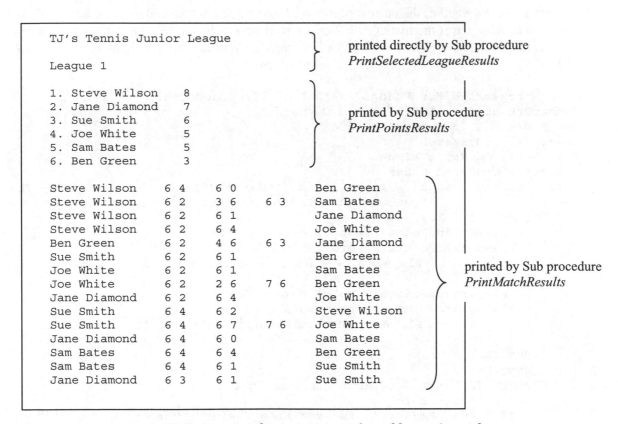

Figure 22.2: Printing the report on a selected league's results

Copy players into array and initialise their points to 0

3. Each record in the Players file is processed by copying the player's name to the array *PlayersAndPoints* if that player is in the league selected from the combo box. This league was sent as a parameter to *PrintPointsResults*. Enter the code below after the declarations in step 2.

```
Open PlayersFile For Random As #1 Len = Len(OnePlayer)
NumberOfRecords = LOF(1) / Len(OnePlayer)
Element = 1
For Index = 1 To NumberOfRecords
  Get #1, , OnePlayer
  If OnePlayer.League = League Then 'is current player in the selected
                                     'league? If yes then
    PlayersAndPoints(Element).Name = OnePlayer.Name    'store name
    PlayersAndPoints(Element).Points = 0            'and set points to 0
    Element = Element + 1
  End If
Next Index
Close #1
```

Calculate points for each player

A match winner scores 2 points. The loser scores 0 points if they lose 2-0 in sets but 1 point if the match goes to three sets.

4. The outer If checks whether the current player is in the selected league and uses the IsNumeric built-in function to work out if the match took 2 or 3 sets. If Scores(5), the winner's number of games for set 3, has numeric data in it then we have a 3-set match. Continue the code below after *Close #1* in step 3.

```
Open MatchesFile For Random As #2 Len = Len(OneMatch)
NumberOfRecords = LOF(2) / Len(OneMatch)
For Index = 1 To NumberOfRecords
  Get #2, , OneMatch
  Winner = OneMatch.Winner
  Loser = OneMatch.Loser
  If (OneMatch.League = League) And (IsNumeric(OneMatch.Scores(5))) Then
                  'there is data for set 3 - therefore match took 3 sets
    For Record = 1 To 10
      If PlayersAndPoints(Record).Name = Winner Then
        PlayersAndPoints(Record).Points = _
                  PlayersAndPoints(Record).Points + 2
      End If
      If PlayersAndPoints(Record).Name = Loser Then
        PlayersAndPoints(Record).Points = _
                  PlayersAndPoints(Record).Points + 1 '1 point for
                                            'losing a 3 set match
      End If
    Next Record
  Else                  'match was won in 2 sets
    For Record = 1 To 10
      If PlayersAndPoints(Record).Name = Winner Then
                  'winner gets 2 points, but no points for loser
        PlayersAndPoints(Record).Points = _
                  PlayersAndPoints(Record).Points + 2
      End If
    Next Record
  End If
Next Index
Close #2
```

Print the league table

5. TJ's naturally wants the league table printed in order of points scored, which makes the coding a little trickier than printing the players in the order they are stored in *PlayersAndPoints*. There are many sorting algorithms you could use (if you know how to code them) but the code below actually does not do any direct sorting. It finds out how many players are in the selected league by calling the function *PlayersInLeague*. If there are 6, for example, then the highest number of points any player in that league can score is 12. So the outer For loop processes each possible number of points from 12 downwards (12, 11, 10 etc.) and picks out the players in *PlayersAndPoints* with that number of points.

```
    NumberOfPlayers = PlayersInLeague(League)      'function call
    Position = 0
    For Points = NumberOfPlayers * 2 To 0 Step -1 'for example if there
         'are 6 players in league, process all possible points from 12 down
       For Index = 1 To NumberOfPlayers
         If PlayersAndPoints(Index).Points = Points Then
           Position = Position + 1
           Printer.Print Position & ". " & PlayersAndPoints(Index).Name _
                              & PlayersAndPoints(Index).Points

         End If
       Next Index
    Next Points
 End Sub
```

Function PlayersInLeague

6. This function returns the number of players in the current league by going through all the records in the Players file and incrementing the variable *Players* if the current player is in the selected league.

```
Public Function PlayersInLeague(League) As Integer
 'Returns number of players in league League
   Dim NumberOfRecords As Integer
   Dim Players As Integer                 'number of players in league
   Dim Index As Integer
   Dim OnePlayer As PlayerType
   Players = 0
   Open PlayersFile For Random As #1 Len = Len(OnePlayer)
   NumberOfRecords = LOF(1) / Len(OnePlayer)
   For Index = 1 To NumberOfRecords
     Get #1, , OnePlayer
     If OnePlayer.League = League Then
       Players = Players + 1
     End If
   Next Index
   Close #1
   PlayersInLeague = Players
 End Function
```

Sub procedure PrintMatchResults

7. The code prints all the match results in the selected league (see Figure 22.2).

```
Public Sub PrintMatchResults(League As String)
'Prints details of each match in league League
  Dim OneMatch As MatchType
  Open MatchesFile For Random As #1 Len = Len(OneMatch)
  Do While Not EOF(1)
  Get #1, , OneMatch
  If OneMatch.League = League Then
    With OneMatch
      Printer.Print .Winner; .Scores(1); " "; .Scores(2); "    " _
            ; .Scores(3); " "; .Scores(4); "    "; .Scores(5); " "; _
            .Scores(6); "    "; .Loser
    End With
  End If
  Loop
  Close #1
End Sub
```

8. You can now try out the second option button on the form. Select a league from the combo box and click *Print*. You should produce printed output that in outline looks like that in Figure 22.2.

Printing all league results

From Figure 19.7 you can see that selecting the third option, to print out the results of all the leagues, calls sub *PrintAllLeagueResults*, which in turn calls function NumberOfLeagues, sub *PrintPointsResults* and sub *PrintMatchResults*. As we have already written these there is not much left to do.

Sub procedure PrintAllLeagueResults

1. A variable, *Index*, is used to pass the current league number to the two printing procedures *PrintPointsResults* and *PrintMatchResults*. The effect of writing Printer.EndDoc inside the loop is that the results of each league will be printed on a new page.

```
Public Sub PrintAllLeagueResults()
'Prints results of all leagues. Calls two procedures - one to print the
'points and one to print the individual match results
  Dim Leagues As Integer
  Dim Index As Integer            'loop counter and parameter passed
                                  '(league no.) to printing procedures
  Leagues = NumberOfLeagues          'function call
  For Index = 1 To Leagues
    Printer.Print "League " & Index
    Printer.Print
    PrintPointsResults (Index)    'send parameter Index to procedure
    Printer.Print
    Printer.Print
    PrintMatchResults (Index)     'send parameter Index to procedure
    Printer.EndDoc
  Next Index
End Sub
```

2. Try out the third option button on the form. You should get each league's details printed on a separate page.

3. Experiment by putting Printer.EndDoc outside the loop (between Next Index and End Sub). The details will be printed continuously down the page.

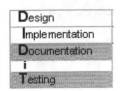

Chapter 23 – Documentation and Testing

Chapters 12 and 13 covered the stages of Documentation and Testing for the Gina's Groceries case study. We will not go over the same ground again, but just highlight some of the differences between what you have to do for Units 7 and 22.

Documentation

The main difference between Units 7 and 22 is that the *Assessment Evidence* for Unit 22 requires only technical documentation and not any user documentation. However before we look at the technical documentation we might consider one thing which would have to be included in a user guide. How does TJ's use the program for the second and later league rounds? After using it for the first league round there will be two full files – Players and Matches. The Matches file would need to be deleted (from Windows since the program itself does not cover this). TJ's could either delete the Players file and enter a completely new set of records or keep the old file and change the data in it from the Players form. For example, if a player was promoted from league 4 to 3 all TJ's would need to do is click the League check box and then OK to change it. Exercise 1 at the end of the case study asks you to implement all this.

The assignment for Unit 22 shows that you can build up your technical documentation from a grade E, through grade C to a grade A standard (see task 4).

Grade E requirement (task 4.1)

This task asks for a printout of your code, which should contain a reasonable amount of commenting. At a minimum the comments should cover the purposes of each procedure and explain some of the more difficult processing. The task also asks you to show your program's modular structure by listing all the event procedures and the tasks they carry out. This looks the same as task 2.3 but really extends it in several ways:

- You will probably improve your first attempt at designing the event procedures as you proceed with the program. The technical documentation must show the finished product.

- Task 2.3 concentrates on events and does not ask you to cover general procedures. For task 4.1 you could follow Figure 19.1 and indicate which tasks are assigned to general procedures.

- The controls in Figure 19.1 do not have Visual Basic names. The technical documentation should use these names.

Grade C requirement (task 4.2)

Task 4.2's first requirement is that you do task 4.1 well. What does this mean? This will very much depend on your assessor, but they will probably be looking for the following:

- How comprehensive the commenting in your code is.

- How easy it is to follow the documentation of your modular structure. Good documentation here does not just mean technical accuracy, but also how readable it is.

The other part of task 4.2 asks for screen prints of your forms in use, including any error messages, and examples of any printed output. Get printouts of each of the three reports from the Reports form to meet the printed output requirement. Ensure that there is enough data in the files to produce full reports. You would need completed matches for at least two leagues.

Grade A requirement (tasks 4.3 to 4.6)

These tasks are:

4.3 Explain clearly all the calculation and manipulation of data in your program

4.4 Draw modular structure charts of your program.

4.5 Document any general procedures you have used.

4.6 Draw diagrams to show how your forms and printout output are designed.

Calculation and manipulation of data

Calculation covers all the arithmetic that is going on in your program. In TJ's Tennis there's not that much. Examples include the calculation of the points scored by each player in the league, and incrementing the *Players* variable in the function *PlayersInLeague* to count up how many players are in a particular league.

Manipulation of data refers to almost any operations that you do on the data. There are many examples in TJ's Tennis.

- Concatenating the various pieces of data into a single string that is then displayed in the list box on the Matches form (to show the result of a particular match). This is done by sub *DisplayMatches*.

- Storing the names of players in a particular league in the array *PlayersAndPoints* in preparation for calculating their total points.

- Going through each record in the Matches file to check that the match details that are about to be stored have not already been stored. (The checking is done by function *ValidGame*).

In short this is really asking you to explain all the trickier parts of your coding.

Draw modular structure charts of your program

Please remember that this is one of the tasks of the assignment in Chapter 16 and is not specifically stated as part of the *Assessment Evidence* of Unit 22. If you have been taught modular structure charts your assessor may well ask you to use these in your assignment.

To answer task 4.4 you would draw the four modular structure charts covered in Chapter 18. These were drawn at design time, and their prime purpose was to help get everything in place before attempting to code. It would be unrealistic to expect all but a small number of students to do these accurately at design time. What you can do, though, is draw them again after you have finished coding. They should now form an accurate document of the structure of your program. If you follow the convention in this book and use general names for the controls in the modular charts at design time, then when you draw these charts as part of the technical documentation you should use their Visual Basic names. Note that you do not need to draw three-dimensional diagrams as in Chapter 18 – simple squares/rectangles will do.

Document the general procedures

Again this is a requirement of the assignment in Chapter 16 and not of the *Assessment Evidence*. Figures 18.4, 18.6 and 18.9 meet this task.

Design diagrams of forms and printed output

Note 3 at the end of the assignment in Chapter 17 suggested that if your original designs (to meet tasks 2.1 and 2.2) are unchanged by the time you have finished the coding then you have more or less done this task already. However, as with the modular structure charts, Visual Basic names were not used for the form controls at design time but for the technical documentation you must use them.

Testing

Testing is possibly the most difficult part of the whole software cycle to do well. For Unit 7 it was a grade A requirement only. For Unit 22 it is a requirement for a grade C (see task 5 in the assignment). What you have to do for a grade C here is the same as you had to do for the grade A in Unit 7. Look back at Chapter 13 to see how to go about testing.

You might also look back at steps 5 – 7 of cmdChange_Click in Chapter 20 to recall how a little testing revealed a fundamental error at design time.

Chapter 24 – Evaluation

What you need to learn

The *What you need to learn* section of Unit 22 states that the evaluation of a program should include the following:

How efficient it is in terms of using resources. For example, if you use a lot of global variables where local variables could have been used instead, more memory will be needed throughout the program. (There is a more important reason than memory for using local rather than global variables, which is mentioned later.) Another example is the use of arrays to store data. Have you declared an array which is much larger than necessary (inefficient use of resources) or one which is just the right size (efficient use)? If you use a dynamic array instead (see Chapter 7) this is also efficient.

How effective it is at meeting its purpose. This means the extent to which the various requirements of the user have been met.

Ease of use. The user is the best judge of this.

Maintainability. Computing textbooks often list three types of program maintenance. *Corrective* maintenance is about fixing run-time errors. *Adaptive* maintenance is changing the program to meet future user requirements. For example, a program may produce exam result grades using a particular set of percentage figures. If these percentage figures are changed the relevant code must be rewritten. *Perfective* maintenance is about improving the code, albeit to produce the same result as the original code. For example, if your program sorted a series of transactions by date it might be that your code takes only a second or two with a few hundred items of data. In the real world perhaps many thousands (or even hundreds of thousands) of items need to be sorted and it might be that your coded solution takes too long for the user. You could rewrite the code using a faster sorting method.

Availability of good documentation or help facilities. Since the Assessment Evidence does not ask you to produce any user documentation this point is hardly relevant to your own work.

Limitations which may affect its use. This relates back to the second item listed above. If you have not managed to code something fully this may have a knock-on effect elsewhere in the program. Not satisfying one user requirement may mean that another one is only partially met.

Particularly good features.

Not so good features. Good and not so good features can be seen from both the user's point of view and the technical point of view. There is a list of technical features you might discuss on the next page.

Any improvements that could be made.

Assessment Evidence and the assignment

Evaluating your program is a grade A task. Criterion A2 of the *Assessment Evidence* is:

A clear, accurate and detailed evaluation of your program which discusses suitability for purpose, identifies good and bad features and suggests possible improvements.

Task 6.1 in the assignment covers this criterion. This task asks for:

- A review of how far it meets the user's requirements
- A review of its good and bad features
- A discussion of possible improvements

It is unfortunate that criterion A2 uses the word 'bad' in referring to the program's features. The *What you need to learn* section uses 'not so good' instead. For your own purposes accept 'bad' to mean everything from 'awful' to 'not too bad but perhaps not so good'!

Meeting the user's requirements

Go through each of the exact requirements that you should have listed in answering task 1.1. State whether it has been achieved. If it has been only partially achieved, say what has been done and what has not.

Good and bad features

You can cover the good and bad features from two viewpoints – the user and the technical viewpoints. From the user's point of view obviously, if any of their requirements have not been met, this is a bad feature and you will already have noted this. Give them the finished program to try out. There may be a number of interface features that could be improved. A note from the user saying what they (honestly) think about the program would be useful to include in your portfolio.

The following are examples of things to consider from a technical viewpoint:

- How much use of general procedures have you made?
- Have you passed parameters where appropriate (or used global variables directly from the general procedures which is poorer programming)?
- Have you used local variables rather than global variables where appropriate? Using global ones that are shared between two or more procedures may lead to unexpected results.
- Is your looping efficient? For example, when looping through a file to find a particular record, does your loop finish when it is found or do you keep looping to the end of the file after you have found it? The latter is poorer programming.
- Are your If structures efficient? If you have several If...EndIfs in succession it might be more efficient to nest them.
- Are your more complex data structures used efficiently? An example of the use of arrays was briefly discussed earlier in this chapter.
- How careful have you been in using meaningful names for variables?
- How well have you commented in your code?
- How consistent have you been in the presentation of your code? For example, have you used the same indent throughout and have you applied it in a consistent way?

Think of this section as an opportunity for you to demonstrate your understanding of a number of programming concepts.

Possible improvements

You can adopt two approaches here. First, what changes could you make to the existing program from the user and technical viewpoints? Your review of the extent to which it meets the user requirements and the poorer technical features you have identified in the previous sections will indicate the changes you could make. Second, what about the future of the program? The item on *maintainability* earlier in this chapter gave one or two suggestions.

An evaluation of TJ's Tennis

Below is the sort of thing you could write for TJ's Tennis to answer task 6.1.

<u>An evaluation of the TJ's Tennis program</u>

<u>Meeting the user's requirements</u>

In task 1.1 I listed the user's requirements. My program meets all these. However I would like to draw together the following points that I confirmed with TJ's Tennis after I started the design stage of the project:

- The printed report on the final league positions does not produce tied rankings if two or more players have the same number of points. The user was happy with this.

- The combo boxes on the Players and Matches forms always display league numbers 1 to 8. The user was sure that no more than 8 would be needed, and if a particular league round has less than 8 leagues the fact that 8 is still displayed would not irritate the user.

- When I demonstrated the Players form and showed that there was no checking that the league number entered by them was an acceptable one, the user said this was OK.

The Appendix includes a letter from TJ's Tennis confirming that all their requirements have been met.

<u>Good and bad features</u>

I do not think the program contains any *bad* features, though I admit that one or two features are less efficient than they could have been. I will review the program's features from two viewpoints – the user and the programmer.

User's viewpoint

An irritating problem can arise when changing the stored details of a player or match. One or more of the check boxes must be selected before the OK button is clicked. When details of a second player or match are changed the user can easily forget that one or more of the check boxes are selected from the previous change. If a check box is selected that the user does not want then the corresponding input box is displayed and the user has to enter the same details as those already stored. If they enter nothing then the stored record will be incorrect. TJ's said that in practice it is easy to be tempted just to press Enter rather than type in the same details again, indeed if they even realise that an unwanted input box has appeared.

Related to the above point, TJ's thought that the message in the input boxes when changing match details was not that clear. It would be better if the name that appears indicated whether this was the winner or loser.

Programmer's viewpoint

I will review the technical features of the program by discussing the following points:

Code presentation

I have included a large number of comments in the code. In particular I have

- stated the purpose of many of the variables.
- stated the purpose of each procedure
- explained many of the selection and loop conditions
- explained the more complex processing

I have used a consistent indent throughout the code.

Code efficiency

I have made most of the selection and looping structures as efficient as possible. For example, cmdChange_Click on the Matches form to find details of the match selected from the list box in the Matches file uses a Boolean value to quit the loop when the match has been found. Another example is the series of nested IFs in cmdSave_Click on the Matches form to validate some of the data entered by the user. Inefficient code here would have separate IF structures.

However there are examples of code that is not totally efficient. For example, sub procedure RenumberMatchIDs renumbers *all* the stored matches whereas only those match IDs greater than the ID of the match that is being deleted need to be renumbered.

Data storage efficiency

I have declared the record structures used for storing details in the Players and Matches files to be economical with storage space – 22 bytes for each player's details and 47 bytes for each match details. I have not stored the points awarded in each match on file as these can be calculated from the data that *is* stored there.

Although I have chosen to delete records from these files physically rather than logically, this was not because of storage considerations. Since the storage needed for either file is small anyway there is nothing to choose between these methods.

For the array to hold details of players' names and total points (which is used when printing the league tables) I have declared a static array of 10 records. The assumption is that a league will have no more than 10 players. TJ's Tennis said this assumption is acceptable. Since the array is reused for each league, rather than having a larger array to store all the league players, I can claim some storage efficiency. Nevertheless it *is* a static array, and if I had wished to be as frugal as possible on storage I could have used a dynamic array instead.

Use of procedures

I have tried to use general procedures where I thought they are appropriate. If the procedure's task is to return one item of data to the calling procedure (event or general), I have written this as a function procedure rather than pass the returned data through a parameter to a sub procedure. Examples of this are ValidMatch and PlayersInLeague.

Where appropriate I have passed parameters to the general procedures. Actually the only examples where this has been appropriate are the two functions mentioned in the previous paragraphs. None of the sub procedures needs parameters.

Scope of variables

Where a variable is used by two or more forms I have declared it on the single standard module. The only examples of this are the two variables for the Players and Matches file names. I could have declared them on the appropriate form and referenced it from the others.

The rule I have followed in deciding whether to declare variables on a form as global or local is this: if the variable is required by two or more procedures then declare it as global unless it can be passed as parameter to a called procedure. In fact none of the variables had to be global; all the variables are local. For example, cmdDelete_Click on the Matches form calls function ValidMatch and passes it the league number selected from the combo box. The variable that stores this league number is declared inside cmdDelete_Click.

The result of imposing this strict rule is that a lot of my procedures seem to have similar lists of local variables. For example I have declared the variable *Index* in 10 procedures and *OnePlayer* in 8 procedures. Why not declare these as global variables on a form? The standard reason for declaring local variables is that there is no possibility of accidentally storing incorrect data, which may have unforeseen results, if you declare them locally. To be honest this argument is not really a valid one in my program, at least for some of the local variables I have used. For example, if I declared Index as a global variable, it would not matter what was currently stored in it wherever it is used. This is because in every case it is used as a control variable in a For...Next loop and therefore is always initialised to a value when first used by the loop.

Possible improvements

Changes to the existing program

Two not so good features from the user's point of view were noted earlier. These can be improved quite easily. First, when the Change or Delete buttons on the Players and Matches forms are clicked, I could add code to deselect any of the selected check boxes. Second, whether the name of the player displayed in the input box when changing match details is the winner or loser can be added to the second (string) parameter sent to the InputBox function.

Although there are several examples of validating data not all data that can reasonably be validated is done. For example, there is no validating the set scores on the Matches form. The following validation could be added:

- The number of games scored by either player in a set must be a numeric digit from 0 to 7.
- If the winner's number of games in a set is 7 then the loser's must be 5 or 6.
- If the winner's number of games in a set is 6 then the loser's must be from 0 to 4.
- If the first two sets have been won by the same person then the other two text boxes for the third set must be empty.

Part of this validation could be achieved by replacing the control array of 6 text boxes with a control array of combo boxes and make each combo box display the values 0 to 7. The Style property of the combo boxes used for the scores in set 3 would have to be different to those used for the first two sets. The first two sets must have scores since a match must be at least two sets long, and so the Dropdown List type of combo box would be needed. If a player wins 2-0 in sets the third set must have no scores and so the default Dropdown Combo would be needed.

Future improvements

There are several improvements that could be made to the program in the future, although the current implementation is acceptable to TJ's Tennis.

- TJ's says that 8 leagues are sufficient for the foreseeable future but what if their membership grows more than they expect and more juniors take part in the league programme? It would be better not to fix the number at 8; this number is built into the List property of the two combo boxes that display league numbers at design time. It would be much more flexible to display only those league numbers that are currently stored in the Players file. The Load events of the Matches and Reports forms could call the function NumberOfLeagues to find this value and a loop used to display the numbers from 1 to this value in the combo box.

- If there are more than 9 leagues in a future league round then a fundamental problem must be faced. The *League* field in the Players file can store only 1 character. This would have to be increased to 2 and the file deleted and created again before being used after this change.

- When a new league round begins TJ's can either delete the two files (from outside the program) or delete the Matches file only and update the Players file from the Players form. It might be better to allow these file deletions from within the program to ensure they are done at the right time and that the right files are deleted.

- The array that stores names and total points for printing the league positions is declared to hold 10 records, i.e. a maximum of 10 players in any league. If TJ's decides to have more than 10 players in a league in the future, although they have said 10 is fine, then the array would need to be redeclared.

Exercises on TJ's Tennis

In the world of software production the user often requires the program to do extra things after they have used it for a while, or perhaps there was something they did not originally wish the program to do but later change their mind. The exercises below ask you to consider examples of this.

*1. The first paragraph under the section *Documentation* in Chapter 22 raised the question of how TJ's would use the program the second and subsequent times a league round is processed. For this exercise assume that TJ's wants the option of starting the Players file from scratch again or using the old file and changing the details as appropriate. On the Main form add a new command button to handle this new requirement. Next to it place two option buttons. One of these deletes the two files and the other deletes only the Matches file and opens the Players form ready to enter new details. Write code in the Click event of the new command button to handle these options.

*2. The printed results of the final league positions have only the players' names. Now TJ's would like their coaches' initials too. Change the code to do this.

**3. TJ's has been using your program for several months now and during that time junior membership has increased far more than expected. The number of players taking part in the leagues has likewise increased greatly. TJ's had thought that eight leagues would be enough for the foreseeable future but not any more. You now decide to automate this part of the program. The league numbers listed in the combo boxes on frmMatches and frmReports will be only those which are currently held in the Players file. For example, if details of players in 10 leagues are stored on file the league numbers 1 to 10 will be listed in the combo boxes. Make any necessary changes to the forms in design view and write code to carry the change you have decided on.

**4. Originally TJ's said that when the league positions are printed it did not matter if two players with the same points were given two different league positions. For example, in Figure 18.8 two players scored 5 points but are in positions 4 and 5. TJ's has now changed its mind and would like tied positions. In the example in Figure 18.8 the two players would be 4= and the last player position number 6. Extend the code in sub procedure PrintPointsResults to handle this.

***5. TJ's would like another printed report. At the end of a league round a list is required of all the players grouped by coach. For each player it should show which league they are in, their league position and number of points. The players (for a particular coach) should be listed in league order. Add another option button to frmReport and write code to produce this report when this option is selected.

Appendices

Appendix A – Visual Basic's debugging tools

Bugs are errors in code when it runs and **debugging** is the tracking down of these errors. The Debug toolbar and Debug menu have a range of methods to help you debug your code. To get the Debug toolbar select **View/Toolbars/Debug**.

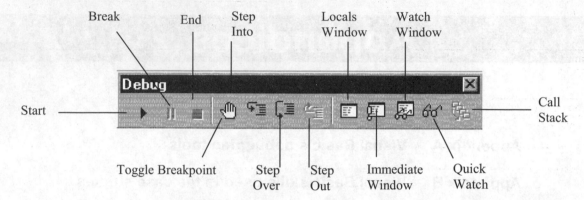

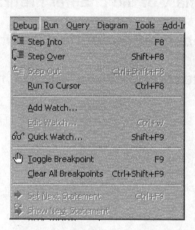

Debug toolbar (above)
Debug menu (below)

Method	What it allows you to do
Step Into	Execute the current line of code, stepping into a called procedure.
Step Over	Execute the current line of code in an event procedure. If this line calls a general procedure it runs the procedure as a unit then goes to the next line.
Step Out	Execute the remaining general procedure code.
Run To Cursor	Execute all the lines of code up the line with the cursor.
Add Watch	Open the Add Watch dialog box. A watch allows you to see the value of a variable or an expression as the program runs. You can use this with Step Over or Step Into to see the changing values.
Edit Watch	Open the Edit Watch dialog box to edit a Watch.
Quick Watch	Open the Quick Watch dialog box. First highlight a variable/expression, click Quick Watch and then click Add to add it to the Watch window (see later).
Toggle Breakpoint	Add or remove a breakpoint. A breakpoint is any line in the code. When the program runs, execution of the code halts at this line. You can then inspect the contents of any Watches you have added.
Clear All Breakpoints	Remove a breakpoint.
Set Next Statement	Specify which statement within a general procedure is to be executed next.
Show Next Statement	Move the cursor to the next line to be executed.

The Debug toolbar has four Window buttons. Generally you need to use one or more of these windows the see the result of using the debug methods described above.

Type of window	*What it is used for*
Watch Window	Keeping track of the contents of a variable or expression for which you have added a Watch.
Immediate Window	Displays the current contents of any variable or expression. You must type this variable/expression into the window and precede it with a '?'. For example to see the value of the variable Total type in ?Total and press Enter.
Locals Window	Displays the current value and data type of all local variables.
Stack Window	Opened by clicking the Call Stack button. It lists all the general procedures that were called in order to reach the current line of code.

Appendix B – Visual Basic skills used in the case studies

Chapter	Topic covered	Relevance to the case study for Unit 7 – Gina's Groceries	Relevance to the case study for Unit 22 – TJ's Tennis
1	The programming environment	All relevant	All relevant
2	Controls	Uses label, text box, command button, combo box, list box, frame. Also uses Line and UpDown controls (not covered in Chapter 2)	Uses label, text box, command button, combo box, list box, frame, check box, option button
3	Data types Variables Displaying output	Integer, Single, String, Currency data types Format	Integer, String, Boolean data types. Format Concatenation
4	If…Then…Else Select Case	If statement	If and Select Case
5	For…Next Do While...Loop Do…Loop Until	For…Next and Do….Loop Until used	All 3 types of loop used
6	Strings Dates Time	General use of Strings Date function	General use of Strings Right function Dates and time not used
7	Arrays	4 ordinary arrays for data storage Control array of labels	1 ordinary array Control array of text boxes
8	Printing	Used to print customers' receipts	Used to print details of players and match results
14	General procedures Standard modules Parameters		Sub and Function procedures used extensively. Standard module used Some parameter passing
15	Records		Used extensively
16	Files		Random access files are very important

Appendix C – Summary of the chapter programs

Program No.	Program name	Main new topic(s) covered
1.1	Display your name	Print text on form
1.2	Change a message	Click command buttons
2.1	A list box of countries	List box
2.2	Option buttons, check boxes and frames	Option button, check box, frame
2.3	Displaying the time	Timer
2.4	Changing a form's colour using scroll bars	Scroll bar, RGB function
3.1	Add two numbers	Variables, Addition, input box
3.2	Illustrating global and local scope	Scope of variables
3.3	Using a static variable	Static variables
3.4	Calculating the average exam mark	Initialising variables, Enabling/disabling controls
4.1	Deciding exam grades	If statement, Message box
4.2	Selecting cutlery	Selecting option buttons and check boxes
4.3	Rent a property	Logical operators AND and OR
4.4	Wards and Patients	Select Case statement
5.1	Multiplication table	For…Next loop
5.2	Addition table	Nested For…Next loops
5.3	Driving test	Do While…Loop
5.4	Password entry	Do…Loop Until
6.1	Ensuring a person's name has one space	String functions Len and Mid
6.2	Extract the area telephone code	Building a string by repeated concatenation
6.3	College library issue desk	Processing dates
7.1	Array to hold numbers	One-dimensional array
7.2	A control array of text boxes	Control array
7.3	A control array with a shared event procedure	Shared event procedure
8.1	Printing exam marks	Simple printing to the printer
8.2	Printing reports on sales staff	Sending data in an array to the printer
14.1	Avoid repeating code	Putting repeated code into a sub procedure
14.2	Calculating interest	User-defined function
14.3	Program 7.1 with a function to search array	Startup Object, Arrays as parameters
14.4	A standard module function	Using a standard module
15.1	Football team players	Records, Array of records, 2 forms in project
16.1	Text file to hold names and ages	App.Path, Reading to/writing from a text file
16.2	Random access file of garden centre products	CommonDialog control, Random access file

Appendix D — Assessment Evidence for Unit 7

You need to produce:

- a working program to meet stated user needs. The program(s) must include most of the data types, objects and events listed under 'program design'.
- user and technical documentation including a test report for the most comprehensive program.

To achieve a grade E for your work you must show:	*To achieve a grade C for your work you must show:*	*To achieve a grade A for your work you must show:*
E1 a clear and accurate specification that meets user needs and defines the input, processing and output needs	C1 accurate technical documentation that defines fully all calculation and manipulation, provides clearly commented program listings of all modules and details all user screens and dialog boxes	A1 a good understanding of programming through an effective modular design and in your imaginative use of events, objects and controls
E2 a modular program design		A2 creation of data entry facilities that are clear, well laid out and suitably labelled, correct validation of input data and provision of appropriate user guidance
E3 suitable data entry facilities in your program(s)	C2 good quality user documentation which makes appropriate use of graphic images and screen prints and includes examples of data input screens, output screens, printed output and error messages	
E4 appropriate use of sequence, selection and repetition in your program(s)		
E5 appropriate use of objects and events in your program(s)		A3 design and implementation of imaginative and customised screen or printed output to provide content and layout that are well matched to user needs
E6 suitable data processing methods in your program(s) including calculation and text manipulation	C3 that you can work independently to produce your work to agreed deadlines	
E7 use of your program(s) to generate screen or printed reports that the user needs correctly		A4 records of thorough module and program testing that checks all major paths, acceptable and unacceptable input and all possible events, and show clearly how any identified problems were resolved to produce a good operational program(s)
E8 clear user documentation that enables a non-specialist to use the program(s) effectively and technical documentation that includes detailed program listings containing suitable comments		

Note: The Edexcel Board does not number the grade criteria. This has been done to make it easier to refer to a particular criterion.

Appendix E — Assessment Evidence for Unit 22

You need to produce:
- one or more programs to solve a given design brief
- detailed technical documentation
- an evaluation report

To achieve a grade E for your work you must show:	*To achieve a grade C for your work you must show:*	*To achieve a grade A for your work you must show:*
E1 a clear description of the purpose of the program(s)	C1 good use of a wide range of techniques which draw together knowledge, understanding and skills to produce designs, write code which is reliable, efficient and clear to read, and programs which are fit for the purpose in relation to the original design specification	A1 precise technical documentation where all calculation and manipulation is fully defined and all procedures and subroutines are clearly annotated in program listings, data dictionary and all other relevant technical documentation
E2 accurate analysis of the processing, constants, variables, output formats and assumptions applicable		
E3 the design and specification of appropriate program(s) to fulfil the stated purpose		
E4 the effective use of suitable programming tools and language to create suitably modularised and structured programs which accurately manipulate data to produce output as defined in the specifications	C2 evidence that your work has been effectively planned and tested, including evidence that the work has been checked and revised to meet some of the problems identified during testing	A2 a clear, accurate and detailed evaluation of your program which discusses suitability for purpose, identifies good and bad features and suggests possible improvements
E5 a clear progression towards your solution	C3 good quality technical documentation making appropriate use of graphic images and screen prints that include examples, where used, of menus, data input screens, printed output and error messages	A3 fluent use of technical language and production of clear, coherent works that have been checked and proof-read to remove most spelling and grammatical errors
E6 clear technical documentation including detailed program listings that are easy to read and are suitably annotated		
	C4 that you can work independently to produce your work to agreed deadlines	

Note: The Edexcel Board does not number the grade criteria. This has been done to make it easier to refer to a particular criterion.

Index

Also from Payne-Gallway:

AVCE Information and Communication Technology Units 1- 3

by *R. P.Richards & P.M.Heathcote*

July 2001   240 pp   ISBN 1 903112 29 X

This book covers the first three mandatory units of the new AVCE in Information and Communication Technology award:

>   Unit 1 - Presenting Information
>   Unit 2 - ICT Serving Organisations
>   Unit 3 - Spreadsheet Design

It is ideal for students, providing them with all the knowledge required to successfully complete these units. Skills are learned by completing sample tasks backed up with further practice exercises. Sample assignments are provided with advice on portfolio evidence.

Unit 2 includes a sample case study as required for the external assessment, discussing the way in which an organisation manages information systems.

AVCE Information and Communication Technology Units 4- 6

by *R. P.Richards & P.M.Heathcote*

July 2001   240 pp   ISBN 1 903112 48 6

This book covers units 4 - 6 of the new AVCE in Information and Communication Technology award:

>   Unit 4 – System Installation and Configuration
>   Unit 5 – Systems Analysis
>   Unit 6 – Database Design

For unit 4 the underpinning knowledge is presented in simple, clear language with step-by-step illustrated guides to installing and upgrading components of a PC system. A sample system specification is also included.

In unit 5, sample case studies are used to illustrate systems investigation and analysis. A sample feasibility study is given and this is developed into a detailed system specification for a database solution. The database is implemented in unit 6 and the student is shown how to write up the technical documentation and user instructions.

Teachers may request inspection copies of books from our distributors:

BEBC Distribution
P.O. Box 3371
Poole
Dorset BH12 3LL
Tel: 01202 712909   Fax: 01202 712913   E-mail: pg@bebc.co.uk

Successful ICT Projects in Word (2nd edition)

by P.M.Heathcote

February 2000   208pp   ISBN 1 903112 25 7

This text, updated for the 2001 syllabus and Office 2000, covers the essential features of Word from basic editing and formatting right through to advanced features such as templates, macros, customised toolbars and menus. It is suitable for students on a number of courses such as 'A' Level or Advanced VCE (GNVQ) ICT, HNC and HND in Business Information Technology and Access to HE.

It gives ideas for suitable projects and explains how to complete each phase from Analysis and Design through to Implementation, Testing and Evaluation. AQA Project Guidelines and a mark scheme are included in an Appendix.

Successful ICT Projects in Excel (2nd edition)

by P.M. Heathcote

June 2000   208pp   ISBN 1 903112 26 5

This book, updated for the 2001 syllabus, will help students to complete a project in MS Excel, using version 2000, 97 or 7. It covers formulae, functions, What If scenarios, Goal Seek, linking workbooks, filtering, sorting and subtotalling, pivot tables, charts, macros, and adding a user interface.

It is suitable for students on a wide range of courses from 'A' Level or Advanced VCE (GNVQ) ICT to degree work, as well as for staff development. A sample project demonstrates how to lay out a complete project report, and the AQA mark scheme is also included. The template for the sample project as well as a sample chapter entitled ''Project Ideas' are available on our web site.

Successful ICT Projects in Access (2nd edition)

by P.M. Heathcote

July 2000   224pp   ISBN 1 903112 27 3

This book, updated for the 2001 syllabus, will help students to complete a project in MS Access, using version 2000, 97 or 7. It covers database design, creating tables, forms and subforms, queries, importing and exporting data to other packages, analysing and processing data, reports, macros and some Visual Basic for Applications. It includes advice on choice of projects and a sample project.

It is suitable for students on a wide range of courses such as 'A' Level or Advanced VCE (GNVQ) ICT, HNC and HND in Business Information Technology, and Access to HE.

Successful ICT Projects in FrontPage

by R.S.U. Heathcote

January 2001   208pp   ISBN 1 903112 28 1

This book is designed to help students on an 'A' Level or Advanced VCE (GNVQ) ICT or similar course to design and implement a Web site using MS FrontPage 2000. It assumes no previous knowledge of FrontPage and takes the reader from the basics such as entering, editing and formatting text and images on a Web page through to advanced features such as writing scripts, gathering data from forms, and making use of active components. A wide range of examples is used to illustrate the different facilities of FrontPage, and a sample project shows students how to tackle and document each stage of project work. Web site resources are available.

Consult our Web site www.payne-gallway.co.uk for latest news on titles and prices.